Enticing Paths

A Treasury
of Norfolk Gardens
and Gardening

Enticing Paths

A Treasury of Norfolk Gardens and Gardening

Edited by Roger Last

Foreword

Few if any counties can boast such a diversity of historic landscapes and gardens as Norfolk; some surviving much as their creators intended, others transformed by later additions and designs, or displaying only vestiges of their past glory. As the family custodian of two historic landscapes and gardens, I have some experience of the complex interactions involved in the creation of such works and have had the good fortune to work with many talented 'specialists' and 'generalists' over a long period of time. I am sure these fascinating accounts will have a resonance for many others who have made or maintain gardens of all descriptions – as well as for those who have no practical knowledge or experience.

Enticing Paths is a compendium of some of the most intriguing articles taken from the Norfolk Gardens Trust's former Journals. These have been chosen by editor Roger Last for their wide range of subject matter, to include parks and gardens of all eras; as well as botanical collections, lakes, follies and fountains, and much else besides; encompassing their design, aspiration and construction, and introducing the extraordinary panoply of characters – designers, architects, horticulturalists and patrons – who conceived or worked on them.

Often garden or architectural history can appear dry and academic. *Enticing Paths* is very different. Although the articles are thoroughly and painstakingly researched, they are aimed at an informed general readership. The inclusion of many additional illustrations and photographs is also welcome, as they contribute so much to our understanding, and help us appreciate atmosphere and context all the more vividly.

Foreword

Since the start of the Coronavirus pandemic in 2020, many gardens and parks have been closed, or have been forced to restrict access; and so, as the country opens up again, they have become ever more essential to our well-being – whether as 'green lungs' in town centres, or as secret worlds to discover in the heart of the countryside – and I believe interest in their history and design will only continue to grow. The varied stories and characters involved in their creation are very much part of this experience, and we should applaud all who have contributed to bringing them to life in this remarkable book.

David Cholmondeley

Contents

Contributors		10
Introduction		14
Chapters		
1	**Norfolk's Switzerland** *Roger Last*	16

Over a period of fifty years, Brundall Gardens, to the east of Norwich, was consecutively in the hands of two dissimilar men: one, the creator – a gifted and visionary amateur gardener – the other, an entrepreneurial showman. Despite their differing responses, they presided over the creation of what was one of East Anglia's finest garden landscapes.

2	**The Leicester Monument** *Christine Hiskey*	34

Flamboyant and rich in its carved detail, derided by some and praised by many, the Leicester Monument in the park at Holkham Hall was built to celebrate the agricultural achievements of T. W. Coke, Earl of Leicester. This grand design had an often-fraught genesis.

3	**My Lord's Garden** *Gillian Darley*	48

The Norwich garden of a duke, romantically approached from the river and designed by a renowned seventeenth-century antiquary, diarist and gardener, My Lord's Garden remained a delightful public open space in the city until overwhelmed by industrial development in the nineteenth century. Now it has been lost forever under a major housing development.

4	**The Eastern Arboretum** *Scilla Latham*	62

'*The Eastern Arboretum* refers not to the vegetable wonders of the Oriental part of our globe, but to a district of our own peaceful and happy England.' So wrote James Grigor, and the district he was referring to was Norfolk. Outside academic circles, the book he wrote, published in 1841, is little known. And until now little was known about the author. The work references Norfolk towns and villages and its primary seats, tree management, and above all is a unique period survey of the outstanding trees of the county.

Contents

5 The Maharajah is Well Satisfied *Roger Last* 84

In need of a cast-iron liquid manure barrow? Many Victorian garden owners were. And they knew that gardens needed more than plants and hard landscaping. A huge range of accessories was required to help maintain and embellish them. Fortunately, mass production was on hand to meet the demand and the Norwich manufacturing phenomenon, the firm of Boulton and Paul, rose to the challenge.

6 George Skipper's Sennowe Masterpiece *Steven Thomas* 104

The impressive campanile towering above the trees at Sennowe Park hints at the grandeur below. And grandeur there is in house, formal terraced gardens and park. The key input for its early twentieth-century transformations came from the East Dereham-born architect, George Skipper.

7 The Business of Gardening *Tom Williamson* 122

Today finding and obtaining plants and seeds could not be easier. With the prolific growth of garden centres, specialist nurseries, mail order, container plants and above all the Internet, if it exists, it can be found. What did estate and garden owners do in the eighteenth century? Searching through the invoices and receipts of the trade reveals surprisingly contemporary answers.

8 The Pleasure Gardens of Norwich *Roger Last* 128

London's Pleasure Gardens of Vauxhall and Ranelagh achieved wide fame and were a huge commercial success. Many provincial cities and towns in England had Pleasure Gardens too, and of these Norwich was very much to the fore. These gardens were businesses and engaged in fierce commercial rivalry to keep the people of Norwich and Norfolk amply entertained.

9 Botanic Connoisseur *Brian Ellis* 146

The greatest botanical collection ever assembled in Norfolk was the lifetime passion of a Norfolk farmer from Fincham, Maurice Mason. A renowned plant collector and impassioned plantsman, he made two large gardens, one of which boasted no less than eighteen glasshouses, the other a large arboretum, a combined horticultural achievement unequalled in the county.

10 Hortus Episcopi *Graham Innes* 166

The oldest and the largest garden in Norwich is the Bishop's Palace Garden. Though it is set within the shadow of the cathedral and once comprised more than six acres, no account has been written of its history and development. A development and horticultural expansion which continues at a pace today.

11 A Parterre by Two Ladies *Roger Last* 188

The great Parterre at Blickling Hall dominates the eastern section of the gardens, looked down on from the Long Gallery. The major garden set piece at Blickling, it is the product of two ages and two garden styles, and of the vision and enthusiasm of two contrasting women.

12 The War Memorial Gardens, Norwich *Lesley Kant Cunneen*   **206**

The austere but original Art Deco gardens standing proud over Norwich Market Place were condemned to play a secondary role to their central feature, the Lutyens-designed war memorial. Subject to many vicissitudes, by the turn of the twentieth century the gardens were boarded up. Restored by 2011, and with the memorial moved, a new phase in the gardens' evolution opened.

13 Lakes in Norfolk Landscaped Parks *Tom Williamson*   **224**

Usually the single most expensive feature of a landscaped park was its lake, the proud boast of the most affluent estates. But not every park had them, and, in this overview of the county's most notable lakes, it is clear not all are products, as is so often supposed, of the eighteenth-century landscape movement.

14 Art and Industry *Roger Last*   **248**

Few people are aware of the work of the Wymondham-born architect, Thomas Jeckyll. Yet for a time he was a leading figure in the Aesthetic Movement of the nineteenth century, and apart from his architecture, was an original and influential designer. Jeckyll collaborated with the prominent Norwich firm Barnard, Bishop and Barnards on the design of two major works, both of which found their way into Norfolk gardens.

15 The Holkham Fountain *Christine Hiskey*   **272**

The *St George and the Dragon* fountain at Holkham Hall is East Anglia's finest, a tour de force of hydraulic display and heroic sculpture. But how in an age before electricity and in the relatively level acres of Holkham, was this spectacular garden addition supposed to work? Somehow the waters had to be made to rise to the occasion. A multifaceted combination of technology and art saw that they did.

16 Carrow and the Colmans *Graham Innes*   **296**

Hemmed in by a multiplex of factory buildings, offices and access roads is an unpromising location in which to find a garden. Yet, amid these many commercial intrusions, the gardens of Carrow House and Carrow Abbey in Norwich, remain. A complex history enfolds this hidden landscape, once the site of a priory and later the home of the Colman family.

17 The Renaissance of Gunton Park *Elise Percifull*   **326**

The decline of the estate at Gunton Park followed a typical twentieth-century pattern. By 1979 much of this beautifully designed landscape was under the plough and in separate ownership. Its restoration, one of the finest of such in the country, is a story of determination and vision.

18 Didlington's Golden Age *Roger Last*   **346**

The mansion and estate at Didlington, eight miles to the south-west of Swaffham, was in the possession of the Tyssen-Amherst family for only sixty years. But under them, both house and gardens reached their zenith in fame and fortune. Unforeseen and dramatic decline was to follow.

19 Some Norfolk Gardens Illustrated by Edmund Prideaux
Tom Williamson   376

Made in the first quarter of the eighteenth century, the garden sketches of Edmund Prideaux are an invaluable visual source of the design and condition of some of the county's important gardens; rare views of 'geometric' garden layouts before the landscape movement overturned them.

20 Templewood *Roger Last*   386

Concealed amid woods is a unique twentieth-century house, which its owner saw as his own Petit Trianon, a villa to which to retreat from the pressures of the high political world he moved in. It sits in a muted but original landscape especially contrived for it.

21 Heyrick 'Tony' Greatorex's Garden, Snowdrop Acre *Richard Hobbs*   406

Though it is one of the smallest, yet in its own way, Snowdrop Acre is one of the most influential of Norfolk's gardens. Little is known of its owner and creator, but it is the *Galanthus* he raised on the site which has brought Mr Greatorex, the founding father of snowdrop breeders, a lasting recognition.

22 James Pulham & Son at Sandringham *Scilla Latham*   420

From the late 1860s to the early twentieth century, the gardens at Sandringham House were extensively redesigned and laid out. Surprisingly, there are few records which survive relating to this intense period of garden activity. Certainly, one of the major firms of designers and manufacturers employed there was James Pulham & Sons, still remembered today for their invention of a convincing, relatively light, artificial rock, 'Pulhamite'.

23 Norfolk's Gardens in Art *Roger Last*   438

Depictions of gardens have long been an invaluable source of information to garden historians. Some of them transcend the mere sketch or record to be accepted as Art. The styles, methods and ambitions of the artists were various. Many of them are unknown, others famous, but their differing degrees of artistic endeavour combine to illuminate and to give pleasure, depicting the gardens of Norfolk over three centuries.

Acknowledgements   466
Sources and Further Reading   467
Picture Credits   473
Index   475

Contributors

Gillian Darley OBE is currently the president of the Twentieth Century Society and a former chair of the Society for the Protection of Ancient Buildings. She is a writer, architectural journalist and broadcaster. She has published biographies of Octavia Hill, John Soane and John Evelyn and with David McKie wrote *Ian Nairn: Words in Place* (2013). Her most recent book is *Excellent Essex* (2019).

Brian Ellis was born in Yorkshire and brought up in Diss. Teacher training at the University of Sussex School of Education majoring in history, followed by Homerton College, Cambridge, and the University of East Anglia, led to teaching in West Norfolk for twenty-one years. He has been a member of and contributed articles to Plant Heritage, the Royal Horticultural Society, the Norfolk and Norwich Horticultural Society, the Norfolk Gardens Trust, and the Alpine Garden, Cottage Garden, and Hardy Plant Societies. His passion is for snowdrops and he grows many varieties and species, subsequently becoming one of the 'immortals' as a *Galanthus* from the Greatorex plot in Norfolk was named by Joe Sharman and Richard Hobbs as *Galanthus* 'Brian Ellis'.

Christine Hiskey read modern history at Lady Margaret Hall, Oxford, and qualified as an archivist at Liverpool University. After four years in the Durham County Records Office, when she also undertook a research degree at Durham University, she moved to north Norfolk with her husband and from 1977 helped occasionally in the Holkham archives. In 1985 the 7th Earl of Leicester appointed her as Holkham's first archivist. Her research there led to the publication of various articles and her book, *Holkham: the Social, Architectural and Landscape History of a Great English Country House* (Norwich, Unicorn Press) appeared in 2016. She retired as archivist in 2017 but continues to do research.

Richard Hobbs is a botanist who worked for many years with Norfolk Wildlife Trust and was its director from 1994 to 1997. He has had a lifelong interest in gardens and was the chairman from 1998 to 2008, and president, in 1991, of Norfolk & Norwich Horticultural Society. He has sat on several Royal Horticultural Society trials committees and holds the National Collection of *Muscari* and related genera. A keen gardener and former gardens advisor to Burghley House, he travels extensively, including leading groups to look at wildflowers all over the world.

Graham Innes' interest in landscape and architecture grew from a long fascination with the castles and fortified tower houses of north-east Scotland. His enthusiasm for garden history and design developed while working with the Plantation Garden Preservation Trust, Norwich, including nine years as their honorary treasurer, and more than thirty years of organising annual visits to historic gardens around the UK. An extended article on the nineteenth-century expansion of Ickworth park and estate appeared in the National Trust's quarterly house journal at Ickworth, 2006–7. He has contributed to the Norfolk Gardens Trust's news and journals and to *Norfolk Gardens and Designed Landscapes* with new research on Shadwell Park, near Thetford, and the Great Hospital in Norwich.

Lesley Kant Cunneen has been a teacher, college lecturer, schools' inspector and local authority director of education, libraries and leisure services. Following retirement, she served as a lay magistrate, chair of Norfolk Mental Health Trust, a council member of Plant Heritage, a trustee of Norwich War Memorials Trust, and completed a doctorate in public green space at the University of East Anglia.

Roger Last worked as a producer and director for BBC Arts in London. Among the films he made were several *Design Classics*, including *The Aga*, *The London Underground Map* and *The Red Telephone Box*. Other series included *Architecture at the Crossroads*, looking at contemporary architecture round the world, *Royal Gardens* with Sir Roy Strong and a documentary on the life and work of Sir Geoffrey Jellicoe. He has designed several gardens including his own five-acre Norfolk garden. He was chairman of the Norfolk Gardens Trust from 1998 to 2001 and edited its Journal from 1998 to 2012. He was co-author and editor of *Norfolk Gardens and Designed Landscapes* (2013). His interests apart from garden design include writing and architecture. He was a founder member of the Norfolk Churches Trust and was also responsible for twice bringing the Monty Python team to film in Norfolk.

Scilla Latham is a garden and architectural historian living in south Norfolk whose career has focused on heritage conservation. After reading history of art at Manchester University, she worked at the Courtauld Institute of Art recording and researching private collections of works of art in many of our great country houses. The study of the conservation of historic gardens and landscapes at the Architectural Association led to a new career researching and advising on historic gardens. Her areas of research include the lost formal gardens at Shaw House, Newbury; the garden buildings of Thomas Archer; Humphry Repton's Red Books of 1793 and the planting records at Blickling Hall. More recently, her research and dissertation at the University of East Anglia on achieving a sustainable future for parish churches – in which she focused on the challenges faced by many rural churches in Norfolk – was the catalyst to return to her lifetime interest in church architecture. She worked in the Diocese of Ely for three years advising on extending the community use of parish churches and is currently the secretary of the Norfolk Churches Trust.

Elise Percifull is a landscape manager and academic researcher with a degree in landscape management from the University of Reading, and a PhD from the University of East Anglia for her work on the influence of the Arts and Crafts movement in East Anglian gardens. Her consultancy practice, HLM Ltd, weaves together practical training with a desire to see historic and heritage landscapes restored and conserved in an appropriate yet dynamic manner. Today HLM specialises in the production of management plans for national heritage landscapes and designed historic parks and gardens and has been privileged to work on many historic sites including Blenheim Palace, Chatsworth House, Houghton Hall and Knole Park.

Steven Thomas trained in landscape management, receiving a first-class degree from Reading University in 1992, where he specialised in the conservation, management and presentation of the natural elements of the rural landscape. His postgraduate diploma, awarded by the College of Estate Management, explored the conservation of historic buildings, which led to a thesis considering the work of the architect George Skipper. Through his preparation of heritage management plans for large nationally outstanding landscapes and buildings, Steven has made HLM Ltd one of the leading consultancies in this field. His particular interests lie in the fields of historic landscape, countryside management, sustainable agriculture, woodland management, and vernacular domestic architecture.

Tom Williamson is professor of landscape history at the University of East Anglia and has written extensively on landscape archaeology, environmental history and the history of landscape design. He has worked closely with the Norfolk Gardens Trust for many years, producing (with Roger Last and Patsy Dallas) its volume on *Norfolk Gardens and Designed Landscapes* in 2013, and co-editing (with Sally Bate and Rachel Savage) *Humphry Repton in Norfolk* in 2018. His publications on garden history more generally include *Polite Landscapes: Gardens and Society in Eighteenth-Century England* (1995); *The Archaeology of the Landscape Park* (1998); and *Lancelot Brown and the Capability Men* (2016). His latest book, *Humphry Repton: Landscape Design in an Age of Revolution*, was published by Reaktion in 2020.

Introduction

Between 1998 and 2012 the Norfolk Gardens Trust produced an annual Journal for its members of especially commissioned articles from experts in their field on a wide variety of garden subjects, all of which were about, or related to, Norfolk. It is a selection from the Journals which forms the basis for this book, enabling a wider readership to access what hitherto has remained hidden within the Trust's archives. Where appropriate the articles have been updated and revised and, in some cases, considerably extended. Whereas the Journals were sparsely illustrated, an aim of this book has been also to bring the articles to life visually, by introducing a large and rich selection of archive and especially commissioned photographs. The book's diversity of subject matter reflects the diversity of the interests of the Trust as it encompasses the study of gardens and designed landscapes from any period, large and small, in town and in the country.

The horticultural components of gardens, flowers, bulbs, shrubs and trees, hedges, and grass, must be to the fore when one thinks of a garden. But their history, development, maintenance, change, decay, their owners, and the people they employed, are all relevant to garden making. As too are the garden designers, architects, plantsmen, and artists in stone and wood who contributed to a garden's appearance. With these rich seams added, a whole new world of garden-related matter begins to open, all of it ripe for study.

Then there is the manufacturing world: who designed and made the machines and appliances the garden relies on, who made the seats, the gates, the decorative fencing? Who supplied the seed and plants, where did they trade in the county? It is worth remembering that garden making in all its forms in this country is big business, and that has been the case for centuries. Vast sums of both private and public money have been lavished on gardens. In part as vanity projects used by their owners to display their wealth, or for commercial exploitation for profit, or money has been spent purely to give aesthetic delight and pleasure. From all facets of the gardening world personalities large and small, some with relish, others fleetingly, begin to reveal themselves. Many famous on the national stage, others known only locally. All of which makes the world of the garden far wider than the world of horticulture.

There is another vital element, the ephemeral nature of the garden. It is living, growing, and ever-changing. Its composition and appearance is often hostage to the whim of new owners and to the blunt scythe of fashion. Gardens are more frequently altered than the houses they surround. The garden is not hermetically sealed as, cosseted, and air-conditioned, paintings can be, it must stand in the full blast of the weather and the seasons. Its life is limited. In the past, literally in their hundreds, ambitious, large, exceedingly expensive, admired and loved gardens have been created which their owners and designers must have looked on as lasting testaments to their wealth and skill. Of so many of these, not a trace remains.

This makes the study of gardens intriguing detective work: how did a garden appear in its prime, what were its owners trying to achieve, who did what, and when, and why, and who altered this and added that, who had vision and who had lassitude? The history of gardens is as much about loss as it is charting what we have. But any hint of regret is soon tempered by the thought that new gardens are always being made, and the relish of opportunities to come. Trying to reveal a garden through the layers of the past, and that can be a very short past, is often no easy task. The veils of time blur and memories fade, knowledge is lost, and speculation can supersede fact. However, in every aspect, and in every detail of the garden there are tales to be told and matters to be discovered. These articles reflect that vast wealth of subject matter. The complex stimuli which charged their creation have ensured that gardens are not, and have never been, mere decorative accessories; they are complexly woven into our lives in so many ways. It is a pleasure to reveal some of them.

1

Norfolk's Switzerland

Roger Last

One of the major tourist attractions in Norfolk in the 1920s was a garden. Today we would expect no less. But in an age before the mass introduction of the car and the arrival of the luxury coach, that 60,000 visitors in one year visited this garden is remarkable indeed. Now the media, books, magazines, and the internet guarantee the coverage of any garden worth its salt, and everywhere is easily accessible. But to attract this number still would be considered highly successful. That it was achieved in the rural Norfolk of the 1920s is down to the entrepreneurial skills of one man, Frederick Holmes Cooper.

Frederick Cooper was a leading figure in the most glamorous industry of the age, cinema. In 1909 he had taken the plunge and forgone a probably secure, even perhaps unglamorous career in estate agency for instead promoting the silver screen. He owned a chain of screens in East Anglia, including the Regent in Prince of Wales Road in Norwich, and he had visited that other Xanadu, Hollywood, where he had

FACING PAGE The Mere at Brundall Gardens.

LEFT Every bit the executive, Frederick Cooper (right) on the set of *The Gold Rush* with Charlie Chaplin (centre) then at the height of his silent era movie fame, in 1925. Chaplin had his own studios in Hollywood, and the delegates from the British Cinematograph Exhibitors' Association were warmly entertained.

rubbed shoulders with the considerable likes of Charlie Chaplin, Douglas Fairbanks and Mary Pickford. This prestigious Californian adventure had been on behalf of the British government, a mission to examine the 'dream machine' up close and to determine why the majority of the films seen in the UK were American and not British; a venture which eventually led to an imposed quota of British films being screened here. Cooper was a cinema magnate of national importance. He went on to become the President of the Cinematograph Exhibitors' Association of Great Britain and Ireland. Back in the slightly less glamorous boulevards of Great Yarmouth and Norwich, Cooper nevertheless still thought big, and decided to turn his Brundall garden, which he had bought ready-made, into a money spinner.

It is extraordinary that anyone then would think of a garden in those terms, but Frederick Cooper, an astute businessman, saw his garden as an exploitable asset. Born in 1866 and then in his fifties, Cooper wisely left the gardening side of this asset to his head gardener, James Strachan, and no less than twenty-two gardeners and marsh men. He knew how to market a product, and his assertive confidence outrageously promoted his acquired garden as 'The Switzerland of Norfolk'. Those naively expecting mountains were doomed to disappointment, but they did get hills, quite considerable ones at that. As many of his visitors approached Brundall across the flat marshland to the west of Great Yarmouth, the Brundall heights must have seemed almost convincingly alpine by comparison. The holidaymakers at Yarmouth were transported to Brundall

The head gardener James Strachan and his wife Alice, at Brundall in the 1920s.

The Mere, called by Cooper the Lily Lake, looking south from the woods, in 1911. By the time Cooper bought the property Beverley's extensive plantings were mature and flourishing.

by a steamer. Cooper owned it, and the promise of a forty-two-mile return river trip and a nice garden at the other end clearly made the three-shilling fare, plus 6d garden entrance seem attractive. Coming from the other direction, Norwich, Cooper pulled off a masterstroke. Brundall lies only five miles to the east of the city. He persuaded the London & North Eastern Railway Company to open a halt immediately outside the entrance to his garden. Brundall had had a railway station since 1844. Cooper argued that the numbers visiting his garden, and those in the future living in the new housing developments he envisaged, warranted the expense of this additional halt. To seal the deal, he agreed to pay the railway company £150 per year for fifteen years to offset costs. The halt opened in 1924. Cooper knew what he was doing when in 1918 he had bought a seventy-six-acre site, boasting a fine ready-made garden, with both a rail track and a river running past the bottom of it.

By 1918 Brundall Gardens was achieving considerable maturity having been started in 1881. Even then the steep escarpment above the River Yare at Brundall was well-

Dr Michael Beverley, c.1880, at the time he bought Brundall Gardens.

wooded. The man who had created the gardens was Dr Michael Beverley. He was an accomplished botanist and became a founder member of the Norfolk and Norwich Naturalist Society, and this dual interest made the Brundall site, rich in wildlife and native plants, very attractive. His gardening, which began as a hobby, clearly grew into a passion, as he devoted thirty years to evolving this outstanding woodland and waterside garden, seemingly undaunted by its huge scale.

Michael Beverley was born in Brooke in 1841, and after graduating as a doctor in 1863 became a house surgeon at the Norfolk and Norwich Hospital a year later, a position he held for twenty-five years. He gradually began to clear the Brundall site

The thatched Museum c.1911.

Michael Beverley and his dog Dick in the Rock Garden, c.1911.

The arid planting in the Rock Garden. Its many yuccas, cordylines and succulents thrived on its well-drained slopes.

and to plant trees, and these, many of them rare and exotic, continued to be planted, and shrubs and bulbs on a mass scale. Later, many choice and tender plants were introduced. Paths were created leading through the emerging garden and to provide river and lakeside walks. On the plunging escarpment he had constructed four spring-fed tiered ponds, which would also enable the introduction of a cascade. While these were being excavated many Roman artefacts were uncovered. So many in fact that Dr Beverley eventually turned one of the numerous marsh men's cottages on his property into a small museum to house them. The excavated area became known as the 'Roman Dock'. Some of the artefacts found there indicated the possibility of Roman boat building, or boat repair, and on the top of the escarpment itself, were indications of a villa. Certainly, the site lent itself to both.

Mass planting of azaleas and rhododendrons on the wooded slopes assured a spectacular late spring display, for summer a Rose Garden and Walk was introduced, many beautiful climbing roses and ramblers were planted and a Heather Garden for winter. In tune with the fashion of the age, a Rock Garden with alpines had to be

On a promontory in the centre of the site the extensive thatched Log House looked out over the gardens and across the Yare valley.

Michael Beverley, aged 70, in the Log House in the last year of his residence, c.1911.

The cover of the brochure for the visit of the British Medical Association in 1890. The gardens were then called 'On the Banks of the Yare'. Beverley's Wishing Spring is shown and some of the Roman pottery finds on the site.

included, as were fountains (gravity fed, the garden being rich with springs) and what were then more exotic plantings of pampas grass, eucalyptus, bamboos, palms, yuccas and gunnera, plus a fiery autumn display of Japanese maples. Added to this were the considerable natural assets of the site, its slopes, its lily-clad lake, Brundall Mere – of some four and a half acres, its marshland rich with bird life – and the River Yare winding through the bottom of the property. Then there were the spectacular views over the Yare valley of unspoilt countryside beyond.

Michael Beverley spent more and more time there, with his wife and six children. A weekend retreat was built called the Log House, high on the escarpment commanding the view. Logs were used to clad the wooden rustic-style thatched house. It was of considerable size, included a servant's room and was organically supplied by spring water. Some of the former marsh men's cottages dotted throughout the garden were converted into summer houses. A boathouse was built on the edge of the Mere and black swans were introduced. In 1890 a garden party for the East Anglian branch of the British Medical Association was held here, when Beverley himself was its president. At its height Brundall Gardens must have been one of the county's most beautiful new gardens, in a small part vying, although not intentionally, with that being created through the same period in the west of the county at Sandringham.

The design, construction and planting of a garden is not cheap. Add to this the

Dr Beverley (seated) his dog, Dick, and a friend Edward Corder, rowing on the Mere, c.1911. The banks are clad with rhododendrons.

Cooper's newly built and imposing Redclyffe House, a symbol of his continuing success, sited on the top of the escarpment above the gardens. The Lily Lake (the Mere) in the foreground.

necessary and continuous maintenance, plus the lavish scale of the Brundall Gardens, and this appears to be an extraordinarily expensive undertaking. With his large family to maintain, how had Dr Beverley been able to finance this huge garden project? It certainly had not been possible even on his generous medical salary. The fabulously unlikely answer is diamonds. He had been left a share in a parcel of land in Brazil which conveniently contained a diamond mine. Eventually extracted stones were turned into cash, which in turn he used to transform his Brundall acres. By the time he retired and sold the property in 1911 at the age of seventy, his regrets about leaving his creation must have been tempered by relief in no longer having to oversee the running and the financing of such a huge and labour-intensive garden. Michael Beverley moved to Scole, and lived until 1930, dying at Overstrand.

The 1911 sale particulars prefigure Frederick Cooper in their unrestrained partisan bombast, declaring the gardens to be 'the most extensive and picturesque in Eastern England'. The 'sloping woods and hills face directly south, thus accounting for the semi-tropical vegetation with which they are covered, justifying the claim to be considered the Riviera of East Anglia'. Up to this point they had not been called Brundall Gardens, instead as the sale particulars made clear, the seventy-six-acre estate was called 'The Banks of the Yare'.

When Frederick Cooper bought the estate in 1918, he did not get off to a good start. He moved with his family into the extensive Log House, which he had adapted as his permanent home. On a cold November night in 1919, a chimney fire set the thatch alight, and although his family was there, the rapidity of the blaze saw the entire building, its contents and the Coopers' clothes, burnt to ash. The inferno took thirteen hours to extinguish. Pitch pine of which the Log House had been built, Cooper now considered fit only for two things: church pews and coffins. Undeterred, he built a new house on the same site, the impressive three-storey, tile hung and brick Redclyffe House. It looked like an opulent mansion in stockbroker-belt Surrey but was clearly fitting for the director of Electric Theatres Limited. In front of it was a terrace with a majestic flight of over sixty steps leading down to the Mere. Although he often looked severe in some of the

Frederick Cooper, president of the Cinematograph Exhibitors' Association of Great Britain and Ireland from 1929.

Cooper's pleasure steamer the *SS Victorious* heading up the Yare to Brundall Gardens from Great Yarmouth, in the mid 1920s.

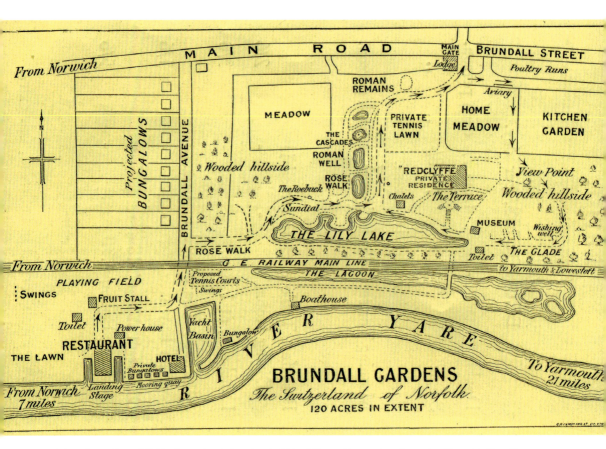

The plan of Brundall Gardens, the Switzerland of Norfolk, and its setting, from the Riverside Hotel's brochure, early 1920s. From the landing stage (bottom left) visitors were sent on a suggested route ascending to the Lodge by Brundall Street and down again, passing all the garden's many attractions. Cooper's proposed residential developments – nine plots for bungalows – are shown to the left of Brundall Avenue.

photographs of him, he was described as 'genial as he is capable' and as 'a man of action rather than words'. At Brundall, action there was as he set about turning these very private peaceful garden acres into a mass tourist attraction.

As the founder of the Brundall Gardens Steamship Company and the owner of the steamer the *Victorious*, moored at Yarmouth, he had a means of mass transport at his command. His requirement for Norwich to Yarmouth trains to stop at Brundall Gardens Halt completed the necessary transport arrangements. Anticipating large crowds, he did exactly what the owner of any comparable attraction would do today: built toilets, lots of them, and a restaurant/tea room, and set up a fruit stall. When the success of the project was assured, he built a hotel by the river with 'unique facilities unsurpassed on the famous Norfolk Broads' for those who wished to turn a day trip into something more lasting.

The gardens proper were entered via the Rose Walk which led to the Lily Lake.

What was a visit to Brundall Gardens like in the 1920s and 1930s for those who came in their hundreds by train and steamer? Both arrived at the base of the gardens. Those coming by steamer moored at a specially constructed landing stage. They were met by the welcoming sight of the toilet block. Anyone already exhausted from the river cruise could head straight for the restaurant. Cooper's acres were 120 in extent including the marshland, with hotel, between the Yare and the railway line. Over the track the garden tour began, on a suggested route. First, to the extensive Rose Walk, on past the Sundial (Beverley had bought the pieces in Bath), then the visitor climbed up the sloping land by the side of the Roman Dock with its tiered ponds and cascade. At the top of the garden near the main road gate lay the Aviary and Kitchen Garden. Skirting away from the private Redclyffe House, the visitors were led to a viewpoint on the hillside with outstanding views over the gardens below and of the Yare valley. Then they descended the wooded slopes to the Wishing Spring, or Well, as Cooper re-branded it. Beverley had used a natural spring in the hillside, building a wall to retain it from gothic fragments, the water fed through a leering gargoyle he had found in a stonemason's yard near Norwich Cathedral. The visit led on to the Museum with its Roman artefacts, passed more toilets (it was a very large site), then to the picturesque acres of Brundall Mere, the Lily Lake in Cooper's terminology.

And so back to the 200-seater restaurant, the very welcome teas were 3d per cup, and eventually on to the waiting steamer or train. Cooper's steamer the *Victorious* left Great Yarmouth at 10 a.m. and did not depart from Brundall until 6.30 p.m., so his captive visitors had to use his facilities. But, given good weather their day should have been delightful, with extensive walks through glades of trees, flowering shrubs, bulbs and exotics, all beautifully maintained, passing hill, lake and marsh. A. H. Patterson in a pamphlet called *Brundall on the Broads* from the 1920s, summed it all up, if in somewhat excited and florid prose: 'The trail to the gardens ... And such gardens. What a wealth of oak, weeping ashes, elms and coniferous trees of many sorts, all so lovingly planted by the dear old Doctor, who spent a small fortune on its beautification. What walks, glades, arbours and leafy nooks lead up from the lily smothered lake to the hilltop, where miles of views hold the onlooker enraptured ... I hardly like the name "Brundall Gardens" it is more like a slice of woodlands borrowed from Eden.'

Mr Patterson styled himself as 'John Knowlittle, Broadland Naturalist'. And his pamphlet, a flagrant combination of garden propaganda and publicity tract, was presented to passengers of the *Victorious* with the compliments of the Brundall Gardens Steamship Co. Ltd. It was no wonder the venue became Norfolk's premier garden tour. However, there were only a few more years left for it to hold this crown. The garden needed a rich man and financial success to keep it all in place.

The Lily Lake from the Dry Garden, looking south over the Yare valley.

The financial disaster of the 1929 Wall Street Crash followed by the Great Depression, led to financial disaster for Frederick Cooper too. The London Stock Market also crashed and as a result of his losses, he suffered a stroke and a nervous breakdown. The family moved to London and the Brundall estate was sold in 1937, Cooper dying two years later. The new owners of Brundall Gardens, the Stringers, wanted the gardens for their private use. Mass invitations and tourists from Yarmouth, or anywhere else, were at an end. Yet they had little time to enjoy their new exclusive slice of Eden. The Second World War saw Redclyffe House requisitioned, and the Stringers had to move out.

In 1945 they returned, but between then and 1968, the land was gradually sold off for development. Cooper from the start had appreciated the development potential of such picturesque land so close to Norwich. He had thirty plots put aside to the west of the gardens for houses and bungalows designed by Edward Boardman. By the late 1960s the seventy-six acres of garden had been reduced to eighteen. Redclyffe House and Brundall Gardens went on the market again. The sale particulars were not much concerned with the gardens, but ominously headlined the development potential of the estate. This soon manifested itself in a developer applying for planning permission to build sixty-two houses. In 1969 Redclyffe House itself burnt down.

Planning delays and changes of ownership meant that for many years what was left of the gardens fell into neglect and decay. Eventually three houses were built on the ridge of the land. Into one of them, Lake House, in 1985 moved Garry and Janet Muter who, together with their neighbours began the long task of restoring the overgrown Roman Dock with its sequence of ponds, and adding to the gardens. Subsequently,

The restored Cascade or Roman Dock, three ponds descending the escarpment, leading to the Mere, in Janet Muter's garden, Lake House, in 2010. Originally there was a higher fourth pond.

three more houses have been built, including in 2000 a new 'Redcliffe' House, for Alan and Linda Jones on the site of the original building, and they also opened up the views to the Mere. Alan Jones built a further new house at the west end of the gardens and continues the restoration and relandscaping of the rest of the estate.

It would have been remarkable indeed if a garden of this size, whose structure and form was nearly entirely composed of plants, with little hard landscaping, could have survived the social and corrosive commercial pressures of the twentieth century fully intact. The gardens exist today in a truncated form but survive despite the number of houses which have been built round them, and the complex ownership of the site. This is helped by no hedges, fences or intrusive boundary markers having been introduced, which allows to a considerable degree the extent and layout of these late-nineteenth-century gardens to be appreciated. What Beverley composed and Cooper so brilliantly exploited has gone, but the choice segments which do remain are a solid reminder of one of Norfolk's former grand garden achievements.

ABOVE The new 'Redcliffe' House, the third property to occupy this prominent position.
BELOW The Mere, Brundall Gardens.

2

The Leicester Monument

Christine Hiskey

Sooner or later, the gaze of visitors in the saloon, the central stateroom of Holkham Hall, is drawn away from the magnificent decor to the views outside. To the south, directly in line with the centre of the hall, stands the Obelisk, designed by William Kent and erected in 1730–32 by Thomas Coke, later 1st Earl of Leicester (1697–1759), as a symbol of his plans to create a great hall and park. To the north, on the same straight line, is the monument, built in 1845–50 to commemorate the achievements in agriculture of his great-nephew, Thomas William Coke, who died in 1842. He had inherited the hall and estate at the age of twenty-one in 1775 and remained plain 'Coke of Norfolk' until receiving the title of 1st Earl of Leicester of the 2nd creation in 1837 at the age of eighty-three, five years before his death. A fluted stone column of 9 feet diameter (2.7 m), rising from a base 44 feet square (13.4 m), and standing 120 feet high (36.6 m), the monument is not quite as tall as Nelson's Column in Trafalgar Square, erected a few years earlier, but its summit is visible, above the trees, from the sea banks at Burnham Overy Staithe and Wells.

FACING PAGE William Donthorn's watercolour of c.1843 of his proposal for the Leicester Monument at Holkham. The monument was built as depicted except that the decorative elements of sheep and ox and the bas-relief panel were turned round to face the hall – visible in the distance.

LEFT The Monument, sited north of the hall, backed by a tree belt.

For at least forty years before T. W. Coke had inherited the hall and estate, Holkham had been known and admired as an architectural masterpiece and treasure house. Coke had little interest in such matters but soon developed an interest in promoting and publicising agricultural improvement, an interest shared by many wealthy landowners at the time. His charismatic character, the potential offered by the estate for farming and the splendour of the hall as the setting for his generous large-scale hospitality, combined to give him a national and even international reputation as a farmer and landlord. At times his innovations were exaggerated: 'Norfolk husbandry' based on sheep, turnips and cereals, especially barley, along with regular marling to improve the land and twenty-one-year leases for tenants, had long been established at Holkham.

BELOW *Thomas William Coke Inspecting His Southdown Sheep with Mr Walton and the Holkham Shepherds.* Detail from the oil by Thomas Weaver, 1808.

Coke's great contribution, apart from his gift for publicity, was his dedication and skill in breeding sheep – replacing the poor Norfolk type first with Leicesters and then with Southdowns – and also cattle, particularly Devons. Tenants were encouraged to follow suit and enjoyed the provision of good houses and premises. At the famous three-day annual Holkham sheep-shearings, starting in about 1800, Coke personally conducted tours of his own farm and those of nearby tenants, showed his sheep and cattle (and took the opportunity for selling and hiring them) and led lively conversations about farming. After dinner on the third day, attended by up to 700 men, 'premiums' or prizes were awarded for the best animals, improved implements, reports on the respective merits of drill and dibble husbandry, ploughing matches, shepherds, and other features of current interest. The last annual shearing was held in 1821, twenty-one years before Coke's death, but the annual audit or rent-day dinners at the hall, liberally accompanied by speeches and toasts, continued to maintain the tradition of mutual goodwill between Coke and his tenants.

The Leicester Monument seen from the south.

Coke died at Longford, his Derbyshire house, at the age of eighty-eight on 30 June 1842. When news of his death reached Norwich two days later, there was an immediate move towards erecting a memorial. One of his leading tenants, Hudson of Castle Acre, a Mr Neave of Wymondham, and Roger Noverre Bacon, editor of the *Norwich Mercury*, took it upon themselves to circulate about seventy of the 'yeomanry' of Norfolk. A subsequent meeting elected a committee from the 'yeomanry and tenantry' and instructed it to seek the involvement of ten representative gentlemen. At the end of the year, when there was already a lengthy list of subscribers, a Committee of Taste was elected to consider the details.

The monument is thus a unique feature at Holkham, not only because all the other decorative structures designed for the park and distanced from the house (the Obelisk, the Temple and, just outside the park, the Triumphal Arch) were Thomas Coke's eighteenth-century creations, but also because it was initiated, organized and financed, not by the Coke family, but through a public committee. Indeed, there was disquiet in some quarters that this essentially public monument was to be erected on private land.

Apart from a portfolio of plans in the Holkham archives, there is little documentation about the origins of the monument. The papers of the various committees are not known to have survived elsewhere, although the chairman said he had presided over three meetings at Holkham, two at Fakenham and twenty-five at Norwich, and had written 800 letters. Fortunately, however, the memorial was of such great public interest that the *Norwich Mercury* and the *Norwich News* gave vividly detailed reports on the various meetings and the celebrations when the first stone was laid. In 1850, as the monument was completed, Robert Leamon, chairman of the committee, and R. N. Bacon, editor and principal owner of the *Norwich Mercury* and secretary of the committee, published a small book, *A Narrative of the Proceedings Regarding the Erection of the Leicester Monument*, detailing the progress of the memorial.

The committee discussed various options and settled on a column in preference to a statue, a model farm or an agricultural institution. It also voted by ten to six for it to be sited in Norwich. The result was a tumultuous general meeting, a week later, at which Mr Young, the surgeon at Wells, proposed an amendment in favour of a site at Holkham. There was uproar as supporters of the Norwich site alleged that 'a large number of new subscribers, many small amounts, had just been added, and brought up from Wells for the express purpose of swamping the original subscribers. (Noise and hisses)'. After heated exchanges, many Norwich supporters left the room, and the vote was carried in favour of Holkham. The *Norwich Mercury*, which was not entirely impartial, condemned 'the very disgraceful expedient resorted to by the inhabitants of Wells' who were 'necessarily benefited by the access of visitors to that noble mansion' – an interesting comment on the spending power of tourists in the 1840s, even before the railways reached the area. The matter was referred to the new owner of Holkham, T. W. Coke's son, the young 2nd Earl. He had been born in 1822, the year after the

last sheep-shearing and ten months after his father's late second marriage, and so had inherited Holkham at the age of twenty. Diplomatically, the young Earl referred the question of the site back to the committee and a postal ballot was held. The result was 322 subscribers voting for Holkham and 281 for Norwich.

After an initial suggestion by young Lord Leicester that the south entrance to Holkham park (not yet adorned with a lodge) might be a suitable site, and with the committee casting a regretful eye at the Obelisk, which occupied the most elevated position in the park, it was agreed to erect the monument on the north lawn, where it would also serve as a landmark for mariners. The chosen site was near the north lodge, which had been designed by William Kent for Thomas Coke some ninety years earlier. Since T. W. Coke's enlargement of the park it had stood incongruously within the park, no longer marking an entrance, and it was now demolished, and trees cleared to restore a view to the sea. Whether or not mariners found the monument a useful landmark as the committee had intended, the Royal Air Force in future years is said to have used the line through obelisk, hall and monument for navigation practice.

The committee then advertised for artists and architects to submit designs for a column to cost £4,000 guineas. Judging took place when members of the committee had gathered in Norwich for the Sessions Week in January 1844. The floors and walls of the Exhibition Room in Exchange Street were 'entirely covered' by seventy-six designs and models but nothing is known of the unsuccessful entries. William Donthorn (1799–1859), a Norfolk architect born in Swaffham, emerged as the clear winner. He had trained under Jeffry Wyatville and designed in a variety of styles: Greek Revival country houses, Tudor-Gothic parsonages, Gothic at Hillington and Cromer Halls and Felbrigg stables, Tudor at Aylsham and West Beckham workhouses, and Italianate at Great Moulton Old Rectory. He was also responsible for church restoration at Stoke Ferry and Bagthorpe. 'The agricultural nature of the design, and its embodiment of leading points of past and cherished scenes and sentiments was', according to the *Narrative of Proceedings,* 'its principal recommendation.'

Details inscribed on the base of the monument explain the reasons for its creation. An inscription pays tribute to the political career of T. W. Coke, 'for more than half a century the faithful Representative of this County in the House of Commons', but it was as the 'Great Promoter and Benefactor' of agriculture that he was chiefly commemorated, 'to which from early manhood to the close of life he dedicated Time, Energy, Science and Wealth'. The other three sides of the base display bas-relief scenes, each illustrating Coke's involvement in an aspect of the improvements for which he was famous and including the figures of specific associates in tribute to his wide circle of influence.

The east side shows the signing of a lease, for it was by granting the security of long leases, incorporating stipulations for rotation of crops and other aspects of farm management, that Coke had encouraged progress among his tenants. The south side depicts Coke and Earl Spencer (1782–1845), a fellow agriculturalist, accompanied by

T. W. Coke is shown seated on the right, ready to sign a lease with one of his leading tenant farmers (John Hudson of Castle Acre) who is accompanied by his young son. Standing behind the desk is Coke's own son, who by the time the monument was erected had succeeded his father as Earl of Leicester. Seated opposite Coke is his solicitor, Sir W. Foster; on the left are two more of his Norfolk tenants (Blomfield and Overman) and to the right, just seen, are senior estate office staff, the agent Blaikie and his assistant and successor, Baker.

T. W. Coke's skill in improving breeds of sheep and his famous annual sheep-shearings are both remembered on this panel. Lord Leicester, always depicted as taller than anyone else, is accompanied by his fellow expert Earl Spencer. There is a hint of self-interest by members of the monument committee in the depiction of the chairman, Mr Leamon, and at least three leading committee members, Sir J. P. Boileau, Lord Colborne and Sir W. Ffolkes. To the right are shepherds and perhaps the farm bailiff.

The *Irrigation* bas-relief relates to T. W. Coke's encouragement of the creation of water meadows to provide early spring grass for grazing or hay. Lord Leicester and his friend and fellow agriculturalist the Duke of Bedford are shown with William Beck, a tenant farmer who introduced water meadows at Lexham, Norfolk.

shepherds, inspecting sheep at a Holkham sheep-shearing. On the west panel he is seen inspecting an irrigation scheme, the water meadows which he promoted as a means of facilitating the early growth of grass. On the corners of the plinth stand large figures representing Coke's interests in animal breeding and improved implements: a Devon ox above the motto 'Breeding in all its Branches'; Southdown sheep above the motto 'Small in size but Great in value'; a Norfolk plough and a seed drill. Other mottoes on the corners echo toasts at the annual audit or rent-day dinners, epitomising Coke's political and agricultural attitudes: 'Live and let Live' and 'Improvement of Agriculture'. The top of the column, supported by other farm animals, is crowned with a massive wheat sheaf.

Donthorn was instructed to arrange contracts with a stonemason, giving preference to Mr Watson. James Watson's stone and marble business at Norwich has left no known records, although the Norfolk Local Studies Library holds a photograph of the works, but between 1845 and 1854 (when his widow sold the business) he did a great amount of work on and around the hall at Holkham in repairs and additions. In 1845 he had 120 men working at Holkham, for whom he gave a dinner after the ceremony for laying the foundation stone of the monument. He and Donthorn had a difficult relationship throughout the next five years. Disagreements over the construction of the foundations delayed work for much of 1844 and 'the greatest care on the part of the Building Committee was necessary to preserve the contracts unbroken'. In February 1845, however, Watson wrote to William Baker, the Holkham agent, 'Mr Donthorn has this morning sent me the papers I require for commencing the column, I am now in hope you will soon see it from your office window, peeping out of the ground.'

The foundations of the monument were 8 feet (2.4 m) deep, excavated, of course, by hand, resting on solid chalk. Borings were taken to another 15 feet before the precise site was selected. The foundations were filled with concrete. They were raised another 2 to 3 feet, making them over 10 feet (3 m) deep in total, for which the Holkham estate agent undertook to supply 67,000 bricks; when it was decided to use stone for the whole structure, the value of the bricks was added to the subscription. The stone for the base came from Lord Hastings' quarries at Seaton Delaval, Northumberland; he had offered to give the stone for the whole monument but, for the column, the architect preferred sandstone 'of a beautiful colour' from Whitby, Yorkshire.

The whole project was a considerable undertaking. According to one report, 'the scaffolding erected for the construction is similar to that used for the Nelson monument, and upon the summit is a travelling machine, like that used in building the New Houses of Parliament. Many improvements have, however, been introduced and the entire height of the scaffolding will be 135 feet.' Originally the plans incorporated a staircase, but this was soon abandoned when it was realized that it would require a permanent attendant.

On 12 August 1845, six months after Watson had started work, a great fete was

held at Holkham to celebrate the laying of the first stone. 'Those who are acquainted with Holkham Park and its noble South entrance,' reported the *Norwich Mercury*, 'can readily imagine the scene from the triumphal arch to the obelisk, when we tell them the procession extended at least two miles.' It was led by Watson's masons, dressed in white with leather aprons and new straw hats, followed by organized ranks of tenants, clergy and gentlemen on horseback; carriages bearing the ladies and dignitaries; Howlett's band from Norwich and Jonas Wright's from Fakenham; and, bringing up the rear, more workmen, all wearing red caps, and people on foot. Numerous banners and flags throughout the procession bore mottoes echoing the traditional political and farming toasts of the Holkham sheep-shearing dinners and regular audit dinners, from 'The Durability of the Constitution' to 'A Fine Fleece and a Fat Carcase'.

After the speeches and ceremony at the site of the monument, the 2nd Earl of Leicester provided a lavish meal, consisting of 'all the delicacies and luxuries which the

The substantial base of the monument.

finest cuisine could supply', served in a huge marquee on the south lawn for 1,000 subscribers and their families. As they left to spend the evening walking and driving in the park and pleasure grounds or sitting in the smaller tents to listen to the bands, 300 workmen and 'numbers of the peasantry' took their place at the tables: 'before sunset the park must have entertained 10,000 people.'

In the meantime, in October 1844, the committee had placed the carving of the bas-relief panels in the hands of John Henning junior (1802–57). Henning had worked with his father, a successful sculptor, on replicas of the Parthenon friezes, seen on various buildings including the Athenaeum in Pall Mall, and had carved the frieze on the screen at Hyde Park Corner. Each of the Holkham figures, apart from the shepherds and the drainage labourers, was identifiable. The scene depicting the signing of a lease shows Coke with one of his leading tenant farmers (Hudson) and the tenant's son, other tenants (Blomfield and Overman), estate office staff (the agent Blaikie and his assistant and successor, Baker), his solicitor (Sir W. Foster) and his own young son (the future 2nd Earl). Many years later, the younger Hudson (Thomas Moore Hudson, of Warham) recalled the exact occasion in 1836 on which the scene was based and asked permission for his sons and their wives to drive into the park as they were 'desirous of seeing my effigy on the Monument'.

An early version of the Irrigation scene, depicting the creation of water meadows, neatly combined entrepreneurs (Coke and his friend and fellow agriculturalist the Duke of Bedford), a tenant (William Beck, who had formed water meadows at Lexham), experts (the geologist William 'Strata' Smith and the engineer Jonathan Crook) and manual labourers. Perhaps there is a hint of self-interest by members of the committee in the *Sheep-shearing* scene, which included the chairman, Mr Leamon, and at least three leading committee members, Sir J. P. Boileau, Lord Colborne and Sir W. Ffolkes. Indeed, there was an intriguing undercurrent about the choice of people depicted on the panels: one of the committee, Mr Beck (possibly the one who appears on the *Irrigation* panel) proposed that no other portraits be added, but subsequently the Duke

BAS-RELIEF—IRRIGATION.
1. Mr. William Beck.   2. The late Earl of Leicester.   3. The late Duke of Bedford.

BAS-RELIEF—THE SHEEP SHEARING.
1. Mr Gurdon.   3. Sir W. Folkes.   5. Lord Colborne.   7. Late Earl of Leicester.
2. Mr. Leamon.   4. Sir J. P. Boileau.   6. Earl Spencer.

BAS-RELIEF—GRANTING A LEASE.
1. Mr. Blomfield.   3. Mr. Hudson, jun.   5. Mr. Baker.   7. The present Earl of Leicester.   9. Mr. Blaikie.
2. Mr. Overman.   4. Mr Hudson, sen.   6. Sir W. Foster. Bart.   8. The late Earl of Leicester.

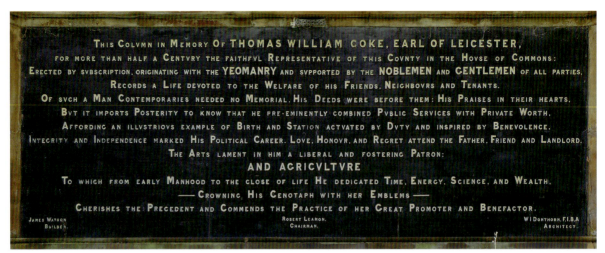

The fulsome inscription, cast in bronze, on the north face of the monument's plinth, in praise of Thomas William Coke: 'Of such a man contemporaries needed no memorial.'

of Bedford was added to the *Irrigation* panel and the 2nd Earl of Leicester and William Baker (the agent in 1845) to the scene of *Granting Leases*. The designs published at the time differed slightly from those executed.

The masonry work was completed by May 1848. The inscription was written by William Bodham Donne (1807–82), who lived at Mattishall and was an essayist, possibly a direct descendant of the poet John Donne. The stonemason was adamant that it was impossible to cut the inscription in the stone provided and, as there were sufficient funds, it was eventually agreed to cast it in bronze.

The monument was at last finished in March 1850, nearly eight years after Coke's death. It was officially handed over to the 2nd Earl of Leicester in August, exactly five years after the foundation stone had been laid. It had cost £5,410, of which about £3,500 was for Watson's work and £970 for Henning's bas-reliefs. It was financed completely by subscriptions, the money given in lieu of Holkham bricks, and bank interest. The subscriptions, of which there had been nearly 1,000, ranging from £105 to less than five shillings, came to total nearly £5,000.

There was an intriguing postscript when, as the monument was completed, the secretary of the committee, R. N. Bacon, a long-standing admirer of Coke, laid claim to the original designs as his own. Donthorn maintained that Bacon had merely furnished him with mottoes from the audits, whereas Bacon claimed that he had sketched for Donthorn the subjects for the bas-reliefs and the animal figures and had written the description for the competition entry. Perhaps Bacon had intended to avoid the appearance of a conflict of interest at the competition stage; now, five years on, he maintained that he had not raised the matter earlier in the hope that Donthorn would eventually acknowledge that Bacon had furnished the design. Donthorn's expertise in the more technical aspects of designing of such a massive column seems to have been overlooked. After hearing both men, the committee declared that 'they were perfectly satisfied with Mr Bacon's statement in proof that he was the author of the design of the monument'.

The monument is impressive but perhaps more interesting in its detail rather than beautiful in its entirety. Coke's daughter certainly disliked it: 'The monument is much too near and frightful, the wheat sheaf looking like a vulgar evergreen flower stuck on the top.' Some of the claims which bolstered T. W. Coke's reputation as a great agricultural reformer, although they persisted for 100 years or more, have been scrutinised by modern historians and found to be exaggerated. The monument, however, stands as striking testimony to the extraordinary influence of Coke's charismatic character, the success with which he implemented, encouraged and promulgated agricultural improvement, and the esteem and affection in which he was held by his contemporaries.

A long axis runs from south of the Triumphal Arch through the park to the Obelisk, and on through the centre of the hall to terminate at its north end at the Leicester Monument. Behind it and the trees is a glimpse of the sea.

3

My Lord's Garden

Gillian Darley

In the 1660s with the Restoration of Charles II, and the dukedom of Norfolk restored, Henry Howard, the 6th duke, was eager to re-establish his family presence in the county. Although his elder brother, Thomas, 5th Duke of Norfolk, was non compos mentis and had been living under restraint in Padua since 1645, the tide was now safe again. Recognizing this, the city fathers of Norwich immediately turned to him for help in establishing their charter. But the family's palatial seat, the Duke's Palace, close to Charing Cross in the parish of St John Maddermarket, was in poor repair after years of neglect, its bad structural condition exacerbated by a site too close to the river, causing the cellars to flood regularly. Though Henry Howard did not inherit the dukedom for many years, he lived in fully ducal style. Built in 1561–67, the Duke's Palace was

FACING PAGE Henry Howard, later 6th Duke of Norfolk, aged 32, by Adriaen Hanneman, 1660. Painted in Holland on the eve of the Restoration and the restoration of the dukedom. Three years later Henry Howard commissioned the creation of his Norwich garden.

RIGHT Henry Howard, later 6th Duke of Norfolk, in ceremonial armour. John Michael Wright, *c.*1660.

approached through a gatehouse giving onto an entrance courtyard with fountains, beyond which were a further two courts. Howard now planned to rebuild the house in the modern style but was determined to retain the same constrained, and patently unsuitable, site. (Robert Hooke has been suggested as a possible architect, but there is no hard evidence and Howard himself was an accomplished amateur). In recompense for the lack of space in which to provide outdoor entertainment, he decided to plan a garden on ground he now owned, some distance away in a more open setting on the banks of the River Wensum. The friary of the Austin Friars had stood on this spot until the dissolution in 1538.

John Evelyn (1620–1706) writer, diarist, founder member of the Royal Society, garden designer and plantsman, by Sir Godfrey Kneller, 1687. Evelyn played a leading part in the development of seventeenth-century arboriculture and horticulture. His *Sylva, or a Discourse of Forest Trees*, published in 1664, became a standard work on trees. He could be looked on today as Britain's first environmentalist. His only visit to Norwich was in October 1671; he was delighted with the city calling it 'one of the noblest in England'. Much to his liking were the fine prospects and the numerous gardens, 'which all the Inhabitans excell in'.

The site, which became known as 'My Lord's Garden', lay off the old street of Conesford Inferior (which first became St Faith's, then Mountebank Lane) in the parish of St Peter Parmentergate. Howard's scheme was for a pleasure garden approached by water. Such open space as there was around the Duke's Palace was entirely dominated by an almost 200-foot-long bowling alley, which stretched from the house to the waterside. He had been forced to look further afield for his garden – hence the acquisition of the friary site. And it was to John Evelyn that Howard turned, even though he was a stranger to the city. However, the reputation that Norwich now had as a centre for expert florists, largely Protestant émigrés from northern Europe, made it a particularly attractive location in which to dream up a 'public' garden, one in which Howard's guests and the dignitaries of the city could stroll, having been rowed to the site.

The man who brokered the arrangement between Evelyn and Howard was Evelyn's steadfast friend and relative, Samuel Tuke, who having been passed over as the Duke of York's secretary, deemed unsuitable since he was a Catholic convert, was now a central figure in Howard's establishment – overseeing the education of the two Howard boys, Thomas and Henry, with whom he would soon move to Paris. Tuke had spent the interregnum years, after his heroic role in the defence of Colchester in the protracted Civil War siege, in a number of European cities – a busy emissary in the exile community. Restive with his confinement in Norwich he wrote to Mary Evelyn, whose Parisian upbringing (her father Sir Richard Browne had been the king's Resident in France) made her more French than English, decrying this '*flegmatique* island'. He would like her to see 'how I behave myself amongst the Gentlemen of the Province, who are a nation as new to mee as the Americans'.

Stranded in the decaying, old Duke's Palace, Tuke was too far away even to build upon his own moment of literary fame in London. His adaptation of a Spanish piece (thought to be by Calderon) was a runaway success of the winter 1662–63 play-going season. Tuke dedicated the published edition of *The Adventures of Five Hours* (1664) to Howard and wrote that it was: 'bred upon the Terrace Walks in your Garden at Aldbury; and, if I mistake not, it resembles the Place where it was Brought up: the Plot is Delightful, the Elevations Natural, the Ascents Easie, without any great Embellishments of Art'. He was, presumably, describing the gardens at Albury as Arundel had left them (and as etched earlier by Wenceslaus Hollar) rather than the subtle but considerable extensions of the Italianate theme for which Evelyn was responsible.

That autumn of 1663 Tuke reported to Evelyn, 'Mr Howard has given 700L for a plott of ground to make a spring garden at Norwich.' He was not looking forward to a long winter in the city, his feeling of isolation perhaps exacerbated after a visit to Henry Jermyn, Earl of St Albans, at Rushbrooke, near Bury St Edmunds, Suffolk, where he met Evelyn's old friend, the poet-politician (and critic of his own writings) Wailer. 'I know of no business to call mee to London; therefore I pray refresh mee sometimes with your Letters.' Evelyn did so, and the men were constant, faithful correspondents.

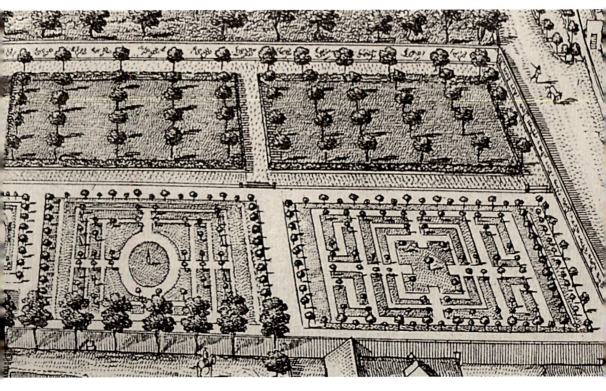

Detail of Sir William Blackett's garden, Newcastle-upon-Tyne, a characteristic garden layout and design of this period.

The first reference to Evelyn's involvement in Howard's planned garden was when Tuke sent a plan of the former Austin Friars site to London on the Norwich coach, for, he told Evelyn, Howard: 'desires your advice how he shall dispose it for a Garden to entertaine the good company in the Towne. He intends to have in it a Bowlingground & the rest to be cast into walks with fruit trees against the walls, with such pert words as you shall judge prupper, the figure is irregular but that is not to be helped. Therefore I pray combine it the best you can'. Presumably the 'words' would be classical mottoes, such as those which visitors remarked upon, scattered liberally over doorways and gates in Evelyn's Deptford garden, Sayes Court, Kent.

In October, Tuke told Mary Evelyn that his patron (Howard) was coming to London soon and wanted to 'speake with Mr Evelyn about the contrivance of his garden; but for my part I shall be frozen up all this winter in Norwich'. But Howard was mercurial and in late October Tuke counsels Evelyn, presumably by then eager to press on with preparatory works before winter set in, to be patient for 'the plott of the garden it will keepe colde'. There are no further references to Evelyn's part in the garden after this, but it is known that it was partially laid out by that January, presumably what was on the

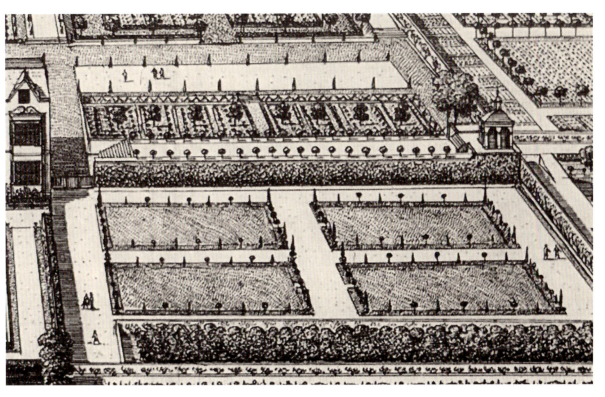

A section of the garden at Beaufort House, Chelsea, drawn by Knyff and Kip c.1707. Although the whole garden was carried out in a grand manner, this section is typical of late seventeenth-century formal gardens. Gravelled paths, rectangular grass beds lined with clipped yews and hollies, formal spacing of larger trees and several varied compartments to discover. In My Lord's Garden instead of a raised pavilion there was Howard House to retreat to. The site gave Evelyn considerable scope and his exceptionally wealthy client would have expected the finest quality and execution in every detail.

ground was the outcome of Howard's requests and Evelyn's experience in execution (albeit at a distance).

Dr Edward Browne, the eldest son of the eminent Norwich-based philosopher, Dr Thomas Browne, was a physician who would, two years later, be one of Christopher Wren's travelling companions in France. He was astonished by the celebrations over Christmas 1663 at the Duke's Palace: 'so magnificently as the like hath scarce been seen; they had dauncing every night and gave entertainments to all that would come & hee build up a roome on purpose to dance in very large, and hunge with the bravest hangings I ever saw, his candlesticks, snuffers, tongues, fireshovels, andirons were silver a banquet was given every night after dancing.' He admired the great collection: 'prints and draughts done by most of the great masters own hands. Stones and jewels ... the more and better than any prince in Europe rings and seals ... all manner of stones and limnings beyond compare these things were most of them collected by the old Earl of

From right to left, the boat journey from the Duke's Palace in crowded Charing Cross to the duke's new garden quickly led to open fields either side of the Wensum before the sharp bend rounding the Cow Tower of 1399. After passing under the medieval Bishop Bridge, and the water gate to the cathedral with its canal leading into the lower close, the countryside began to open up before reaching the site by the sharp bend in the river (left). Here a high wall screened the garden from King Street behind.

Arundel who employed his agents in most places to buy him up rarities, but especially in Greece and Italy.'

In addition, he continues, Howard 'hath lately bought a piece of ground of Mr Mingay in Norwich by the waterside in Cunsford'. The Mingays were mayors of Norwich and Howard must have bought the land in Conesford ward, towards the outer limits of the city, following Robert Mingay's death in 1660. It is from Browne that one learns that the outline of the garden was already sketched out on the ground, presumably following Evelyn's plan. Howard, wrote Browne, intended: 'a place for walking and recreations, having made already walkes round and crosse it, forty foot in breadth. If the quadrangle left bee spatious enough hee intends the first of them for a fishpond, the second for a bowlinggreen, the third for a wildernesse, and the forth for a Garden. These & the like noble things bee performeth and yet hath payed 100,000 of his Ancesters debts'. On 16 January Browne went to look at the site for himself. If one trusts his evidence, and he seems to have been a very accurate witness, My Lord's Garden was taking shape over the winter of 1663–64.

Soon after, Howard left Norwich and Tuke headed for Paris, where he was in charge of Howard's sons. But a few years later the prospect of a visit from Charles II brought Howard's attention back to East Anglia and his property in Norwich. In autumn 1671, the court extended the annual visit to Newmarket with a detour to Lord Arlington's Euston Hall, Suffolk (where Evelyn was also giving advice on planting), as well as

Yarmouth and Norwich. The king spent just one night in Norwich, but the queen extended her stay in the Duke's Palace to three nights, before returning to Euston. Was she, perhaps, rowed along the Wensum to the riverside pleasure garden? Evelyn, himself, thanks to Arlington's patronage, was also caught up in the royal progress and, at Howard's invitation, was able finally to visit Norwich.

On their journey Evelyn learned from Howard that he was hoping his son might marry one of the king's daughters (an ambition he did not achieve). He also confessed to his dalliance with Jane Bickerton, an actress, of whom even the king disapproved. When they reached the Duke's Palace, it was still hardly visible beneath the recent hasty conversion of the house and outbuildings to accommodate no less than three royal courts, those of the king, the queen and the Duke of York: the tennis court became the kitchen; the bowling alley the dining rooms. Now Howard 'advised with me, concerning a plot to rebuild his house, having already as he said erected a front next the streete, and a left wing, and now resolving to set up another wing and pavilion next the garden'. Nevertheless, Evelyn thought the Duke's Palace a 'wretched building, & that part of it, newly built of brick, is very ill understood ... it had ben much better to have demolish'd all'.

Evelyn, who (a true Vitruvian) always emphasized the crucial importance of a carefully chosen site, suggested an entirely different location, nearer the castle. Howard took no notice, although he rebuilt it at the cost of some £30,000 (oddly the same figure given for Berkeley House, London), nor is there any reference to My Lord's Garden. It is not known whether Evelyn saw the garden he had laid out on paper: the lack of comment may have been more a reflection of Evelyn's growing distaste for Howard. By the 1690s, in his additions to William Camden's *Britannia*, Evelyn no longer even claimed the remodelling of the gardens at Albury for himself. But in 1671, Evelyn's stay

The Duke's Palace fronting onto Charing Cross in Norwich. It was rebuilt by the 6th duke in 1672, possibly to the design of Sir Robert Hooke. A cour d'honneur is accessed through an arched gateway set into a screen abutting the street. Four columns on its main façade support a large pediment with a small central cupola above. Hipped roofs and pedimented dormer windows are visible on the side wings. Etching by J. Basire, 1710, after John Kirkpatrick.

The river frontage of the Duke's Palace, enriched with alcoves, pediments, ornate carving, cupola and no less than forty-one windows. Before it lay an enclosed garden of grass plats leading down to the river and to boats to reach the duke's new garden downstream. Despite its external splendour, internally the remodelled palace was never finished. The building was demolished in 1711 by the 8th duke, Thomas Howard, except for the domestic wing. Etching by J. Basire, 1710, after John Kirkpatrick.

in Norwich was made memorable by the pleasure of finally meeting the newly knighted Sir Thomas Browne, one of those few people to whom, many years before, he sent the outline of his ambitious manuscript, the *Elysium Britannicum* – still unpublished in 1671.

As the years passed, Henry Howard came to epitomize for Evelyn the decadence and untrustworthiness of those in court circles. Tuke, knighted in 1664, had died in 1674, and despite her pleas for help, Howard gave Lady Tuke and her three young children no financial help whatsoever. When in the mid-1680s Evelyn visited the 6th

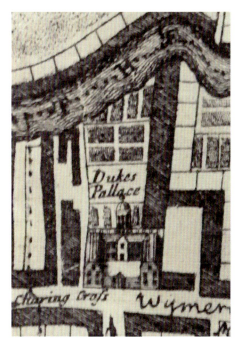 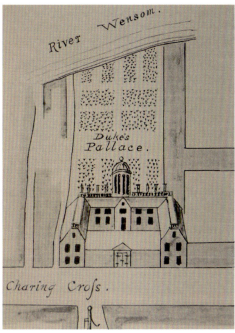

1696 map by Thomas Clere, with a clarified sketch taken from the map. Despite the small scale of the depiction, the Duke's Palace is remarkably faithfully portrayed. Perhaps the layout of the garden stretching down to the River Wensum, can be relied on too? Four rectangular grass plats set in gravel led from the palace, next lay an open area of gravel; or was this a convenient space for Clere to label this site? Beyond, set in gravel with cross paths, lay four rectangular beds of grass, and beyond this a triangular termination of the garden as it followed the curve of the river, containing four elongated beds of varying length. St Andrew's multi-storey car park and the apartment blocks of Duke's Palace Wharf now lie over much of this site.

Duke's house at Weybridge, Surrey (originally belonging to his mistress, Jane Bickerton, now the Duchess of Norfolk), he commented that 'never in my daies had I seene such expense to so small purpose'. By then the Howard estates were in flux. There was a crumbling (though almost new) palace in Norwich; Albury had been sold in 1680; and Arundel House, the rambling townhouse on the Strand, London, demolished. For all the expenditure the duke had lavished on rebuilding his Norwich mansion, in 1681 Thomas Baskerville described it, though 'sumptuous', to be sited in a 'dunghole place'. The topographer found the Duke's Palace with 'little room for gardens and is pent upon all sides both on this and the other side of the river with tradesmen and dyers's houses who foul the water by their constant washing and cleaning of their cloth'.

He was, perhaps, all the more shocked by the flawed grandeur of the Norfolk family house after his pleasant impression of the 'fair garden' to which the boatman had first rowed them. It had 'handsome stairs leading to the water by which we ascended into the garden and saw a good bowling-green, and many fine walks'. On arrival, they were plied with 'good liquors and fruits' by the gardener, who was evidently always ready

ABOVE Henry Howard, 6th Duke of Norfolk (1628–1684) aged 49, by Sir Peter Lely. He succeeded to the title after his insane unmarried brother's death in 1677, when this portrait to mark Henry's accession was painted.

LEFT The remaining wing of the Duke's Palace in use as a workhouse. The hipped roof has been replaced with a pitched one studded with a double row of dormers, maximizing the attic space. In 1805 around 550 people were living there in appalling, degrading conditions. It was mostly demolished a year later.

Howard House, in King Street, Norwich, photographed in 1934. Built for Henry Howard, in 1664, as a 'Summerhouse' it stands at the north-west corner of the site, on its highest point, commanding a view across the garden to the river. It could provide shelter and may have been used as a banqueting house. The building underwent alterations in the 18th century, and after a period of neglect was restored in 2017.

to welcome admiring guests. Despite his many distractions, Howard apparently still retained and maintained the mature and congenial pleasure garden on the Wensum in fine style. In Baskerville's opinion, it was there that the Duke's Palace should have been rebuilt since 'From this garden for the rest of the city down stream, and about a furlong up Stream, there are no houses built on the other side the river to hinder that prospect into the country'.

Eventually – and inevitably – the extravagantly rebuilt Duke's Palace was demolished in 1711–14, its materials reclaimed and sold for a fraction of the original cost. Only Duke Street, a nineteenth-century route to a new bridge, commemorated Howard's costly folly. My Lord's Garden, which seems on the available scant evidence to have been largely Evelyn's achievement, long outlasted the palace. The strength of Evelyn's disapproval of the 6th Duke of Norfolk led him to disown his connections with the family and his role there probably remained unknown beyond Howard's immediate circle. Francis Blomefield recorded the garden in the 1730s as 'some time sold', but its high stone walls (probably remnants of the friary) with 2 acres of orchards and gardens were still intact.

The slender evidence for the garden and the fact that Evelyn does not mention it more

Part of the site of My Lord's Garden, 2016, cleared for redevelopment. Howard House, under a protective cover, awaiting its restoration, is at the bottom of the site on King Street. The bend in the River Wensum is the probable site of the landing stage and steps leading up into the garden. Until the Dissolution, this had been the site of an Augustinian friary, and after the duke's withdrawal from Norwich, it became a successful pleasure garden. From 1848 to 1961 it was the site of Morgan's brewery, later Bullards and Stewart & Patteson, finally taken over by Watney Mann. Brewing ceased here in 1986 and the buildings were demolished three years later. In the seventeenth century this was a particularly beautiful site, elevated to the rear and looking out across the river to meadows, the hills of Mousehold Heath, to woods and the Yare valley stretching away to the east. The potential for this to have become a twenty-first-century inner city green open space is now lost forever.

Part of the site of My Lord's Garden under redevelopment, 2019. King Street runs beside it on the left. Howard House stands at the top of the site with underground parking constructed in front of it. To the right, the riverside area of the site is already developed with multi-storey apartments and an eight-storey tower.

do not detract from the importance of this lost city garden. It is known that he considered it with care and was even growing impatient for work to begin on his scheme, surely the garden that was being laid out within weeks of Howard's request? Evelyn's diary (written up long after the event) can be misleading, and many of the people and places which figure in Evelyn's correspondence and papers pass without mention in its pages. Equally as men revealed themselves, Evelyn tended to change his view of them and their works (e.g. his judgement on Clarendon House, London, in the light of the earl's fall from power) and to distance himself from men whose reputations had become unsavoury – from Charles II to the 6th Duke of Norfolk. It is odd, but not uncharacteristic, that he did not record visiting My Lord's Garden when he visited Norwich in 1671 – it may have slipped his mind or been a deliberate omission. The correspondence with Tuke, Edward Browne's note of the new garden, and finally Baskerville's description are conclusive that Evelyn's garden, designed on the basis of a plan of the site, was the very one that was delighting visitors to Norwich many years later.

The tower of the St Anne's Quarter residential development stands on the lower south-eastern corner of My Lord's Garden site. It was probably here, at the bend in the river, that the 'handsome stairs' (Thomas Baskerville) led up from the water.

4

The Eastern Arboretum

Scilla Latham

The Eastern Arboretum, written by James Grigor and published in 1841, appeared in a period of ever-increasing availability of affordable books, part-works and magazines dedicated to bringing all aspects of gardening to a wider public. Whilst the idea of a paper arboretum is generally credited to John Claudius Loudon (1783–1843) with the publication of the *Arboretum et Fruticetum Britannicum* in 1838, which Grigor acknowledges as the great book of knowledge on this subject, however this was not the first book of this sort. In 1830, Jacob George Strutt published *Sylva Britannica; or Portraits of Trees, distinguished for their Antiquity, Magnitude or Beauty*. Published through subscriptions, the descriptions and engravings of the trees established a model for similar later books. It is interesting how many trees across Britain described in all of these books have names such as the 'Winfarthing Oak' or the 'King of Sprowston', which underline their enduring significance to their communities.

The aspiration to spread both scientific knowledge and practical advice on horticulture can be related to the growth of museums, galleries, zoological gardens and public parks which were all intended to educate and inform the masses. *The Gardeners Magazine* first published in 1826 by Loudon, was intended to disseminate new and improved information on all topics connected with horticulture and to raise the intellect and character of those engaged in this art. During the 1830s a number of other monthly gardening magazines were set up to challenge the position of *The Gardeners Magazine*: the most successful being the weekly *Gardeners Chronicle* first published in 1841 by Joseph Paxton. These publications brought printed advice and extended the availability

Willow – Sandlings Ferry (Pull's Ferry) Norwich
'Strange though it may appear, we think it probable that in the east of England few people have seen a full-grown willow-tree. It is generally so pollarded and metamorphosed, that the form and expression of the natural object cannot be recognized. This specimen, so far, forms an exception ...' — 'We confess we care little about the species in general: ... the purposes to which its timber is applicable are very trifling.' — 'The triumphs which it achieves over what is generally termed bog land, are, we believe, accomplished by no other ligneous object – a feature in its character which, after all, places it very high.' — 'We observed a variety of it (*Salix a. caerulea*) growing round the lake at Felthorpe park, which fully establishes its claim to a place in the most polished landscape.'

THE EASTERN ARBORETUM,

OR

REGISTER OF REMARKABLE TREES,

Seats, Gardens, &c.

IN THE COUNTY OF NORFOLK.

WITH POPULAR DELINEATIONS OF THE BRITISH SYLVA.

BY JAMES GRIGOR.

Illustrated by Fifty Drawings of Trees,
ETCHED ON COPPER BY H. NINHAM.

London:
LONGMAN, BROWN, GREEN, AND LONGMANS.
JOHN STACY, NORWICH.

MDCCCXLI.

The title page of *The Eastern Arboretum*.

of plants to an ever-wider audience and frequently carried advertisements for stock available from Grigor's own nursery in Norwich. Both of these publications carried complimentary reviews of *The Eastern Arboretum*. In particular, the opening words of the first review in *The Gardeners Magazine* suggest that Loudon both knew and admired Grigor: 'We have great pleasure in noticing this publication; partly from our regard for the author, and partly from the genuine love which he exhibits for a subject to which we ourselves are so much attached.'

In June 1840 the first of fifteen instalments of *The Eastern Arboretum or Rural Register of all the remarkable Trees, Seats Gardens etc. in the County of Norfolk* by James Grigor (1810–1848) was published. Evidently the part-work was a success and it was published as a single volume in the autumn of 1841 in London and Norwich. In the Introduction Grigor declares his intention 'to notice all the trees of Norfolk that are interesting on account of their age, size, rarity, historical association, or in any other respect; and, in order to make it complete as a book of reference, we shall annex directions as to sowing, transplanting, pruning, and felling all our English timber trees; the whole forming a popular dictionary of everything relating to this interesting department of Natural History'. In fact, the book does even more than this, since it combines the role of a gazetteer of Norfolk trees with a survey of the seats and gardens belonging to the great and good of Norfolk, descriptions of many towns and villages across the county, and fourteen chapters on the history and management of individual species of trees. The book is illustrated with etchings of portraits of fifty of the trees by Henry Ninham (1793–1874), a member of the Norwich school of artists who is possibly best known for his watercolours of views of Norwich.

In the Introductory Remarks, Grigor justifies his humble pretensions on the subject by informing the reader that 'out of love to the science, we have devoted an apprenticeship of about twenty years to practical botanical pursuits'. Where he had served this apprenticeship is hard to identify with any certainty but since he came from a family of Scottish nurserymen who were based in Forres, Morayshire this is where he almost certainly learnt his trade before moving south. His elder brother John (born c.1806), took on the family nursery and became an acknowledged authority on the cultivation of trees. Loudon refers to Grigor's brothers, the highly respected nurserymen of Elgin and Forres, in his review of the third part of *The Eastern Arboretum* in December 1840. It is possible that James Grigor worked for one of the London nurseries before moving to Norwich since throughout the book he makes detailed observations about specific areas of London and trees growing in the London area, which appear to be based on first-hand knowledge. He remarks that 'some of those delightful scenes met with about the great metropolis of England, especially in the neighbourhood of Kensington and Bayswater, Notting Hill and Camden Hill are very like Thorpe; the villas are of the same style, and the inhabitants of a similar grade – men generally of refined taste, who carry their wealth out of the city with them, and beat it out at leisure ... in the shape of gardens, trees and flowers ...'

Little is known of James Grigor or why he settled in Norwich. His reference to a tree 'about ten years old of our own planting, which is big enough to attract the attention of magpies, and if it continue to thrive as it has hitherto done, we do not despair of soon seeing some of the loftier-minded fowls of the air lodging among its branches', suggests that he had been living in Norwich for at least that long by 1840, but equally it may have been planted elsewhere. Census records of his brother John record that he was born in Elgin and it is likely that James was also born there. There is no definite census record for James, which suggests that in April 1841 he may have been abroad. In early 1843 he married Matilda Cattermoul (c.1824–1890), the daughter of a prosperous Norwich builder; in the same year he took out a life insurance policy of £100 with Norwich Union, no doubt a reflection on the responsibilities of married life. They lived in Mount Pleasant Lane, Heigham not far from his nursery on Newmarket Road.

From the numerous advertisements for plants in his nursery it is possible to get some idea of the extent of his business. He refers to his agent in the Himalayas who sent him seed of rare species of trees, which were raised at his nursery and would have fed the demand for new species to be planted in fashionable arboretums. He supplied young trees in huge quantities for country estates requiring plantations or for windbreaks in coastal areas and gave copious advice on their planting. As well as the Norfolk resorts of Hunstanton and Yarmouth, he also lists Harwich, Aberystwyth, Brighton and Bridlington as places where his advice on seaside planting has been followed with success. The scale of the business suggests he was doing well and had he lived longer, would no doubt have been better known today. At least one advertisement regretfully announced that the potted-up stock of specific species of trees of a particular size had sold out, but they would soon have more potted and ready for sale. Simply managing healthy stock and the dispatch of sales of tens of thousands of young trees and other plants across the country must have required a good business mind in addition to his undoubted horticultural skill.

In the Preface of *The Eastern Arboretum*, Grigor explains the origin of his book and reflects on some of its shortcomings, which become more obvious as the book progresses. We are told it was undertaken chiefly as an amusement, and that it has been hurriedly written in the hours of relaxation from business, which suggests that it developed from a journal of observations made whilst visiting clients and passing through towns and villages on the way. The part-work title described it as a register of all the remarkable trees, seats, gardens etc. in the County of Norfolk, whereas the book title more realistically omits the 'all'. He welcomed suggestions of trees to be included in a possible future volume: 'All notices of remarkable trees within the county, not here recorded, will be most thankfully received, as heretofore, at our publisher's in Norwich.' His acknowledgment of the contributions of 'the few friends who have so kindly furnished us with dimensions of trees in various parts of the county' makes

Anthony Sandys' portrait of Henry Ninham (1796–1874) whose fifty etchings illustrate *The Eastern Arboretum*. Unfortunately, there are no known images of James Grigor himself. Ninham was a painter in oil and watercolour, an etcher and a lithographer. He trained under his father John and was taught by John Crome. His subject matter was mainly landscape and antiquities, particularly of Norwich. He published his *Views of the Ancient City Gates of Norwich* as they appeared in 1722 after sketches by Kirkpatrick, in 1864.

it clear that the huge number of statistics of tree sizes were not solely Grigor's own efforts. The acknowledgement of the pre-eminent botanist and horticulturalist John Lindley that, 'few artists have been so successful as Mr Ninham in representing the characteristic features of trees' may have been included in the Preface as a wider recommendation of the authority of the book. The illustrations are modelled on those in Loudon's *Arboretum Britannicum*, very often including a human figure, or cows to provide an idea of the scale.

The structure of the book reflects the piecemeal nature of its origins, having no contents page and the list of etchings in the first edition appears to have been included by accident, since it is sub-titled 'Directions to the binder'. The complicated balance between manual of arboriculture and topographical guide is anticipated in the Introduction: 'In order to break the monotony of a continued treatise on the same class of subjects, the reader will be occasionally relieved by general descriptions of such gentleman's seats as are considered worthy of particular notice.' Not content

LIST OF ETCHINGS.

DIRECTIONS TO THE BINDER.

ENGLISH ELM	St. Peter at Hungate, Norwich	to face p. 16
POPLAR	St. Faith's Lane	18
OAK LEAVES & FRUIT		23
POPLAR	Chapel-field	24
SNOWDROP-TREE	Town Close	28
ENGLISH ELM	Cossey Park	34
SILVER FIR	Taverham Park	58
SCOTCH PINE	Keswick	67
POPLAR	Holkham Park	74
BEECH-TREE	Stratton Strawless Park	86
OAK	Blickling Park	100
CEDAR	Stratton Strawless Park	104
BEECH-TREE	Wolterton Park	113
ARAUCARIA	ditto	114
LIME-TREE	Barningham Park	121
SWEET CHESTNUT	Felbrigg Park	124
SILVER FIRS	ditto	124
WALNUT	ditto	125
YEW-TREE	Gunton Park	132
SCOTCH PINE	Horsford	136
ELMS	Haverland Park	151
ALDER	ditto	152
OAK	Thorpe Market	157
BEECH	Sall Park	159
SWEET CHESTNUT	Heydon Park	161
OAK	ditto	161
ASH-TREE	Scottow Park	164
DITTO	Hillington Park	180
LIME	Sprowston	200
SCOTCH PINE	Wroxham	213
WEEPING ASH	Pottergate Street House, Norwich	220
CEDAR OF LEBANON	Beeston Park	226
DECIDUOUS CYPRESS	ditto	226
SILVER FIR	Honing	229
WILLOW	Sandlin's Ferry, Norwich	239

with restricting himself to this mission, Grigor devotes an early chapter to making the case for a new public botanical garden to be laid out in Chapelfield, Norwich. 'Such gardens are now being established all over England; ... at present Norwich possesses nothing of this description; for Chapel-field, from its being so much the resort of loose and idle boys, ... seems to be in a great measure deserted by the respectable citizens ... To have trees and flowers collected together, and planted for the purposes of being seen and studied, is to many people as interesting as a collection of beasts, or birds, or insects; so apart from its advantages to the mere arboriculturist and florist, a Botanical Garden would facilitate the important researches of the scientific naturalist, and store the minds of youth with pleasing and interesting associations; it would engender better propensities amongst the community in general, and lead them to leave off their unprofitable and useless habits.' References to his promotion for provision of allotments for rural populations, some of whom at this time were frequently living in conditions of severe deprivation, provide evidence of his concern for improving the lot of society as a whole.

Before setting out to describe trees, seats, towns and villages across Norfolk, Grigor dedicates the first topographical chapters to the city of Norwich and its environs. From the start Grigor not only identifies the locations but also the owner's names, providing an interesting additional social commentary to his tours. The first tree to be described is a hawthorn (later identified as his favourite species) in the churchyard of St Michael's at Thorn, Ber Street; followed by a list of trees in a number of other Norwich churchyards – this sparks a typical burst of Grigor prose. 'There is something far from being unpleasant in the idea, that, after we shall have put off this mortal coil, we shall be laid down to sleep through the last days of the world beside those trees, which will be our companions in all weathers, and which will in spring-time gladden the spot by their blossoming, and court for us the balmiest breezes, and allure the birds to sing over our sepulchres, which our friends will often revisit for our sakes.'

The first seat he describes is 'Cossey' Park where he is moved to declare: 'We thank God for his trees, and the green sod he has laid out around them! They are his gifts; and we look upon them as so many invitations to us to be good men!' From here he continued along the road to Dereham, where he devotes most of his energies to a eulogy to the poet William Cowper who is buried there. There follows a leisurely tour around estates great and small across much of Norfolk; as the book progresses the style of the topographical descriptions occasionally varies from one place to another which may indicate that some reports were sent to him rather than being made from his own observations. Grigor himself could see little point in economy of words, his style closely resembling that of Humphry Repton with passages of unctuous praise, which he applied equally to the great estates and beautifully kept village gardens. At Stratton Strawless, the seat of Robert Marsham, son of the great eighteenth-century tree planter of the same name, Grigor devotes a page and a half to the almost mythic wonders

Cedar of Lebanon, Stratton Strawless

'This tree has in all ages been reckoned one of the princes of the vegetable kingdom.' — 'But in order to fully satisfy those who find it hard to reconcile the language of Scripture with the dwarfish specimens of the cedar they have met with, we annex an etching of a tree of this species, growing at the seat of Robert Marsham, Esq., at Stratton Strawless, in this county, which sufficiently illustrates the character of it being tall and towering; ... planted when one foot and a half high in 1747, now, in some respects at least, the handsomest tree of the species in the kingdom. Its stem is forty-four feet in height, free from branches, and measures at two yards from the ground, twelve feet two inches in circumference. The height of this tree, which contains ten loads of timber, is seventy-nine feet.' — ' ... let us remember, that though this is a noble upright object, it bears but a remote comparison to those which grew on the elevated ridges of Syria in the days of Solomon.'

of the place before actually mentioning a single tree. 'It is with a delightful feeling that we have to notice this eminent and interesting seat. It is one of nature's ancient dwelling-places, where she has long worn the garbs of settled majesty; a residence, too, associated with men who have been for successive generations distinguished for planting and general improvement. Comparatively speaking; such names are but few in our country; but when found they fail not to awaken in the mind a high admiration of their character. They are linked to deeds which the multitude perhaps care little for, but which the wise and good appreciate as dispensing blessings of incalculable value ...' The great cedar of Lebanon at Stratton Strawless that illustrates the chapter on this species is one of the few trees described by Grigor that survives into the 21st century; today its trunk is entangled in a thicket of laurel and only the top of the tree can be seen from across open fields. In the village of Northwold, Grigor praises the garden of the Revd C. M. R. Norman: 'It is all that can be wished for. It excels not only in one or two respects, but in all: for it is equally perfect whether we regard its flowers, its shrubs, or the grandeur of some of its arborescent objects. Too much praise cannot be bestowed upon the gardener ...'

He could also be an unflinching critic of decaying estates as in the case of Salle Park, the seat of Sir Richard Paul Jodrell, Bart: 'We regret that a seat possessing so many advantages, – in the midst, too, of a country which is rich almost beyond parallel, – should be allowed to wear so little that is interesting in garden scenery. We know nothing of the circumstances connected with it, but the entire place, and especially the scene in the immediate neighbourhood of the hall, looks as if the proprietor had been long from home, and as if the owl and the bittern would soon possess it.'

---

40   THE EASTERN ARBORETUM.

OUR TREES.—No. I.

THE BRITISH OAK—*Quercus Robur*.

Do you see that gnarled and scraggy-headed tree, that watches yonder roofless pile so faithfully—embracing its mouldering turrets—lending a solemnity, as it were, to a scene naturally grave? It is verily of the olden time, you will say. Aye, it was there when you were an infant: when your father's father was a youngster, it was reckoned old-fashioned and antique, and nobody knew then " aught of its age "—it was " old a century before *their* day." Well may

The fourteen chapters headed 'Our Trees' that are interspersed between the topographical descriptions, fit awkwardly into the structure of the book. Written in a more bookish style than the rest of the text, they generally include more general information about the origins of the trees and their place in biblical and classical writing than practical advice on the cultivation and maintenance of the tree. The British oak is

Oak – Thorpe (Market)
'We never saw a finer tree, and we have seen all the fine trees around London, where they are really prized and preserved ... ' — ' ... We have alluded to the esteem in which it is held by those who live in the neighbourhood. Common people, who never talk about trees in general, have many things to say regarding this object – a proof of its unusual attractions. Many have come from a great distance for the purpose of seeing it, and all have expressed their astonishment of its noble structure. So full of grandeur is it, that by real lovers of trees long and perilous journeys might be undertaken for the sole purpose of viewing it, without the slightest risk of their being attended by any disappointment!'

the first tree to be discussed in detail and with it Grigor sets the tone for the chapters on trees. 'As a specimen of vegetable beauty, this imperial plant is perhaps the grandest that rises in our county ... We venerate it ... By its noble outline and bearing it is universally recognized as the monarch of the woods, holding sway over all the others, which, compared to it, appear to be but the saplings of yesterday.' What is interesting in this chapter is that Grigor fails to mention any oaks in Norfolk, nor is there an illustration of one, although in the course of the book it is the most illustrated and one of the most frequently admired trees in the topographical sections. The finest oak tree illustrated is the Thorpe Oak, so special that Grigor devoted an entire chapter to it.

The chapter on the yew, which Grigor describes as a tree of the night rather than of the day, reflects on the changing tastes in gardening: 'During the seventeenth century, this tree was generally used in curious gardens for being clipped into globular and conical figures, and in some instances, into that of beasts and birds; but this questionable taste has in a great measure subsided, and the practice is now seldom adopted in the gardens of our nobility and gentry.'

Grigor's evident fondness for hawthorns is demonstrated by them being singled out wherever he could. In the 'Hawthorn' chapter, Grigor devotes seven pages to the history, traditions and cultivation of the tree. He states that he spent a whole day at Hethel collecting anecdotes about the age and traditions associated to the Hethel Thorn, his 'text tree', which then had a girth of fourteen feet three inches and the circumference of its spread was thirty-one yards. The double size etching of it that illustrates the chapter is one of only two etchings which are inscribed 'Drawn and etched by H. Ninham', the other being the Winfarthing Oak, which may indicate they were also available as individual pictures. Undoubtedly one of the most venerable of trees in Grigor's time, it continues to survive over 160 years later, fenced off from the attentions of cattle in a quiet field.

As well as remarking on trees, Grigor frequently comments on flower and kitchen gardens of the places he described. On occasion a particularly rare or recently introduced plant caught his eye and some of these descriptions give an insight into the early cultivation of what are now common garden plants. The collection of unusual plants in the gardens of Middleton Hall encouraged him to be even more extravagant in his praise than usual: 'We are almost tempted to say that there are few spots on the earth's surface, at least few under an English sky, more richly decorated with all that is elegant amongst floricultural objects.' He recorded a *Garrya elliptica* growing there that was already 4 feet tall which he considered to be as tall as any in England. He noted that *Garrya elliptica* had been discovered by Douglas in 1828 and flowered for the first time in the Horticultural Society's gardens in 1834, and that Lindley considered it was probably the greatest botanical curiosity sent home by Douglas.

Apart from running his nursery in Norwich, Grigor also wrote essays and articles on a wide range of related subjects that were published in gardening magazines and

The Hethel Thorn
'*Crataegus oxyacantha* – Norfolk is rich beyond parallel in these objects ... by far the greatest interest in this part of the country ... is the one known by the title of the "Hethel thorn" or, as it is termed in the immediate neighbourhood, "the Witch of Hethel".' — ' ... though it still greets the May-morn with its profuse and odoriferous blossoms, and bears a plentiful crop of fruit like the others, it is invested with a character differing materially from that of the species in general, arising from its extreme old age. In looking upon it, one would suppose it had been here for thousands of years; and indeed, if the common tradition of the place is to be relied upon, it must be acknowledged to be in a high degree patriarchal.' — ' ... its very appearance justifies us in allotting to it an age of more than five centuries ...' — 'It is covered all over with lichen, and crowned with mistletoe, adding still more to the effect which age confers upon such objects.' — 'The boys of the village, too, are in the habit of going a-Maying to the "old thorn," and robbing it of large bunches of spray every season, a practice which as to this particular tree should be at once discontinued.'
BELOW The Hethel Thorn today.

agricultural society journals in England and Scotland. He is frequently described as a land improver. His prize-winning essays on tree planting, coastal screening and even an essay on effective methods of fencing in Nottinghamshire – which was published in the Journal of the Royal Agricultural Society – would have reached a wide audience and indicate that the nursery was just part of his business. His advertisements increasingly refer to great estates, including Holkham and Welbeck, where he had given advice and supplied trees: a glowing reference from the Duke of Newcastle in relation to Clumber appears in several of them. His lengthy detailed essay entitled 'Report on the Trimmingham and Runton Plantations in the County of Norfolk belonging to Sir Edward North Buxton Baronet' won a gold medal from the Highland Agricultural Society of Scotland and was published in the Society's Transactions in January 1847.

A tantalizingly short fragment of a letter to Grigor from William Wordsworth, printed in one his advertisements in 1844, praises what was then called the 'Highland Pine' and demonstrates their mutual love of the species. The letter appears to acknowledge the safe receipt of a drawing of a Pine tree and possibly Grigor had visited Wordsworth at his house in the Lake District. 'Now that we are on the subject of trees, I may mention what I have very likely told you in some of my previous letters, that I prefer the Highland Pine to all other trees except the Oak, taking into consideration its beauty in winter, and by moonlight, and in the evening. December 7th 1844. Rydall Mount.'

James Grigor died young, aged thirty-eight, from tuberculosis on 22 April 1848. Two obituaries in Scottish newspapers indicate that although he had set up business in Norwich, his ties to the country of his birth remained strong throughout his life. His final weeks must have been fraught with worry as the last published references to his business are two advertisements in *The Gardeners Chronicle* in March 1848 which state that 'At an immense sacrifice in price ... in consequence of work of re-development of a strip of his nursery he was forced to have a sale of stock'. He is buried in the Rosary Cemetery, Norwich: a private burial ground founded in 1843 where many of the large non-conformist population of the city were buried. His widow and in-laws were also later buried in the same plot.

Grigor's will, dated 18 April 1847, provides detailed instructions relating to his published works and for the care of his stock until the disposal of his nursery business, which he instructed should either be sold by private tender as a business, or failing that, the stock should be sold by public auction. Advertisements for the auction of stock appeared both in the *Gardeners Chronicle* and the *Norfolk Chronicle & Norwich Gazette* in November 1848. The scale of his business can be assessed from the numbers of plants indicated in the advertisements – well over 500,000 trees and several thousand shrubs, roses and soft fruit bushes, as well as a quantity of seed potatoes most of a very rare sort... amongst them 'Grigor's Prolific'. The auction was held on the site of his business on the Ground, Town Close, Newmarket Road – this can be identified with Townclose Nurseries which is marked on the 1st Edition Ordnance Survey map of 1883.

The Eastern Arboretum has long languished in the background of mid nineteenth-century horticultural literature and for many, trying to read it may convince them that this is its proper place. However, as a historical document of Norfolk in the 1840s, it provides a fascinating insight into a different world: not only giving a record of trees and gardens but also the houses they surrounded and the people who lived and worked

The Winfarthing Oak
'This remarkable tree, so long the pride of the county, ... is invested with all the characteristics of a grand old ruin. Its size is extraordinary; and, perhaps, in examining it, the only feature which in a painter's eye would be found deficient, is the rough and gnarled workings so common in the oak tribe.' — 'Notwithstanding the loss of all its boughs, its head, which is splintered in several parts, is highly picturesque; and at eventide its singular frame is said to be somewhat startling. The villagers, naturally enough, speculate as to the noble sight it must have presented in the days of its prosperity ... ' — 'Now, an inscription on a brass plate attached to the Winfarthing oak gives us the following as to its dimensions: – "This oak, in circumference, at the extremity of the roots, is seventy feet; in the middle forty feet, 1820."' — 'Now, I see no reason, if the size of the rind is to be of any criterion of age, why the Winfarthing should not ... be upwards of 700 years old at the Conquest; an age which might very well justify its then title of the "Great Oak". It is now a mere shell – a mighty ruin, bleached to a snowy white; but it is magnificent in its decay ... ' — 'A correct idea of this tree will be had from the subjoined etching of Mr. Ninham; but we should advise all those who are anxious to see the original, to lose not many seasons before repairing to it.'

there. This is particularly true in the final chapter a 'Miscellaneous Summary of Trees, Gardens etc.' which gives wonderful accounts of small towns and villages describing the gardens and praising the owners and, in many places, their gardeners by name.

The past is a foreign country but Grigor's words bring long forgotten people back to life, on account of their horticultural skill or even simply because a fine tree grew within their grounds. James Grigor remains a shadowy figure, but by writing this unusual book he carved a small place for himself in the annals of nineteenth-century horticulture.

Spanish Chestnut – Heydon
'The trees here are remarkable for their picturesque beauty. Several specimens of the sweet chestnut-tree, growing beside a small lake on the north side of the building, with "great rugged horns", are particularly fine.' — 'They form the remains of an avenue which once stood here and are equally interesting with those of Hevingham. There are likewise some magnificent specimens here of that tree which, of any great size, is so scarce in Norfolk – the ash ... ' — 'The visitor of Heydon will at once be impressed, we think, with the peculiar feature by which we have considered it is so much characterized – that of pensive grandeur.' — 'The entire place is a testimony of the wonderful effect which trees produce on a surface like that of Norfolk, which in general is naturally uninteresting.'

Poplar (Lombardy Poplar) – St Faiths Lane

' ... there is a host of writers who condemn this tree.' — 'Muskau says "it is too fluttering." Cobbett represents it as "a great ugly tree;" and Sang, in similar language, says it is ugly. We have little hesitation in stating, that what is here said as to the tree, should have been applied to the disposition or mode in which it is planted in the landscape, which in many instances, is tiresome and uninteresting.' — 'To talk of the ugliness and uninteresting nature of the poplar is absurd.' — 'Its whole life may be said to be a hurried effort to add dignity to the spot where it rises; for no tree grows faster, and few attain to a more lofty stature.' — 'The proudest works of men's hands are in imitation of it; and we may refer to the spire of our Norwich cathedral, and the cathedrals of England generally, for examples, on a magnificent scale, of the outlines borrowed from this beautiful tree.'

Weeping Ash – Pottergate Street House

'Norfolk ranks very high for specimens of the weeping plant (*F. excelsior pendula*), a variety of the common tree … ' — 'The most of our villages abound with specimens of it, which form delightful arbours in the summer months. At the residence of C. Turner, Esq. Pottergate Street, Norwich, there is an elegant tree of it growing on the lawn in front of the house … For the richness of its verdure and the regularity of its spray, which falls gracefully around it on all sides, we fancy it is not surpassed in the county.' — 'The timber of the ash is beyond all comparison applied to a greater number of purposes than that of any other tree … there is scarcely any implement in the farm-yard, but is more or less of ash … it is superior to oak in enduring "the unquietness of ponderous rolling stones," and those sudden concussions which take place in cider-mills, flour-mills, and other engines.' — 'a tree which has divided the opinions, perhaps, of more writers than any other similar object; for whilst some have gravely told us that it should never be allowed to appear near to a dwelling, others have discerned in it a very graceful character, and have termed it the "Venus of the Woods."'

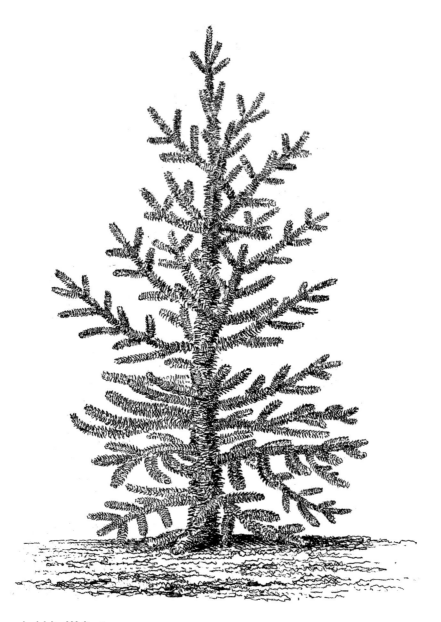

Aracauria (sic) – Wolterton

'It is well known that the surface of this estate, as well as the generality of those in Norfolk, is but very little varied; and that its charming and diversified appearance arises entirely from the elements of wood and water. The great use of trees especially, is here strikingly illustrated, maintaining, over scenes naturally deficient in expression, a very interesting picture.' — 'The present noble proprietor, whose taste for trees is well known, has distinguished this place above many others, by forming in it collections of trees and shrubs belonging to the genera *Pinus*, *Abies*, *Cupressus*, *Schubertia*, *Araucaria*, *Erica*, *Crataegus*, and *Ilex*. The collection in the Pinetum is very complete, including specimens of the Deodora pine nine feet in height. The *Araucaria excelsea*, or Brazilian pine, as it is called here, rises to the height of nine feet nine inches, and bears the rigour of winter with a very slight protection.'

Scotch Pine – Horsford

'We like the appearance of this seat (Horsford Hall) beyond many. The trees of the park, and those of the neighbourhood of the church, of the elm tribe, sufficiently testify the venerable character of the place, whilst their dense and lofty growth throws an air of stillness and tranquillity about it, which, to the contemplative mind, constitute one of the greatest charms of rural life.' — 'Those of most noted character here are Scotch pine (*Pinus Sylvestris*), some of which are of exceeding beauty.' — 'The specimen represented in the etching ... may be said to possess the excellence of its kindred on the northern hills – in every respect a fit accompaniment to the bold scenes which it was originally formed to adorn. We are sometimes surprised to find this tree accommodating itself so well to the flat and fertile plains of Norfolk; for, in its native habitations it has to seek its support amid rocks and ravines, and in some instances of sandstone; situations in which it attains to its greatest beauty.'

Weeping Ash – North Runcton

'North Runcton, the seat of Daniel Gurney, Esq., is one of those exceedingly elegant places, which, although not abounding in large trees, is remarkable for the neatness and propriety which prevail throughout. The humble green-sward, so justly the pride of England, is here in its perfection, and its embellishments are scattered with a judicious hand. In short, amidst the various materials which compose this picture, the eye of taste is at once reconciled; a thing which we can but rarely state with regard to our county seats.' — 'The finest tree here is a weeping ash, which is a tree indeed. It is unquestionably the finest specimen of its kind we ever beheld; ... the circumference of the space over which the branches extend is over eighteen yards.'

Lime – Sprowston

' ... close by the road to Rackheath, is an extraordinary lime-tree (*Tilia Europaea*) which has attracted the attention of many a spectator.' — 'Allowing a few years for its age when planted, this lime may now be reckoned two hundred years old. Near the ground, the circumference of its trunk is twenty-four feet seven inches; its extreme height is sixty-six feet. The inhabitants of Sprowston called it "The Seven Brothers," from being divided into this number of large limbs ... '

Kett's Oak – Wymondham

'We visited this tree on the ninth of April last, and found it to be nine feet in circumference from the base, and five feet from the ground seven feet seven inches. It stands on the path for foot passengers, and, though almost reduced to a shell, bids fair to live for many years. With a praiseworthy feeling, some one has had it clasped in iron about nine feet from the ground; but we are of the opinion that if it is not yet further supported by having stakes set around it, it will be soon overthrown by the tempest.'

RIGHT Kett's Oak today.

BOULTON & PAUL, MANUFACTURERS.

IMPROVED GARDEN ROLLERS.

For Tennis Courts, Lawns, Drives, and Gravel Paths, Fitted with Counterbalanced Weights.

These Rollers are superior to most in the Market, being heavy and well finished. The cylinders are bored and faced, and spindles turned in the lathe, which adds considerably to the value of the Double Cylinder Rollers, friction and noise being thus reduced to a minimum.

DOUBLE CYLINDER ROLLER WITH BALANCE HANDLE

The Cylinders are cast in two parts, and have rounded edges, which admit of the Rollers being turned sharply with the greatest ease, and without injury to the surface of the ground. Painted green and black, with varnished wood handles.

Reduced Cash Prices.

Size	Approximate Weight cwt. qrs. lbs.	Price £ s. d.
18 in. long by 16 in. diameter	2 0 0	£1 18 6
20 in. ,, 18 in. ,,	2 1 0	2 3 6
22 in. ,, 20 in. ,,	3 0 0	2 11 6
24 in. ,, 22 in. ,,	3 2 0	3 2 6
26 in. ,, 24 in. ,,	4 2 0	3 10 6
28 in. ,, 26 in. ,,	5 1 6	4 12 6
30 in. ,, 26 in. ,,	5 2 0	4 16 9

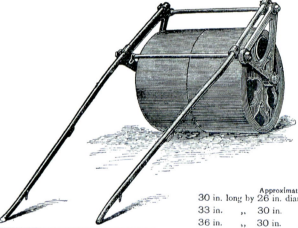

IMPROVED ROLLER WITH BALANCE SHAFTS.

For Parks, Drives, Cricket Fields, or Bowling Greens.

Constructed as the Hand Rollers. Self-acting Scrapers can be fitted to these Rollers at a slight extra charge.

Cash Prices

Size	Approximate Weight cwt. qrs. lbs.	Price
30 in. long by 26 in. diameter	5 2 16	£5 15 0 for Donkey
33 in. ,, 30 in. ,,	6 1 0	6 10 0 for Pony
36 in. ,, 30 in. ,,	6 3 8	7 10 0 for Cob

CRICKET FIELD ROLLER.

In Two Parts.

Cash Prices.

Diam.	Length.	Approximate Weight. cwt. qrs. lbs.	Price £ s. d.
30 in.	by 32 in.	9 2 0	£8 11 0
36 in.	,, 42 in.	14 2 0	12 12 0
36 in.	,, 48 in.	16 1 0	14 8 0
42 in.	,, 48 in.	20 3 0	18 0 0

Carriage Paid on all Orders above 40/- value to the principal Railway Stations in England and Wales.

5

The Maharajah is Well Satisfied

Roger Last

Rose Lane, in the medieval curtilage of Norwich, running roughly parallel with Prince of Wales Road, derives its name not directly from the romance of the rose, but prosaically via a pub, the Rose Tavern of 1688. By the second half of the nineteenth century any idea of romance had been comprehensively eliminated, for here was a large assemblage of industrial buildings with chimneys billowing out smoke. Taking place within them, however, was something of a manufacturing revolution, certainly a horticultural one. Prefabricated wood and iron garden buildings of all kinds were being produced, and a host of garden accessories, ranging from melon frames to lawn sprinklers. These found their way into gardens throughout the country. Queen Victoria was a customer. And, taking their cue from her, so it seemed was everyone else. This small quarter of the

ABOVE Bolton and Paul's Rose Lane works, Norwich. The high glazed roof of the joiner's shop is seen below the castle. A section of the elaborate foreground wall in Mountergate still survives.

city was responsible in part for changing the appearance of Victorian and Edwardian gardens, and how they were gardened, on a national, and to some extent, international scale.

The Industrial Revolution of the eighteenth century, which gathered momentum in the nineteenth, led to an outpouring of manufactured goods. These were showcased in spectacular fashion at the Great Exhibition of 1851, forced into being by Prince Albert despite hostile opposition and housed in Joseph Paxton's vast prefabricated Crystal Palace. The Exhibition was such a success that the notion of a prefabricated building at once gained acceptability and fashionable kudos. The social changes of the nineteenth century led to a vastly increased and, among the middle class, affluent population. Many in this new group of property owners had gardens, and the money to spend on them. With an increasing array of tender plants arriving in the country from Britain's colonies, and from remote corners of the globe not coloured red on the map, an ornate conservatory, especially if it was heated, was essential. Full of expensive plants, it was a sure sign of horticultural prowess, of status, and certainly of wealth. The entrepreneurial Norwich firm of Boulton and Paul saw the market, and its mass production techniques rose to the challenge, satisfying the exacting expectations of its affluent gardening clients, and setting an unrivalled standard of excellence.

Joseph John Dawson Paul (1841–1932) Mayor of Norwich, 1900–01. Born at Thorpe Abbots Hall near Diss, his great-grandfather had been a manufacturer in Norwich, and his father, although a farmer, was an inventor having patented various agricultural implements. The investment in one of them, which he had not perfected, led to a large financial loss. An astute businessman, Dawson Paul was described as having a genial and easy manner. He died aged 91; only two months earlier he had been out motoring.

Here the netting is to protect the rabbits to the bemusement of the hapless fox.

No. 53. A New Rabbit Fencing for enclosing Warrens, &c.

The company had started with the opening of an ironmonger's shop in Cockey Lane, Norwich in 1797 by William Moore of Warham. Moore died in 1839 and the firm was joined by John Barnard and later by William Boulton. A twelve-year-old apprentice, John Joseph Dawson Paul was taken on in 1853. After serving his apprenticeship, he took over the managership of the works department of the firm's London Street and Castle Street shops. When a small factory was opened in Rose Lane in 1864, he was made its manager. The business was then called 'Boultons'. After the death of John Barnard, Dawson Paul was taken into partnership, and the firm became Boulton and Paul in 1874. On the death of William Boulton in 1879, Dawson Paul became the sole proprietor. His association with the firm was to last for seventy-nine years, and he relinquished his position as chairman only four years before he died.

By 1869 an extensive range of products was being produced, mainly agricultural and horticultural implements, but also kitchen ranges, fencing and every kind of railing, iron bedsteads, even mincing and sausage machines. Wire netting production was started, a product which became profitable and in increasing demand. It was eventually claimed that 7,500 miles of Boulton and Paul wire netting was sold in Australia to control rabbits. The Rose Lane site underwent considerable expansion, stretching down King Street. With the manufacturing know-how in place, it was applied to the growing product demand of the Victorian gardener.

Thirty years later the firm's 1898 catalogue was a testament to the outstanding success of the Norwich manufacturer. It was particularly proud to advertise its patrons, and considering the roll-call, it is no wonder. Headed by Her Majesty the Queen, the list descended through the Prince of Wales and other royal princes, His Imperial Majesty the Sultan of Turkey, His Grace the Archbishop of York, twelve dukes, two duchesses, and then a long list of marquesses, earls, viscounts, lords, honourables, and sirs, some 300 in total. Added to this was the patronage of the Board of Works, Kew Gardens and the Royal Horticultural Society. Notably absent was the Archbishop of Canterbury, who clearly took his patronage elsewhere. Nevertheless, the Norwich firm were pre-eminent in their field. The 1880 catalogue claimed the patronage of 'upwards of 12,000 leading families in the United Kingdom'. Certainly 'The Maharajah is well satisfied' was a testimonial hard to beat.

Among the patrons who gave permission for their names to appear in the catalogue however, it was the wealthy middle class who came to the fore. No doubt pleased and encouraged by the company they kept, company who helped to dispel any nagging doubts about having to deal with manufacturers. Boulton and Paul were not the artisans of old England, but a thrusting enterprising firm prepared to make whatever would sell and make a profit. Allowing people from manufacturers into one's garden for days, if not for weeks, clearly struck a doom-laden chord with the Victorians. Unreliable, unruly, loud and surly workmen were as much a concern to them as they are to us. It was vital for Boulton and Paul to stress equally the quality of their product, and of the men who would be dispatched to erect the various constructions. It was not the trusted local carpenter who would be tramping past the new evergreens and carpet bedding, but a team of construction workmen sent by a manufacturing company from a provincial city. It may be an old cathedral city, but that guaranteed nothing. This prospect of the workmen from hell was clearly alarming.

Boulton and Paul had addressed itself to the problem. Its men were custom picked to respect their betters, and particularly their property. They were trained to go about their work as quietly as possible. Reliability was also key. The firm compiled testimonials ringing with reassurance. 'Their conduct throughout was excellent' (the Bishop of Ely); 'your men were in every way reliable and trustworthy'; 'very satisfied with your men'; and 'the workmen deserve a special word of praise for the quiet manner in which they carried out their respective parts'. Theodore R. Saunders, pleased with the extensive range of forcing houses constructed for him at Ventor on the Isle of Wight wrote: 'The men you sent gave especial satisfaction being both intelligent and industrious.' Norfolk men clearly rose to the challenge.

The mainstay of this horticultural manufacturing was the conservatory. Boulton and Paul had their own range of designs, with models of every possible dimension to suit any affluent purse. They boasted: 'Surveys made in any part of the country. Ladies and Gentlemen waited upon. Plans prepared, adapting designs to suit any situation.' Flexibility and an accommodating approach were to the fore. In addition, carriage was paid by the firm to any railway station in England and Wales, also to Edinburgh, Glasgow, Dublin, Belfast and Waterford.

The conservatories were made of cast iron, forged in the Rose Lane works, and of timber and glass. The variations on a theme seemed boundless. Some could range for hundreds of feet if required, and the treatment of the floor plan and finish could be so varied that no two conservatories need be alike. The glazing could be straight, or more expensively curved, and ornamentation supplied to cresting on the roof ridge, to barge boards, spandrels in simple or elaborate patterns, to cast-iron gutters and

CONSERVATORY.

This design is admirably adapted for placing in the angle of a building, and could be entered either from billiard or reception room.

CONSERVATORY AND FERNERY.

Erected for Mrs. Monins, Ringwould, Dover.

RANGE OF LEAN-TO PEACH HOUSES.

This form of roof is intended to be placed against a fairly high wall, say 12 ft. A fine example has been erected by us at Twickenham for W. Cunard, Esq., 170 ft. long; also one for His Highness The Maharajah Prince Dhuleep Singh, at Elveden Hall, &c., &c.

stained glass – particularly in doors and transepts. These constructions were not cheap. But they became much sought after.

All forms of 'glass house' were exploited; span roof greenhouses, the lean-to greenhouse, the lean-to conservatory, the three-quarter span roof vinery, or the lean-to peach house. His Highness the Maharajah Prince Dhuleep Singh of Elveden Hall had a lean-to peach house, to his great satisfaction. The standard of workmanship was high, and testimonials verified that the glass houses had 'withstood all the gales of the past few weeks, not one drop of water having entered'.

The Norwich firm was also manufacturing forcing houses, plant preserves and plant frames to any size. Its small greenhouse it claimed was 'priced fearless of competition'. The 1880s catalogues quite rightly boasted of the Royal Horticultural Society gold medals the firm had won for its conservatories. One satisfied customer wrote: 'The Lean-to greenhouse or vinery is a great ornament to my garden and I am sure will be much admired by my friends.'

A great coup was the commission of a Flower Court at Sandringham House for the Prince of Wales. This was nine bays long with a rectangular central lantern. The detailing was elaborate throughout. The lantern boasted iron hammer-beam supports with ornate spandrels and the Court's side glazing was in a fashionable chinoiserie style. The Flower Court was not over-planted in the usual Victorian manner but was left open, with room to stroll and admire the many choice climbers and specimen plants in pots. As it adjoined the Ball Room, it allowed for a perfumed retreat from

the heated activities next door. A second Sandringham commission was for an aviary.

Boulton and Paul was the natural choice of supplier for the gardening gentry and middle class of Norfolk. The firm supplied 1,500 feet of piping for the Plantation Garden in Norwich, as well as manufacturing the large conservatory and boiler. A conservatory was supplied to Carrow House in Norwich for the Colmans, and a three-quarter span glasshouse to Lord Hastings at Melton Constable Hall. His gardener, Mr J. Clarke, considered it 'splendid'. The Norwich-made products were also dispatched abroad. Mr A. W. van Beeck Calkoen of Utrecht was pleased that the lean-to greenhouse he had ordered 'had arrived in perfect order' and was 'to the entire satisfaction of his daughters'.

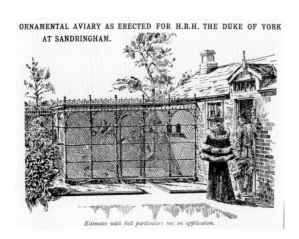

No. 400. Galvanized Iron Church or Chapel-of-Ease,
With Nave, Chancel, 2 Transepts, 2 Vestries & Porch, Turret & Bell.

Cool in Summer.

No possibility of damp.

Can be used immediately the workmen leave.

REGISTERED DESIGN, No. 5946.

CONSTRUCTED of strong wood framework, covered on the outside with galvanized corrugated iron, lined inside with varnished matchboarding. Roof principals fitted with curved braces, sheet felted between the wood and the iron, strong wood flooring. Eaves gutters, down pipes, and locks included. Carriage paid to nearest goods station. Erected by our men on purchaser's light brickwork foundation, he providing assistant labour. Outside woodwork painted three coats. Windows glazed with 21-oz. sheet glass.

Size 67 ft. by 26 feet. Width through Transepts 46 ft. ... Price, about £500.

Conservatories were not the only large prefabricated item produced. Although not strictly for the garden, if one had an estate and therefore the space, the options were tantalizing. If you wanted a galvanized iron gymnasium, with lavatory and visitor gallery – and who wouldn't – Boulton and Paul were your men. Miss Palin of Tallwylan declared herself 'much satisfied' with her iron Chapel of Ease. A galvanized iron infectious hospital was there for the taking, and if you were unfortunate enough to be in some distant disease-prone colony, the product made sense. There were pavilions suitable for concert halls or casinos, and even a racecourse grandstand. The boundless inventiveness epitomized by the Great Exhibition found its way into the rapidly expanding world of garden accessories. Boulton and Paul's output was extended to include iron gates, garden seats, cast-iron urns and every conceivable horticultural accessory down to iron plant labels. The firm of course made and installed complete boiler systems for their conservatories, saddle, combustion and slow combustion boilers, including all the values and pipes, and cast-iron ornamental gratings.

Under the heading of 'Appliances for the Garden and Pleasure Grounds' could be found espalier fencing and wall trainers, wrought-iron espaliers, diamond-wire trellis, improved pea-trainers and hurdles made with netting which could be used instead of pea sticks, and then moved off to enclose poultry. There were strawberry protectors, the improved garden roller for the tennis courts, or for the lawn, drive and gravel paths.

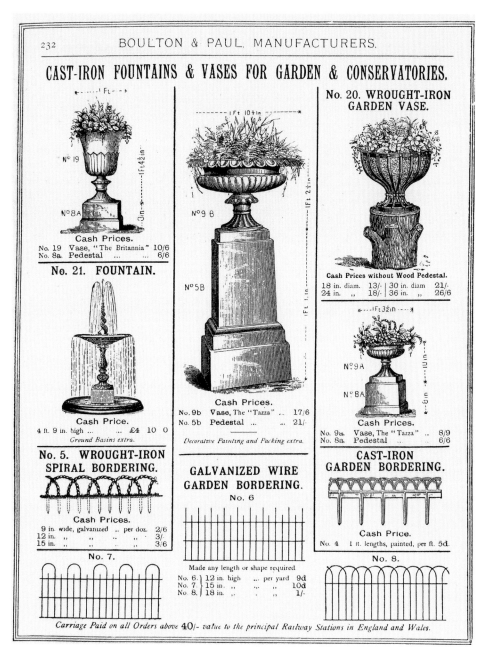

And for the man who had everything, there was the portable iron billiard room, complete with porch bay and lavatory.

For exhilaration in the garden 'The Hamburgh First Prize Watering Machine', (£5.10s) took some beating. This could throw water at the rate of three and a half gallons a minute for a range of up to sixty feet. There were water and liquid-manure barrows,

No. 7. WROUGHT-IRON TREE SEAT.

This illustration represents a seat 4½ ft. in diameter, to fix round a tree 18 in. in diameter, back 3 ft. high from the ground, made in halves, and fitted with bolts and nuts.

Cash Prices.

As illustrated, painted green	... ...	£2 10 0
Without elbows and back		2 0 0
Circular foot rest	...	1 10 0

Any size made to order.

No. 7. RUSTIC TABLE.

Cast-iron legs and wood top, 24 in. in diameter; legs painted in imitation of birch; top grained oak or stained.

Cash Price, 15/-

Carriage Paid on all Orders above 40/- value to the principal Railway Stations in England and Wales.

wrought-iron ashes and offal barrows, garden benches and seats. The Paris seat was suitable for balconies and porticoes. There were Rustic tables, 'The Lady's Lounge', the Tennis armchair, the Arboretum seat, the 'double croquet chair with awning', cast-iron fountains, and beehives. There was a full range of entrance, carriage and wicket gates, these in iron or pitch pine, garden tents, and the sportsman's and explorer's tent (£5), and a garden swing, (£4.10s). For enclosing flower beds and shrubberies, what could be better than ornamental game-proof hurdles.

No. 87.
THE HAMBURG FIRST PRIZE WATERING MACHINE.
WITH POWERFUL GARDEN ENGINE.

This Implement is very complete, and most useful in large gardens. The engine is of entirely new design and improved construction; all the working parts are brass, and the barrel being brass-lined throughout, rust or corrosion is impossible. By a simple arrangement of the valve, which is regulated by the wheel shown, the pump will draw water from the barrel or direct from a pond or cistern, which can be delivered either into the barrel or distributed through the spreader as shown in illustration (it will easily throw with great force 3½ gallons of water per minute in a continuous stream to a distance of 60 feet). When required, it answers as a water barrow, from which, with the same valve, water-pots and pails can be filled. The barrel is fitted with valve and spreader for watering garden paths and lawns, and special spreader for the distribution of liquid manure for irrigation, etc.

The barrel is of oak, and will hold 36 gallons. The framework is of wrought-iron, and the wheels of steel with broad tyres The whole is made of best materials, and highly finished.

Prices, Carriage Paid.

To hold 36 gallons, fitted with galvanized water spreader, pump, and 10 ft. length rubber suction pipe, complete ... £6 0 0
If without pump 3 10 0

Longer lengths of suction pipe can be had, if required, at 1/3 per ft.
An extra galvanized spreader, especially adapted for distributing liquid manure, 5/- extra.
The extreme width, outside wheels, is 3 ft. 2 in.
Width of tyres 2½ in.

Registered.

In an age before engine propulsion the lawnmower, which could be heavy, had to be matched to its user, regardless of physique. There was a product range and size suitable to be used by a lady, or a boy; a lad; a man; a man and a boy; two men; and for those with extensive swards, a pony. Although after the pony had mown the lawn, Boulton and Paul's 'Water Ballast Double Cylinder Garden Roller' was probably needed to rectify matters.

No. 23.
ORNAMENTAL BRIDGE.

For connecting Park with Garden. Supported on arched lattice girder. Kiosk in centre, with curved roof projecting on brackets over the sides of bridge, to shelter the rounded bays enclosing the seats. Finished in any style of decoration.

Special Designs prepared for Rustic Work or other Bridges.

Gentlemen waited upon in any part of the country.

REGISTERED DESIGN.

No. 20.
WOOD FOOT BRIDGE.

BRIDGE constructed of wood, with supporting posts in centre. This style of Bridge is very suitable for crossing streams having marshy borders, as it can be made to any length, being supported at intervals on posts.

REGISTERED DESIGN.

No. 21.
REGISTERED DESIGN.
This design can be made up to 20 ft. span.

No. 22.
REGISTERED DESIGN.
Garden Bridge can be made up to 30 ft. span.

Estimates on application.

There were also bridges for the garden. The larger and more ornate bridges clearly were not for the suburbs for they were to 'connect park with garden'. Such large and elaborate structures were only for those with money and acreage, and perhaps not much taste. The kiosk in the centre featured roofed, rounded bays, which enclosed seats. At less cost was a wooden footbridge. Yet this too could be on a grand scale,

No. 448. FISHING TEMPLE AND BOAT-HOUSE.

REGISTERED DESIGN.

This building is specially constructed for erecting near a river, but can be arranged to suit any situation.

Estimates on application

for it could be supplied at any length and was 'suitable for crossing streams having marshy borders'. Special designs could be prepared for rustic work. For the really adventurous, there were several substantial offerings: a fishing temple, a boathouse and the 'comfortable' galvanized iron two-storey cottage, or suburban residence. It seems that the infinite enterprise and drive of the Norwich firm could meet any demand. And there was something to suit every purse. Any size of house or garden outbuildings could benefit from the 'Sudden Death' mousetrap. 'They simply run into it for shelter' ran the sales pitch. This humanitarian approach hid a duplicitous endgame. Sparing Victorian sensibilities, what happened next was not detailed: the tripping of a wire and the alarming descent of a heavy block of metal, which splattered the rodent. With so

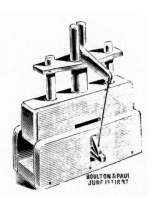

SUDDEN DEATH MOUSE TRAP.

THIS is the most certain trap ever invented for the destruction of rats and mice, they simply run into it for shelter, and none escape.

Cash Price 2/6 each.

Place trap against the wall, and the mice will run into it for shelter.

Larger size for rats, 4/6 each.

If there is a mouse in the house this trap will catch it.

many products available, Boulton and Paul can be said to have made a major impact on the appearance and the running of the late Victorian and Edwardian garden. Somewhere throughout the United Kingdom a garden roller, iron urn, garden seat, melon frame, veranda or conservatory from the Norwich works was likely to be found, although not, for whatever reason, in the grounds of Lambeth Palace.

By 1879 the firm employed 350 men. Its garden products had turned Boulton and Paul, if not into a household name, then certainly into a horticultural one. As demand increased so did the size and ambition of the factory buildings. In 1876 the joiner's shop was rebuilt at the Rose Lane works. This was truly impressive. Of iron and glass and of course manufactured by the company, it was of seven bays and two storeys in height and rising above that was a vast glazed roof. Here even the largest conservatory could be assembled before being taken apart and prepared for dispatch. The upper of the two galleries was used by the painters and glaziers who needed good light, and the area below it for the assembly of smaller units. The spacious main floor was full of work benches and products in course of construction – a scene of industry and activity.

There are many unanswered questions in this story of horticultural enterprise, notably where did the design and aesthetic element of the products come from. A large product design team was required with detailing in wood and ironwork, stained glass, and in every architectural element. The extent of these products originating from Norwich imposed a design aesthetic on the nation, for better or for worse. Some of the items like lawnmowers were designed primarily by the demands of their function. The more decorative items reflected the standard Victorian aesthetic of their times, notably a love of the ornate, particularly in finials, spandrels and stained glass. Still, collectively the Boulton and Paul catalogue represents a large body of product design, all of it by unnamed designers.

The second half of the nineteenth century saw the apogee of conservatory and garden manufacture. By 1935, for Bolton and Paul, and other competing firms, that age was over. The post-war demand was more for wooden buildings – sports pavilions, clubhouses, huts for holiday camps, poultry houses. The company still produced greenhouses, but there was a shift in emphasis to commercial greenhouses, garden frames and a demand

FACING PAGE One of the reasons behind the success of Boulton and Paul was the enlightened and philanthropic approach of its owner. Business was brisk in the 1880s and as a token of his appreciation of his workforce Dawson Paul invited all his employees and their wives to a Christmas dinner and entertainment. 'Love and health to all' was not the most apt quote chosen for the programme card, the words spoken by Macbeth as one of Banquo's murderers, still with blood on his face, slips into the banquet, as does Banquo's ghost. Appalled, Macbeth tries to rally himself and toast the company. However, in an especially decorated St Andrew's Hall, 700 sat down to a meal of roast beef, boiled mutton, roast turkey and sausages, plum pudding, mince pies, cheese and celery and dessert, all provided by Mr A. Levett of the Market Place. Toasts and speeches were enlivened by the Norwich City Amateur Minstrels and Campling's Orchestra Band, with ballads, and humorous, comic and Irish songs. The evening concluded with an Offenbach operetta in one act, *The Blind Beggars*.

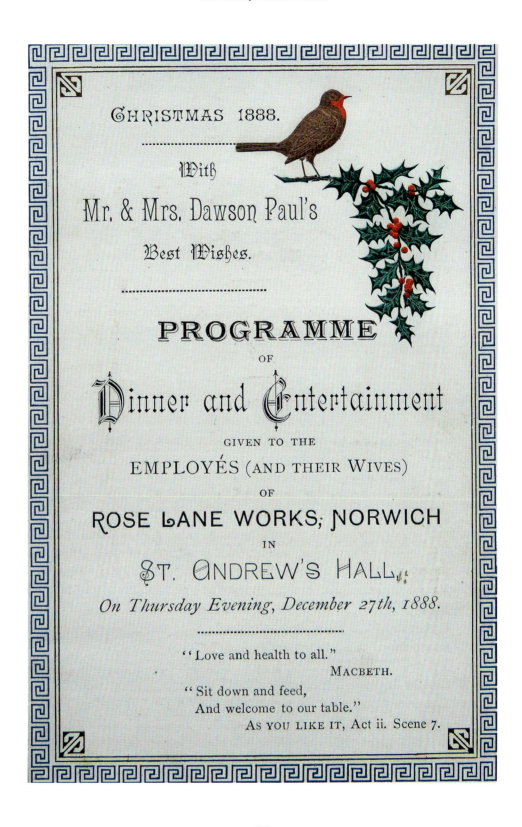

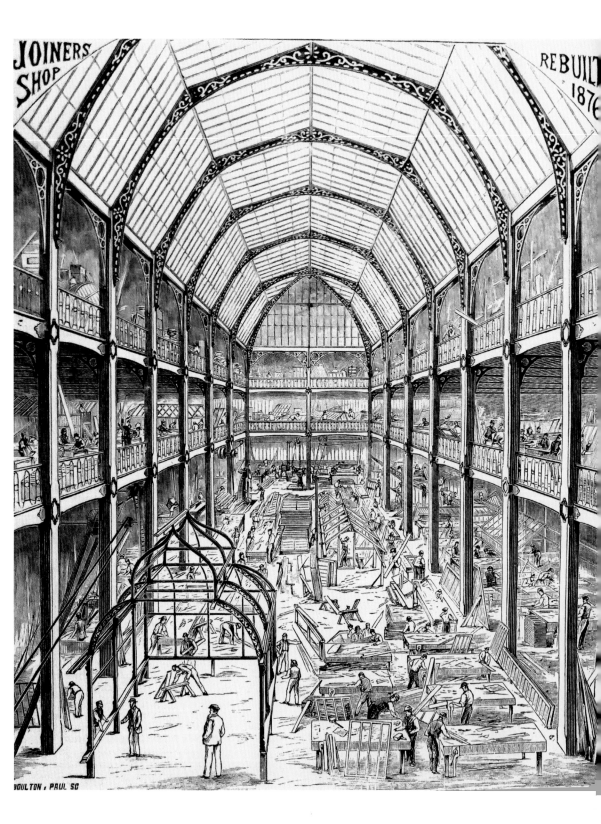

for timber village halls. However, even churches were still manufactured, as well as other portable buildings. 'Motor car houses' had been added by 1909.

The catalogues, or rather by now, product pamphlets, 'Distinctive Buildings for Garden and Estate', were more modest in size and the social elitism had vanished. Conscious of the changing age and of the middle-class preoccupations, added to the list were 'Sunshine Rooms', timber summer houses marketed as 'The Way to Health', inducing their owners to spend more time out of doors. Here one could write, read, laze, dine and play cards, and they were 'the very thing for outdoors sleeping'. The rooms could be revolved to capture maximum sunlight. Not a new idea: Kensington Gardens had a revolving summerhouse in 1733. Now a more modest version was available for everyman. Whereas the Georgians no doubt turned theirs out of the sun, the health-seeking early twentieth-century family turned theirs into it, uniformly bronzing, blissfully unaware of the dangers from melanomas.

In 1915 Boulton and Paul were commissioned to build aircraft and an even larger manufacturing site was needed. One was acquired over the river at Riverside, eventually covering fourteen acres. All the company's manufacturing was moved there. Eventually, as the century progressed, products for the garden gave way to the commercial ascendency of the plane. The Rose Lane site was sold to the Cooperative Wholesale Society for use as a shoe factory. The only remaining building from the original works

ABOVE The twentieth century brought a new catalogue style in addition to new products.
FACING PAGE Boulton and Paul's great glazed joiner's shop at their Rose Lane works. With double galleries, its size allowed for even large commissions to be assembled here to satisfy quality control before being taken apart and despatched to the client for installation.

is The Tudor Hall, built as company offices in 1899, and, facing Mountergate, a section of the ornate brick wall which bounded the site. As for the impressive joiner's shop, not a trace remains, one of the great lost treasures of Norwich. Much of the area is now covered by housing.

As for the firm's products, one must scour the country to find what remains. Examples, like the restored Carrow House conservatory in Norwich and greenhouse at Raveningham Hall are splendid testaments to the quality of the work. Elsewhere conservatories, seats, urns, and fragments from the Norwich works do exist, but as yet no fully comprehensive national or county records have been compiled, not even for Norfolk, so the extent of this important Victorian and Edwardian horticultural legacy is unknown.

FACING PAGE An Invoice heading of 1899 labels the component parts of the Rose Lane works: stockrooms, foundry, galvanizing shop, joinery shop, forwarding department, wire weaving shops, stores, and smiths' forges, with the Mountergate wall in the foreground.
BELOW The elaborate wall of the works remains facing Mountergate, with housing on the works site.

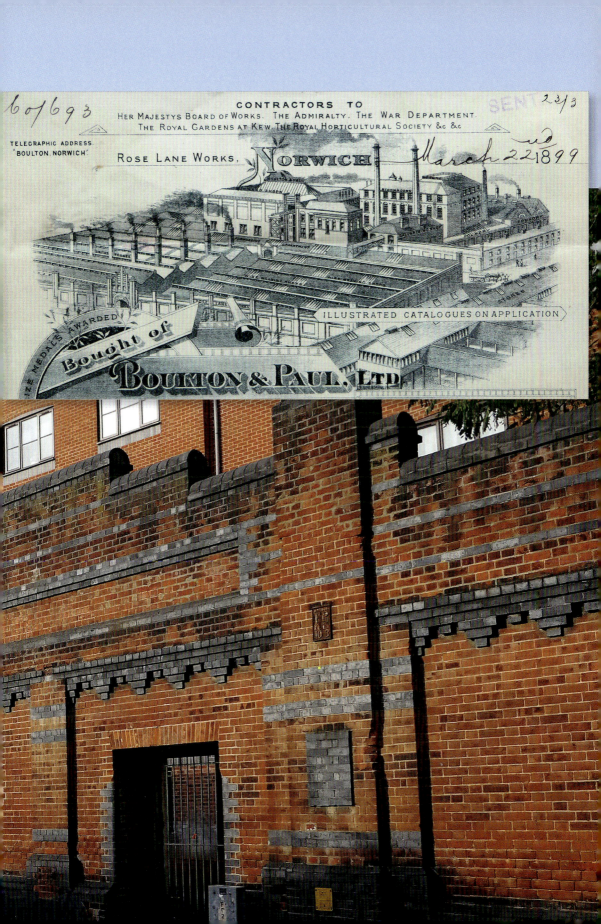

6

George Skipper's Sennowe Masterpiece

Steven Thomas

Although its early history is somewhat obscure, it is possible that there was a building of some kind at Sennowe in the early fifteenth century. There is a record of Prior Hugh of Walsingham leasing a convent's rabbit warren and hut ('garyte') at 'Senhaw' to Roger Skynnere of Lycham. However, the origins of the landscape park and grand house we see today lie more than 100 years later when a substantial property (the bones of which survive in the present one) was built in 1774 for Thomas Wodehouse, the third son of Sir Armine Wodehouse of Kimberley in Norfolk. A map of the parish of Guist, surveyed in 1785 shows that the eastern section of the park had already been created by this date, and the walled garden built in its present position. The Wodehouse family did not

FACING PAGE The Boathouse at Sennowe, constructed c.1910. Originally thatched, the building is timber framed with large projecting wrapped round balconies, internal rooms and with cavernous openings at water level for mooring boats. Artist unknown.

ABOVE Sennowe House, built in 1774, as remodelled by Decimus Burton, 1855–56, with its new bays and upper storey on the east front, to the right. To the left of the house is a three-bay conservatory, which although large is smaller than Skipper's replacement. Part of William Barron's 1850s garden layout is complete with a fashionable monkey puzzle tree, next to the urns on the left.

ABOVE Thomas Albert Cook. (1867–1914). An oil painting based on photographs.
ABOVE RIGHT George John Skipper (1856–1948). He was born in East Dereham and trained as an architect in London. He set up his own business in Norwich in 1879. His best known work of excellent quality and design was carried out between 1890–1910.

appear to lavish a great deal of time or attention on their new residence because for the first part of the nineteenth century the estate was leased out and by 1851 was the residence of one Colonel Fitzroy. Although the woodlands in the western half of the park were increased around this time, the more interesting period in the development of both the house and the landscape was yet to come.

Edward Wodehouse died in 1855 and this heralded an era of great change. The trustees engaged the architect Decimus Burton to enlarge the house by adding an upper storey, following which the Morse-Boycott family came into possession. Some time during the 1850s (the exact date is not recorded) William Barron was commissioned to create a more up-to-date landscape to accompany Decimus Burton's remodelling of the house. He laid out gardens and carried out work in the park, including the planting of the West Drive. In 1887 the estate was sold again, this time to Bernard Neve-Foster who remained for eleven years before putting the estate back on the market.

Bernard Neve-Foster's purchaser was Thomas Albert Cook, grandson of Thomas Cook who had founded the travel agency. The family had made a fortune in the travel business and after the death of his father in 1899, Thomas Albert, known as Bert, sold out of the business to buy and finance his new estate in the country. Cook was a bon viveur and his flamboyant nature was reflected in the elaborate nature of the house and gardens he was to create at Sennowe. The architect he chose to help him, who had a flamboyance of his own, was George Skipper.

By the early twentieth century Skipper had become a prominent architect with many Norfolk commissions of note, including striking city properties such as the Jarrolds building in London Street, Norwich. Part of that complex was his own office, where highly decorative use of terracotta included figurative relief panels, two of which, typical of his extrovert approach, portrayed himself. Also in Norwich were Surrey House (now part of the Norwich headquarters of Aviva), whose opulent main hall is clad with various coloured marbles originally intended to face part of the interior of Westminster Cathedral, and the Royal Arcade, with its confident Art Nouveau styling and playful tiling, as well as several large and elaborate hotels in Cromer. Sir John Betjeman, noting Skipper's love of decoration and exuberance, decided that 'He is altogether remarkable and original. He is to Norwich rather what Gaudi is to Barcelona'.

Skipper was commissioned by Cook in 1905 at the height of his career and worked

Details from the terracotta friezes, possibly by James Minns, on Skipper's London Street office, now part of Jarrolds. George Skipper himself, in top hat, being shown the cartouche which is similar to the one seen behind in situ in the pediment of his office building for Norwich Union, Surrey House, 1903–04. He also appears in a bowler hat examining architectural plans on site. His second wife, Rachel, is with him on both friezes. She died in 1904, and he later married for a third time.

on Sennowe on and off until 1910. During this time, he remodelled and enlarged the original house and added a grand Winter Garden. In the grounds he built an impressive free-standing red brick Italianate campanile clock and water tower close to the western façade. The Clock Tower is listed Grade II* and forms an important element of the architectural composition at Sennowe, especially on the approach to the house from the east drive. It is free-standing of five storeys with stone dressing. There is a Doric entablature and frieze with a series of windows set between the triglyphs and under a projecting cornice. An octagonal belfry tempietto carries an octagonal copper roof. Internally there are white glazed bricks. The Clock Tower clearly 'borrows' from other architectural work and has many classical references. It is, however, unique in Skipper's work. Below the south front he laid out grand Italianate gardens. Beyond the gardens Skipper embellished the main drive with a bridge over Decimus Burton's drive and added ornate lodges at the entrances to the park.

When Thomas Cook returned from abroad, he found that his architect had given him a large Edwardian Baroque country house, which looked both east and south across its parkland. In remodelling the house Skipper had used red brick and mathematical tiles with stone dressings, topped by a slate roof with some copper details. The design incorporates Doric, Ionic and Corinthian columns and it is richly embellished with exceptionally fine decorative carvings and statuary. The entrance front faces east across the park while the five-bay south front overlooks the terraced gardens. The design of the south front is closely linked to the gardens, including as it does a ground floor stone loggia with Ionic columns and statues, which returns at the western end to join the magnificent five-bay Winter Garden.

The Clock Tower. The massive brick and stone five-storey tower is also a water and observation tower and can be seen rising above Sennowe Park's tree canopy for miles around.

George Skipper's watercolour of his design for the east front of Sennowe, as executed.
The Building News, August 1911.

The Italian Gates.

Thomas Cook driving his family through the park at Sennowe, with his newly remodelled house in the background. Oil painting by A. de Faxthorn, c.1910.

George Skipper's influence on Sennowe was extensive and elaborate, and it is his legacy which survives to the present day. The extent of the work demonstrates that it was his most important country house commission, one of probably only four major houses he undertook, and it remains the best surviving example of his work for a private client. The designs are full of echoes of devices he himself had used elsewhere, as well as borrowings from buildings by other architects he admired. He was essentially a classical architect, and this remains at the core of his design, but he was also happy to use a variety of other architectural devices, provided he had seen them working effectively on other buildings. He was not an architect who created entirely new styles – rather, he created his own style by using a unique blend of the classical put together with many other influences.

Sennowe Park lies to the middle of Norfolk, beside the village of Guist. It covers about 66 hectares (163 acres), with the house sitting centrally between the east and west lodges. To the east, north and west the park is completely enclosed by nineteenth-century ornamental woodlands which form a strong landscape feature, and the River Wensum which forms the southern boundary adds to the beauty of the park, set, as it is, beside a sinuous lake. The landform is gently rolling, falling from north to south down to the Wensum valley and the lake, with the house taking advantage of the high ground overlooking the water. Beyond the Wensum river to the south of the park lies

ABOVE Excavating the lake at Sennowe, c.1909. The men are digging with forks and loading the spoil with shovels into linked metal containers on tracks, a steam engine with winching gear stands on the bank (top left) to pull the load out. One horse stands by. Despite the site being waterlogged from winter rain, the men are in ordinary working boots.

LEFT The Boathouse from the rear. The original thatched roof was replaced with pantiles.

BELOW The Boathouse. The projecting balcony wraps round three sides.

ABOVE The Norwich Drive. Skipper's bridge over Decimus Burton's drive is marked by the four pillars at its corners.

TOP Sennowe Park. The Clock Tower rises over the well-wooded park at Sennowe. The huge foreground lakes were formed after twentieth-century gravel extraction. Above them winds the River Wensum with the Edwardian lake above that. The Kitchen Garden lies between the tower and the lakes. The main drive, the Norwich Drive, enters from the right, curving behind a block of trees to arrive at the entrance on the east front of the house.

an area of land on rising ground which has, to some degree, been embellished as part of the park scenery and yet has always remained outside its boundary.

One of the special features of Sennowe is the elaborate lodges and gates into the park. The main approach is called the Norwich Drive, which enters the park from the A1067 in the east. Here George Skipper built a pair of identical lodges interconnected by ornate iron railings and stone gate piers with overthrow. They are known as the Italian Gates. Skipper used brick with ashlar dressings and slate and copper roofs, together with copper-topped towers on the drive side, to create an Italianate style. The long straight drive runs south-west down a gentle dip and is flanked by wide grass verges bounded by mixed woodland underplanted with laurel and rhododendron. As it enters the open park, the drive is carried over an Edwardian Baroque style bridge of

brick with stone dressings, which Skipper added in about 1910. After the bridge, the landscape opens out into parkland, although the drive continues to follow the edge of the woodland bank until it swings south to arrive at the carriage court on the east front.

Prior to Skipper's involvement in the site, the principal entrance had been from the west. The West Drive is still in use, but it became the secondary entrance. It enters the site from a minor country road, past twin lodges, the northern one being of an earlier date. Skipper enclosed its fabric in the early twentieth century to match the new one he built on the southern side of the entrance. This long meandering drive is very picturesque, as it winds up a steep climb, through woodland planted with mixed exotics, including pines, cupressus and cedars, planted by William Barron in the 1850s.

TOP The eastern domed temple. Steps from the park allow access through it to the lower terrace.

ABOVE The house from the lower terrace. The imposing steps are repeated either side of the terrace. Recessed beneath the upper terrace is a loggia.

Thomas Albert Cook, 'Bert' (1867–1914) standing in front of his newly redesigned house. The youngest of the three grandsons of Thomas Cook, the founder of the eponymous travel agency, he inherited part of the family fortune in 1899. An oil painting based on photographs.

He is said to have moved many of the trees as mature specimens from the Earl of Leicester's Holkham estate.

The drives lead eventually to the core of the park around the house and the lake. This is the only open area of parkland and it is sparsely ornamented, mainly with nineteenth-century oak, beech and sweet chestnut, scattered in small groups. Three very mature trees appear to pre-date the creation of the park – namely a sweet chestnut of *c.*400 years; an oak of *c.*350 years and a fine-layered beech.

The majority of the park at Sennowe is heavily wooded, from a variety of periods of planting. Today much of the character comes from the early twentieth century when a mix of species was planted at wide spacing for amenity and shooting value. Recent thinning has begun to favour Corsican pine and Douglas fir with natural regeneration of the hardwoods being encouraged. However, in the late eighteenth century, when the park covered an area of around 130 hectares there was already a high concentration of woodland along the north-eastern edge and some mature trees survive here. The 1785 parish map shows that the West Drive was in position, but the southern sections of park were partly under the plough and carr vegetation with no evidence of ornamentation. By 1850 the layout had changed but the size remained constant – the woodlands had been increased all around the perimeter and the mansion was described as being set in 'rich park-like grounds' (sale particulars, 1850). During the second half of the nineteenth century William Barron's work on park and woodland planting increased

The western temple.

their ornamental nature and by the end of the century Norris's Plantation had been added to the east. The lake appears in the park at the same time as Skipper was working on the house, and it was given a very fine rustic timber-framed Boathouse, with an upper balconied storey extending out over the water. Whether this was to a design by Skipper is possible, but not clear from the records.

The extensive terracing of the gardens below the south front formed a major part of George Skipper's contract at Sennowe in the early years of the twentieth century. He arranged them on two levels, which were surrounded by brick retaining walls, and decorated them in the Italianate style with stone quoins, balusters, coping and urns. At the mid-point of the east and west walls great cedars of Lebanon spread their boughs over two stone temples with Tuscan Doric columns and hemispherical domes, forming entrances to steps to the park below. The upper terrace has further stone staircases to east and west and in the centre of its retaining wall is a three-arched stone loggia with shell-headed niches and balustrade at the upper terrace level. The lower terrace is laid to grass beside which run deep, exuberantly planted herbaceous borders along the base of the retaining wall. On the open lawns stand two, fluted and swagged, stone urns.

On the top level of the garden terraces, at the western end of the house, stands the recessed Winter Garden. This magnificent building with its ornate decoration and luxuriant tumble of vegetation, survives almost exactly as Skipper designed it. It is said that when Thomas Cook returned from abroad to see his new house, his only

Brick bastions of the lower terrace.

Skipper's Winter Garden, and the interior soon after completion.

disappointment was that he did not have a ballroom, so Skipper made the Winter Garden big enough to use for dancing. It must have been a marvellous setting for a ball!

George Skipper made much of the location of the gardens, which today still give panoramic views south and east from the raised terrace over the park towards the lake. The eye is caught by the impressive Boathouse at the eastern end of the water, from which point there are views back up the park to the house.

To the west of the Italian Garden, and at a lower level, is a semicircular lawn, backed by yew hedging and a balustrade, which makes a viewpoint west into the Woodland Water Garden. Tennis courts once lay to the south of this lawn, but these have long since been abandoned. The Woodland Pleasure Garden runs between the west side of the house and the eighteenth-century walled Kitchen Garden, which lies about 150 m to the south-west. It is planted with mixed species including sweet chestnut, monkey puzzle, holly, box, yew and many conifers and it is cut through with paths and a watercourse which runs from a semicircular grotto pool below the balustraded viewpoint through narrow rough-stone lined channels and pools, bridged occasionally by larger stones. The sale particulars for the 1850 sale suggest that this Woodland Pleasure Garden already existed in some form by the mid-nineteenth century.

At the end of the main walk a wide brick archway leads to the outer east wall of the Kitchen Garden, where a long flower border once ran along its entire length beneath a wooden pergola (probably the work of George Skipper, but no longer surviving). Within its walls, the ground slopes gently from north to south, providing the perfect growing conditions for fruit, flowers and vegetables. The walled garden has been in the same position since Thomas Wodehouse built the first house in the late eighteenth century although the present brick walls are mid nineteenth. A substantial amount of

The lake from the Boathouse balcony. The house and tower are visible to the right.

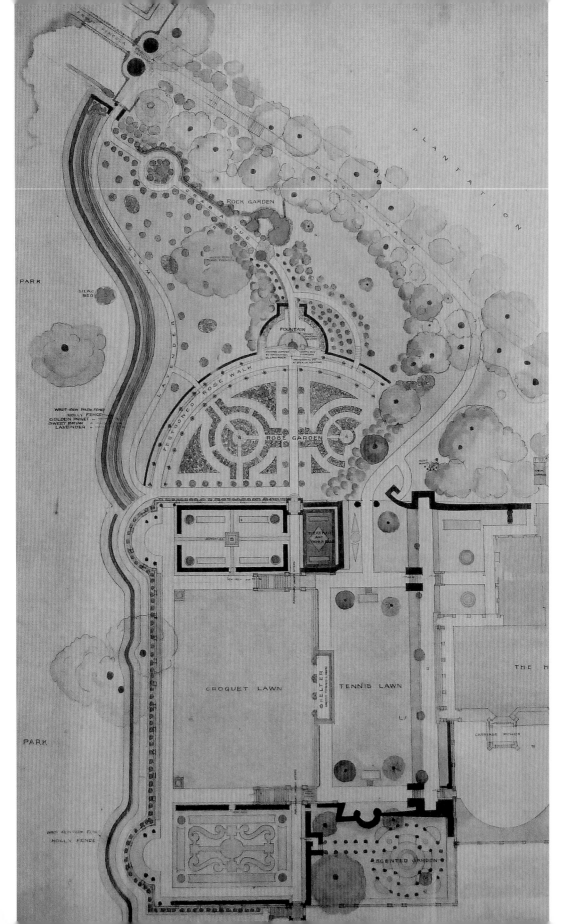

work must have been carried out here at this time because the garden still contains a mid nineteenth-century glasshouse along the inside of the north wall (which has recently been renovated), while on the outside of the same wall are a series of frames and garden storage buildings, together with the mid nineteenth-century red brick gardener's cottage.

Some traces of the old ornamental layout of the Kitchen Garden survive. The brick base of the peach house runs south centrally from the glasshouse and ends in a curved retaining wall with central steps down to a circular dipping well. The early twentieth-century pattern of box-edged paths has now gone but the area is still given over to vegetable production.

FACING PAGE George Skipper's master plan for the layout of the gardens at Sennowe.
The house, with its large, attached conservatory or Winter Garden, is on the right, coloured pink. In front and below it, to the south, on the first terrace, is a Tennis Lawn, leading down to a second terrace with a Croquet Lawn which includes a three-arched shelter or loggia with shell-headed niches set under the terrace above. At the bottom of the plan, to the east, adjoining the upper terrace, is a concealed Scented Garden which adjoins a formal Parterre with a strapwork design. Shown above the two lawns, to the west, is a formal rectangular lawn with a central sundial, four rectangular beds and trees in each corner, now called the Italian Garden. To the right of this is a Heather and Gorse Garden. Steps lead down to a large and complex semi-circular Rose Garden, based on two circular layouts with twenty-one planting beds and an outer Festooned Rose Walk. The land slopes down at this point and set into the retaining wall of the Rose Garden is a wall fountain with pool. The water from this was led by the side of a curving avenue of crab trees, then under it to feed an irregular elongated pool forming a Water Garden, behind which was a Rock Garden. From the upper terrace the curved Pergola Walk leads directly to the formal brick entrance to the long Pergola (top left) and the Kitchen Garden. The walled Kitchen Garden with its sequence of glasshouses, is not shown. A third walk, the Lavender Walk also links the main sequence of gardens with the Kitchen Garden. The suggested hedging for the area below the Rose Garden is for a four-tiered hedge of lavender, sweet briar, golden privet, and holly. Because of the contours of the site the plan incorporates fourteen separate sets of steps of various sizes, as well as balustrading and two large pavilions with hemispherical domes and tall supporting columns. Some of the gardens are enclosed by yew hedging and the main terraced area is retained by high brick walls incorporating two semi-circular bastions topped by balustrading. Below the wall is suggested a long line of spaced and topiarized bushes, a gravel path and an outer holly hedge, beyond which is the sloping park, which eventually leads down to the new lake with its Boathouse.

7

The Business of Gardening

Tom Williamson

The late eighteenth century was a period of immense gardening and landscaping activity in Norfolk. Country houses were provided with spacious parks, and also with serpentine pleasure grounds, planted with flowers and specimen trees; while among the middle classes, in town and country alike, a wide variety of flowers and shrubs were planted in gardens and trained against the walls of houses. This was an increasingly commercial age, and the plants required for all this were supplied by an expanding nursery industry.

Of course, the selling of plants and seeds was not in itself a new development in this period. In the seventeenth century Norwich was already renowned as a centre of horticultural excellence, and Evelyn wrote of 'the flower gardens which all the inhabitants excel in of this city' – something which Fuller, writing in 1662, ascribed to the Dutch immigrants who had settled here in the previous century. There were annual 'Florists feasts', horticultural shows for professional cultivators and enthusiastic amateurs, and these continued to be held throughout the eighteenth century. Nevertheless, for a long time, commercial nurseries seem to have been fairly small concerns, like that run by William Sadler in St Swithin's parish, who died in 1696 leaving five beds of tulips, 57 pots of gilly flowers, 15 'glasses', and 'a diall and a diall post'. Major landowners, and some minor squires, seem to have acquired many of their plants (especially fruit trees) from London nurseries. When Roger Pratt of Ryston laid out his new garden at Ryston Hall in the 1670s he bought many of the trees from the noted nursery of Leonard Gurle at Whitechapel in London, while at Thwaite in the 1720s, and at Honing in 1754, fruit trees were purchased from Henry Stevenson's nurseries at Brompton Park. In 1747, the Jerninghams of Costessey Hall were buying cypress, larch and Scots pine from metropolitan nurseries. Even in the second half of the century some landowners preferred to buy London stock, especially those with a house 'in town',

Extract from a map of 1833, showing the main 'public' area of Mackie's nursery ground in Lakenham, which extended over some 48 acres (c.19.5 hectares). Much of the land is laid out on a functional grid plan but around the entrance is an area of curving drives and fashionably serpentine planting. This was evidently designed to display plants to the best advantage and thus to tempt potential purchasers.

or who visited the capital regularly. In the 1770s Thomas de Grey of Merton received regular deliveries of both exotic trees and shrubs, and larger quantities of deciduous native trees, from London nurseries, while at Hillington in 1770 Lombardy poplars were being purchased from Eaton's nursery in Chancery Lane. As late as the 1790s the Bulwers of Heydon Hall were buying large numbers of trees and shrubs from London nurseries like Gordon Dermer Forsyth of Fenchurch Street, and from Hairs, Hairs and Co. of Ham Common, Surrey.

By this time, however, some very large businesses had emerged locally, capable of supplying most horticultural needs. One key figure in this development was William Aram, who set up business in Norwich in 1759. In May 1760 he advertised in the *Norwich Mercury*: 'Gentlemen and others may be supplied with seedling Scotch Firs 2 years old at 10sh/1000. Will. Aram, Nurseryman in Norwich, where may be had ... Fruit and Forest Trees, Flowering Shrubs, Greenhouse Plants, Pine Apple Plants, Bass Matts etc.' Aram was almost certainly the son of John Aram, head gardener and surveyor at Holkham in the 1720s and 1730s (his brother, another John, was still regularly advising on the gardens there in the 1760s). William Aram's name appears with monotonous regularity in the accounts of Norfolk estates in the 1760s and 1770s. He not only supplied plants to places in the immediate hinterland of the city, but also made deliveries as far afield as Hunstanton and Heacham. Like many businessmen in this age of the 'consumer revolution', he had a keen eye for advertising and self-promotion. In January 1762 the *Norwich Mercury* reported his proposal to the Earl of Orford, the Lord Lieutenant of the county, that the 'whole declivity of Castle-Hill' in Norwich should be planted 'with larch, Scotch Firs, &c.'; which were to be supplied, one presumes, by himself. The offer does not appear to have been accepted.

In 1773 Aram's daughter married John Mackie, who at or around the same time joined the business, which a few years later moved to a new site in Lakenham, just to the south of the city. Thenceforth payments to 'Aram and Mackie' appear routinely in estate accounts. Mackie ran the enterprise (now referred to as the 'Norwich Nursery') alone after his father-in-law died, and after his own death in 1796 it was run by his son, William Aram Mackie, subsequently joined by his brother John Mackie junior. Following their deaths, in 1817 and 1818 respectively, the business continued to be run by members of the family: first by Sarah Mackie, William's widow; and subsequently, after 1833, by her son Frederick. The Mackie family's clientele was if anything even more widely distributed than that of Aram: estate accounts show them supplying flowers, shrubs and trees as far north as Sheringham and, once again, as far west as Heacham. Almost certainly, however, the bulk of their sales were to members of the middle class, especially those living in and around the city of Norwich.

The nursery at Lakenham covered a substantial plot of ground – over 83 acres (c.33 hectares) in all – and this not only allowed a wide variety of plants to be cultivated in considerable numbers, but also gave opportunities to display them in an attractive

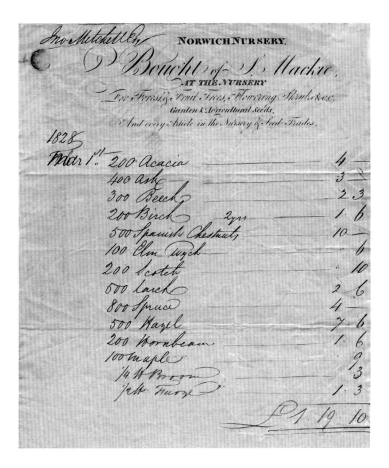

An 1828 invoice, printed on headed paper, from Mackie's 'Norwich Nursery' for the sale of over 4,000 trees for under £2. Cost comparisons are impossible as there is no indication of the size of the trees supplied.

and appealing manner. Indeed, one of the striking things about eighteenth-century commercial life is the feeling of modernity often conveyed by contemporary descriptions: and such large commercial nurseries often sound remarkably like modern garden centres. They supplied various gardening accessories, including pruning gloves, as well as plants. On 24 May 1780 James Woodforde, parson of Weston Longville, recorded in his diary one of his rare visits to Norwich, and described how he walked 'Out of St Stephens Gates to Aram and Mackie's Garden. Walked over the Gardens and then paid him a bill for Fruit Trees &c. Gave also to the men working in the garden 1sh and 6d'. Similarly, on September 29 in the same year, he attended the service at the Cathedral, and 'from thence took a long Walk to Mackays gardens and bespoke some Trees &c'. Visits did not have to be on foot. In October 1811 Nicholas Styleman 'drove round both Mackie's nursery grounds and on towards Lakenham'. On such visits, customers would be tempted by an extensive array of plants. They often succumbed. On Woodforde's second visit to Mackies in 1783 he bought twenty Turin poplars, ten plane trees, ten acacia, two vines, ten laurels, two 'double blossom thorns', two moss roses, ten evergreen cytisus, ten Weymouth pine, six guelder rose, two Old Newington peaches, and an Old Red Roman nectarine. The nursery produced a number of printed catalogues, that for 1790 running to more than 100 pages. It included no less than 111 different varieties of apple alone.

There are hints that the nursery ran a kind of mobile gardening service which ranged widely over the county. Thus, on a number of occasions in the 1780s and 1790s James Coldham of Anmer in west Norfolk recorded in his memorandum book how 'Mr Mackies gardener', or 'Mackies man', 'came to prune my fruit trees'. Anmer, it should be noted, is some fifty kilometres from the Lakenham nursery. Certainly, members of the family visited some clients in person. James Woodforde recorded in his diary how on 13 July 1781,'Mackay, Gardener at Norwich called here this Even', and he walked over my Garden with me and then went away. He told me how to preserve my Fruit Trees &c. from being injured from the future by the Ants which was, to wash them well with Soap Sudds after a general washing – specially in the Winter.'

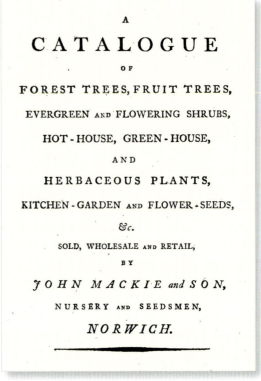

Mackie's printed catalogue for 1790.

More surprising than this trip – Weston Longville is, after all, only fifteen kilometres from Norwich – is William Mackie's visit to Nicholas Styleman in 1813, again apparently to give advice: for Styleman lived at Heacham, over sixty kilometres from the Lakenham nursery. Such careful attention to the needs of important customers may, in part, explain the phenomenal success of the Mackies' nursery business.

By the end of the eighteenth century there were a number of other large nurseries operating in Norfolk. One, at Hoveton, was run by Frederick Fitt during the 1770s, 1780s and early 1790s and supplied a wide variety of plants to estates in north east Norfolk. Fitt seems to have gone bankrupt in 1793, and his stock, as advertised for auction in the *Norwich Mercury* in February, included 'upwards of 20,000 forest and fruit trees, a large quantity of shrubs, greenhouse plants etc' (all to be sold 'exceedingly cheap, the proprietor being under the necessity of clearing the ground'). Another important nursery was established at Mundford by one William Griffin in the 1760s and provided trees and plants for a number of west Norfolk estates. Griffin's most noted achievement was the planting of the great perimeter belt at West Tofts in the heart of Breckland, a vast area of woodland enclosing both the park and much of the home farm. The firm was still run by the Griffin family in 1809, when it supplied laurels for the pleasure ground at Holkham, but by 1829 seems to have been taken over by one William Kedie. Other prominent businesses include Fifes at Thetford, which supplied forest trees throughout the county, and into Suffolk, in the decades either side of 1800. And as well as large nurseries, the late eighteenth century saw a steady proliferation of seedsmen, not only in Norwich but also in some of the market towns. In an age eager for novelty rival firms vied with each other to be the first to procure and sell new varieties, usually described as freshly arrived from London. In September 1787 for example John Mackie announced in the *Norwich Mercury* the arrival of the 'large yellow Antwerp Rasberry' at 5/- per plant. The following January he was selling them off at half price, their place in the novelty stakes clearly taken by the 'Dwarf prolific pea which grows only about 9" high'.

Some of the larger nursery firms not only supplied enormous numbers of trees but also operated a complete planting service – preparing the ground, establishing the young plants, and guaranteeing and maintaining them for a certain number of years – usually five or ten. The practice was established as early as the 1770s – William Griffin planted the West Tofts belt under such an agreement – and was quite common by the early nineteenth century, when we find William Windham of Felbrigg using the services not only of William Mackie but also of William Falla, whose nursery was based as far away as Gateshead in County Durham. Windham's timber book reveals the problems he experienced in dealing with both contractors, but especially with Mackie. In 1827 the latter contracted to plant 13 acres (c.5 hectares) of Gresham Mill Common at £6.10.0 per acre: 'It was well done but cost too much money.' The following year he gave up using Mackie altogether and noted with some feeling: 'After the long trial and expense we have undergone, I never advise anyone to purchase trees of Mr Mackie.' Windham was not alone in his dislike of contract planting. In 1813 Abbot Upcher of Sheringham agreed a contract for planting three acres (c.1 hectare) of trees on the edge of the park with Fife's nursery at Thetford. They were to 'warrant them good for four years, replacing such as may die, for £10 per annum'. But he noted: 'This I already repent, finding I can plant much better and cheaper myself.'

The development of nurseries and seed merchant businesses in Norfolk in the course of the eighteenth and early nineteenth centuries is a fascinating subject; one which certainly requires more detailed examination than I have been able to give it. How large were the various nursery grounds? To what extent did nurserymen combine their businesses with other activities, especially land surveying and garden design? How unusual was the mobile advice service apparently provided by Mackies? These are important questions for scholars – both 'professional' and 'amateur' – to address.

8

The Pleasure Gardens of Norwich

Roger Last

Before 1800 the only English provincial cities with Pleasure Gardens of any consequence were Bath, Liverpool, Newcastle-upon-Tyne, Birmingham and Norwich, and of these Norwich excelled. London, over a period of time, had more than sixty lesser spas, tea gardens and resorts. Its most famous Pleasure Gardens were Vauxhall and Ranelagh, followed by Marylebone. Norwich, for several centuries England's second city, and not overtaken in population until the mid eighteenth century, boasted no less than four competing Pleasure Gardens.

These gardens, first appearing in the capital in the seventeenth century, came to dominate the social scene throughout the eighteenth century and into the nineteenth. The gardens became an essential part of urban living, and in the age before the municipal park, they provided large green open spaces, usually well maintained and managed. They presented all the elements expected from a garden: tree-lined walks, arbours, trellised alcoves, flower beds, decorative use of water with fountains, canals and pools, and ornamental buildings. But they were so much more, with areas in which to take breakfast, to dine, to listen to music, and to stroll safely on clean gravel or grass. They became the fashionable resort of all classes of society, although entrance fees

ABOVE A detail from Samuel and Nathaniel Buck's *The South-East Prospect of the City of Norwich*, 1741. '9' marks the centre of the Spring Gardens, its paths shown in the form of the union flag. Behind it, with more mature trees is My Lord's Garden with its many tree-lined walks.

BELOW A detail from Samuel and Nathaniel Buck's *The South-East Prospect of the City of Norwich*, 1741, showing the elevated ground towards Bracondale, the city walls and the Black Tower, which still stands, marked as '3'. Beneath the shelter of the walls two Pleasure Gardens were established, first the Wilderness, followed by the Richmond Hill Gardens, both benefitting from the impressive views over the city and the Yare valley to the east.

and charges tended to do their own social vetting. These gardens were called upon to form the fashionable core of public entertainment. Divertissements of all kinds were introduced, in particular, firework displays, and music, both instrumental and vocal. To the fore was theatrical illusion with huge illuminated set pieces and cunningly devised 'stage' machinery. But perhaps the greatest draw of all was the opportunity to leave the confines of home, to dress up, to promenade and to socialize, to see and to be seen.

The first of the Norwich Pleasure Gardens was very early, My Lord's Garden, constructed as a private garden in 1663–4 for Henry Howard, later the 6th Duke of Norfolk, and designed by John Evelyn. It was also the first Pleasure Garden outside London. Sited on sloping ground between King Street and the River Wensum, it was a place of recreation, with walks, bowers, a bowling green and a flower garden. As the Duke was rarely at his palace in Norwich, his garden further downstream, was soon open to visitors and particularly after the demolition of the Duke's Palace in 1711, open for public use.

In 1739, 200 yards upstream, between St Faith's Lane and the river, gardener John Moore, opened the New Spring Garden. It was named after the New Spring Garden south of the river in London, which already by this time had been renamed Vauxhall Gardens. Apart from the pleasant layout and nature of the site, Moore offered pleasure-boat trips on the river and more to the point various wines, ales and cakes, all served in genteel surroundings.

By the middle of the century, the concept of the Pleasure Garden and what it had to offer was gaining ground. In 1749, Samuel Bruister opened the Wilderness, as it came to be called, on an elevated site, part of Butter Hills, below the city walls between Ber Street gate and the Black Tower. Extensively planted with trees to create a wilderness for walks and shelter, the gardens commanded delightful prospects over the city, the river and the surrounding countryside. Bruister opened his gardens with the publicity of a grand wrestling match, which attracted much attention.

Pleasure Garden lighting. A detail from Thomas Rowlandson's *View of London's Vauxhall Gardens* of 1785.

A Triumphal Arch erected in 1746 to the side of the Guildhall in Norwich to celebrate the victory of the Duke of Cumberland at Culloden which crushed the Jacobite rebellion. A wooden frame was covered with silk, painted, and at night was illuminated from behind by lights. Similar constructions installed in the Norwich Pleasure Gardens enabled elaborate topographical and historical scenes to be depicted.

This forced Moore at the New Spring Garden to up his game. The London gardens had introduced illumination, so were able to extend their entertainments into evenings, and into the early hours if there was the demand. Moore would do the same. Glass globular oil lamps filled with whale oil, on which floated lighted wax wicks dipped in sulphur, were strung through the trees. Some were attached by brackets, others hung from the branches in wire baskets. Vauxhall at this time dazzled with 1,000 lamps. Moore engaged an orchestra to give Tuesday evening concerts and now too firework displays could be mounted. During Assize Week, in August, four public breakfasts were held, serving tea, coffee, chocolate and French rolls. A further attraction was a transparent arch built in the Gothick taste, lit from behind by lamps. Often lightweight linen or calico was used stretched across a frame; front lit it produced one image, lit from behind, especially with the use of translucent dyes, a different image appeared. Theatre scene-cloth artists were often employed, and certainly in the capital, artists of considerable standing could command high prices for their depictions.

A fourth Pleasure Garden opened in 1766, Smith's Rural Gardens outside St Stephen's gate, on the site of a former nursery garden. By now illumination was an essential prerequisite (in 1769 Vauxhall dazzled with 5,000) as was food and drink and both cider and nog were served. In case this brought in the wrong type of clientele, perhaps coming up from the Norwich slums and eighteenth-century sink estates, two bouncers were employed to keep out 'such Persons as may be thought disagreeable'. Clearly the need for the men showed that some disagreeable elements had been causing upsets. These gatherings would have been highly productive fields for pickpockets and for ladies whose wares were not of the manufactured kind. For entertainment, fireworks inevitably had to follow. The one shilling charge, on par with its rivals, was offset by 8d being allowable against drinks and fruit. In line with their former use, the gardens also boasted magnificent flower displays. Norwich now had four pleasure gardens in fierce competition. The rivalry to tempt the public grew more intense, with each garden adding new attractions, which in turn spurred on yet more.

By 1768 the Wilderness had changed hands and the new owner, Samuel Stebbing, introduced his own public breakfasts with music being played, and again in the evenings, when the gardens were illuminated. Two years later My Lord's Garden had a new tenant, William Curtis, who added public breakfasting and more pyrotechnics with line rockets running from 'the Top of the Summer-House to the Top of the Booth'. Three years on the Wilderness changed hands again and new owner, Joseph Hammond, had the Long Walk under the city wall gravelled, the garden decorated with lamps, more fireworks introduced, and musicians hired. At the Assize Week breakfasts, the assembly danced cotillions and country dances. William Curtis responded with large transparent paintings of topographic views, sparklingly lit at night by lamps, revealing such marvels as the Duomo in Florence, the Quirinal in Rome and Ranelagh gardens, plus there were the wonders of an ingenious grotto and shellwork.

Back at Smith's Rural Gardens, the widow of the founder had taken over and she brought in William Quantrell as her engineer, who in 1771 produced something which must have been hard to resist, the largest 'Piece of Firework that ever was seen in Norwich', six vertical wheels, all moving at once. My Lord's Garden countered with the construction of an artificial cascade, copied from Vauxhall, including a watermill. Curtis claimed his version was far superior to Vauxhall's as 'Swans will appear on the Water, and the Sun and Moon appear to move in the Element; which is not in the Cascade at Vauxhall'. Visitors who wished to avoid the crowds could view this phenomenon privately for half a guinea. There was much interplay here between the theatre and the Pleasure Gardens, both using machinery to create illusion and wonder.

In 1772 William Quantrell took over at the Rural Gardens and the fireworks, his speciality, became an ever more elaborate and crowd pulling feature. My Lord's Garden was taken over by Mr Graves who, not content with a cascade, installed an elaborate piece of machinery 'representing a Sea-Fight, with Five Ships, &c. also the Method of storming a Castle' with martial music, and with 'a beautiful Transparent Painting, representing a Sea God, drawn in a Triumphal Carr ...' This was soon embellished by mermaids and dolphins. As if this was not enough, he added a view of Mount Vesuvius, and a new machine called the Man of the Mill. The Wilderness too was adding machinery, theirs running on a line for 680 yards. Further mechanical and theatrical enhancement saw the addition of a waterfall, a working watermill, sheep, presumably mechanized, swans, and a heron. All these attractions involved water effects, rather than the real thing.

At Quantrell's Rural Gardens firework displays designed by Italian artists, clearly considered Europe's top-notch pyrotechnicians, were announced, with 36 ft high palm trees and 'Dragons to go to different parts of the Garden'. Graves at My Lord's Garden, brought in another Italian pyrotechnic expert, Giuseppe Gatti. This sparked even further competition with William Quantrell enlisting the invaluable talents of

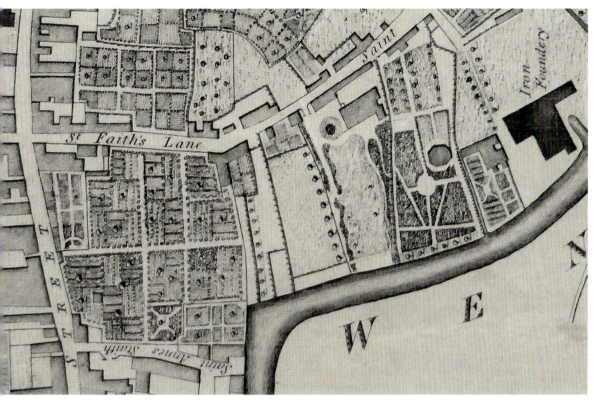

ABOVE A detail from Anthony Hochstetter's map of 1789 shows the position of the Spring Gardens by the River Wensum, by this date complete with its octagonal rotunda called the Pantheon. Between the bend in the river, and King Street on the left, is My Lord's Garden, formerly the private garden of the dukes of Norfolk, and throughout much of the eighteenth century a successful Pleasure Garden. Here it is shown as an elaborate sequence of gardens, some of them formal, within a cross of paths.

Baptista Pedralio, an assistant of the famous pyrotechnician Giovanni Battista Torré (known as 'Fireworks Macoroni'). Torré had staged remarkable fireworks displays in London's renowned Marylebone Pleasure Gardens. Pedralio revived one of these by producing a globe 21 ft in circumference which turned on its axis before falling apart into four pieces to disclose Vulcan 'attended by his Cyclops ... with Vulcan's Cave and Forge and the Eruption of Mount Aetna'. Something it can be comfortably assumed Norwich had never seen before.

By 1776 the Spring Gardens were in the hands of James Bunn. 'The great resort of Company to this garden bespeaks at once it's preferable Situation to all others' ran the advertising. And clearly Bunn had bought a successful concern, for it was claimed that for several seasons in Assize Week upwards of 2,500 tickets at 1s. each were sold in a single night. The Spring Gardens in the hands of Bunn and the Rural Gardens in the hands of Quantrell became locked in intense and serious rivalry.

Bunn considerably upped the game. He took his cue from the highly fashionable Ranelagh Gardens in London which as early as 1741 had built an astonishing Rotunda, 555 ft in circumference, (its interior famously depicted by Canaletto). Bunn decided on a Norwich version, in the middle of the gardens, calling it the Pantheon after the example then in Oxford Street. The advantages were obvious: now he could give shelter to 1,000 people in inclement weather and extend his season into the autumn and winter months. Who designed his octagonal Pantheon is not known, but it was heated, which allowed for a winter concert to be attempted. Until then the vagaries of the climate made musical performances problematical especially in wet weather, even though marquees could be erected for the players. At last, concert performances could be guaranteed. Local instrumentalists, singers and militia bands were enhanced by star performers from the London stage or gardens. Bunn also acquired the old artificial waterfall and landscape from the Wilderness which closed in 1778 when Hammond retired.

At Quantrell's there was already a cascade. In 1780 a bowling green was added, and flower shows continued to flourish. Although sited in Norwich, the whole of the county was drawn to the Pleasure Gardens, at least those who had the means and time to travel. Parson James Woodforde records in his diaries a visit to Quantrell's in June 1780: '... walked about the City by myself till near 5. in the Afternoon & in my walk saw Quantrells Gardens. At 5. drank Tea at the Kings Head – after that went to Mr Buckles there stayed & talked with him and Mr Sterling till near 6. o'clock – from there walked to Quantrells Gardens by myself, heard a sad Concert and saw the Fire Works, which were very good & worth seeing – gave on going in 0:1:0 for which have 6. worth of any thing at the Bar. I supped & spent the Evening there & stayed till 12. o'clock. For my Supper and Liquor – paid 0:1:6. A very heavy Storm fell about 9.o'clock. A prodigious Number of common Girls there & dressed – The Fire Works began about 10. o'clock and lasted about an Hour – In it, a representation of the

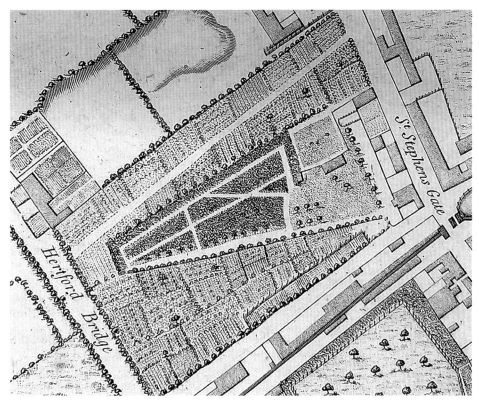

Hochstetter's map of 1789 shows the site, by St Stephen's gate, and layout of 'Quantrells', formerly Smith's Rural Gardens, later Ranelagh, and finally the Royal Victoria Gardens.

Engagement between the English & French Fleets under Sir George Rodney. About 12. I came away.' Two months later he was back and commenting that Quantrell's was much larger than Bunn's, but Bunn's put on a much better firework display. It was in the splendour and novelty of their fireworks that the two gardens now locked horns. These were, however, dangerous pursuits. While he was preparing a display at Bunn's, an explosion killed one of the workers and instead of a display, a memorial concert had to be given for the benefit of the widow.

Fortunately, more novelty and immense crowd-pullers were on hand: balloons. Unmanned ascents had taken place in Paris in 1783, followed swiftly by manned flight. Europe was hooked, and so too was Norwich. London celebrated a manned flight in 1784. Although small balloons soon rose from both Quantrell's and Bunn's, it was a manned ascent which would draw the crowds. In 1785 Quantrell's struck first. A Norfolk man, James Decker would attempt a flight. Spurning any nascent concepts of Georgian Health and Safety, he resolutely put personal profit to the fore. That summer two Frenchmen were killed trying to cross the English Channel, possibly the first fatal aviation accident.

Prior to the planned ascent, the balloon could be viewed daily for one shilling, although 'Working people, Children and Servants' got in for half that. The 'Royal Balloon' had come from London and from it hung an elegant gondola on which stood, so the Norwich press extolled, a 'beautiful Chinese Temple, richly embellished and decorated in a Style of unparalleled Elegance'. Such a prodigal event as this, attracted mass attention and expensive prime-spot seats (ten shillings and six pence) were sold to the eager gentry for the sensation of a close-up view of the extraordinary, and no doubt highly dangerous, take-off. The large silk balloon was filled with hydrogen, the highly flammable gas labouriously produced by pouring sulphuric acid on to large quantities of scrap iron, but poor weather (wet and stormy), ruptures in the fabric, loss of gas, hail, and everything else a normal early June day can produce, meant that Decker had to jettison his fourteen-year-old travelling companion. She, described as, 'a young lady from London', no doubt clambered from the 'Chinese temple' basket with much relief, and Decker had to attempt the flight alone. At ten to four the moment came, and the balloon and brave Decker rose with 'considerable rapidity'. Both were lost in the cloud after eight minutes. One can imagine the excitement, the wonder and foreboding of the onlookers as the hapless man, who by accident of birth clearly was not acclimatized for altitude, disappeared into the unknown. A fatal plummet from an inconceivable height seemed inevitable. Parson Woodforde had watched from Bracondale and saw the balloon pass over his head. He comments in his diary on the 'vast Concourse of People' who had assembled to see it and the courage of Decker to have ascended so soon after the 'violent Tempest ... very loud Thunder with strong white Lightening with Heavy Rain ... ' and the ominous fact that the balloon had 'bursted twice' on filling.

Incredibly Decker was seen again. He landed unscathed in a meadow near Loddon. That night, back in Norwich, the hero was feted. The populace took the horses from his carriage and dragged him in 'great pomp' to the theatre, where he was received with 'unbounded marks of applause'.

It was difficult to replicate this level of excitement. Both gardens added more variety turns to their entertainments. Bunn brought in equestrian circus companies. In 1789 he sold the gardens to John Keymer. Keymer rearranged the hundreds of lamps in the gardens, cambered the walks to improve drainage, and had the Pantheon painted. But success required aggressive show business. Keymer staged an enactment of a royal progress to St Paul's using models, which was an immediate success. Quantrell countered by commissioning John Ninham, (who is particularly remembered today for drawing the medieval gates of Norwich city wall) to design a pasteboard replica of the Bastille. So, only a year after its fall, the hated fortress fell again in Norwich, after the usual concert and fireworks. Norwich citizens could witness the Bastille prison cells being exposed, with their torture chamber and skeletons, while the governor was beheaded (at least in dumb mechanical display) and prisoners were released. It was up-to-the-minute momentous European events brought right to the heart of the

A similar balloon ascent, in 1811, to James Decker's earlier flight. Mr Sadler with Captain Paget of the Royal Navy ascending from the gardens of the Mermaid tavern in Hackney. Although twenty-six years later than the Norfolk ascent, judging by the numbers who took to roofs for a better view, including the church tower, this was still an event full of spectacle and potential danger, which attracted large crowds and excitement. And no doubt, as planned, the Mermaid tavern did a roaring afternoon's trade. The pair landed safely at Tilbury Fort after a flight of one hour and twenty minutes.

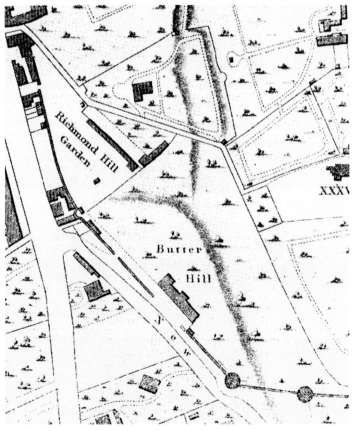

ABOVE *Merry-making with a View of Norwich from Richmond Hill Gardens*, from an oil by Robert Ladbrooke, c.1816. Its spectacular setting was draw enough, and the newly ornamented gardens in 1819 offered free entrance with a painting of a Don Cossack, (the Don Cossacks had helped in the defeat of Napoleon) by the gates in the costume of his country, being 'an object of general attraction'. This and 'Bacchanalians and other subjects' were deemed 'fully appropriate to the mirthful scenes the Gardens are so well situated to draw forth, when the minds of the citizens wish to unbend from their daily toil'. Judging from this, something the citizens were not slow to fully embrace.

LEFT Richmond Hill Garden at Bracondale from Millard and Manning's Norwich Plan of 1830.

city – little could top that. Keymer tried, with a pantomime, which included his own version of the Bastille with the inevitable torture instruments and wretched chained victims. In fact, the daunting fortress had only held seven prisoners, and of these one was a 'lunatic' imprisoned at the request of his family and another a 'deviant' aristocrat, the Comte de Solages, who had been imprisoned by his father.

Clearly such entertainments were near ruinous to mount. Quantrell faced financial problems. Eventually he was forced to move and to work for his old rival at Spring Gardens. Both gardens decided that rebranding might help and taking their cue from London, the Spring Gardens were now renamed Vauxhall, and the old Rural Gardens became Ranelagh, which was taken over by yet another proprietor. But in 1799 Keymer retired, leaving, for a time, Ranelagh supreme.

But Samuel Neech at Ranelagh soon faced competition from the Prussia Gardens which opened in the Ipswich Road. Neech acted with confidence, and went for a knockout blow, erecting his own rotunda, capable of holding an impressive 2,000 people. On one occasion in 1801 more than 3,300 people flocked to the gardens. The 'peculiar beauty' of the gardens was commented on, and Neech continued to attract huge crowds both to the morning breakfasts and evening promenades and concerts.

The first quarter of the nineteenth century was the apogee of the Ranelagh Gardens. Other lesser gardens came and went.

However, the Prussia Gardens continued successfully, and a new contender appeared, Richmond Hill Gardens, on the western end of the former Wilderness Gardens. Apart from its extensive and romantic views over the city, the gardens were fitted up at 'very considerable expense'. Breakfasts, concerts, illuminations, and fireworks all followed.

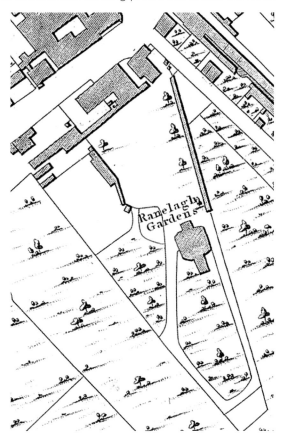

Ranelagh Gardens, showing the Pantheon. From Millard and Manning's Norwich Plan of 1830.

A poster advertising the appearance in the Pantheon at Ranelagh Gardens of a 10,000 square foot painting of the three decisive battles between 16 and 18 June 1815, which saw the defeat of Napoleon. In Norwich, after touring the nation and before departing for Europe, the huge panorama, with eleven changing scenes, was brilliantly illuminated and could be viewed four times daily accompanied by the excitement of a full military band. The proprietors were at pains to point out that the panorama was entirely novel and was 'not the one from Leicester Square, London'.

In 1817 W. Finch took over at Ranelagh. His improvements boosted attendance. In Assize Week 1819, 9,000 people came. Ranelagh boasted two Chinese walks festooned with lanterns, an arch erected in the Long Walk, the interior of the impressive Pantheon was redecorated, and now three bars served refreshments. An octagonal military bandstand was built, refreshment boxes to hold 600 and an amphitheatre for circus performers. But despite all of this, by the end of the 1820s critics were finding fault.

Still new gardens opened. Page's Greyhound Gardens in Ber Street run by Alfred Page began to attract attention. In 1841 there were three bands here together with rope-dancing and fireworks. 'The disposition of the comparatively small plot of ground is really creditable to the ingenuity and taste of the proprietors, for it is laid out in terrace walks, arcades, and grottoes, while the centre affords excellent scope for the entertainments and promenade of the company.'

Page took on bigger things, in 1842 becoming proprietor of Ranelagh Gardens, now renamed the Royal Victoria Gardens. These had been sold by auction in 1835 described as being 'six acres including stables, a Coach House, a Pantheon, Saloon, Bowling Green, Flower and Vegetable Gardens, Alcoves, Mound for display of Fireworks, and Pleasure Gardens with a great variety of Ornamental Trees and Shrubs'. An emphasis on buildings to contain circuses, pantomimes, romantic dramas, and ballets, reflected the shift in public taste. All began well and in 1842 Page was congratulated for his entertainment provided over the two race days in July. The grounds were visited by some thousands and those from the country who had not seen anything like it before, were amazed at the dazzling brilliancy of the illuminations and the illuminated painting of the young Queen Victoria. Performances commenced in the newly and splendidly decorated 'Olympic Temple'. It was reported that Mademoiselle Reikee danced admirably and the gymnastics of Mr Cotterell and his son delighted the juveniles. The fireworks went off with much *éclat*.

In August 1844 an evening of ballet was mounted with military, brass, and concert bands, and 'Mr. Frampton and his celebrated Juvenile Ballet Company'. A selection from the then new ballet *Ondine* was performed and a variety of dances from Irish to Chinese. The evening concluded with the essential fireworks. And all of this for 6d. But it was not enough. An inevitable decline of, and reaction to, the Pleasure Garden, with fashionable social gathering at its core, had already set in. The higher echelons of society no longer wished to parade, certainly not in the highly mixed company who now frequented these places. A stylish venue had now become an over-popular one. Neither was the new Victorian middle class in tune with the flamboyant robustness of the Georgian, whatever the latter's veneers of the genteel.

In 1849 the Victoria Gardens closed. The land was bought by the Eastern Union Railway Company and soon trains were pulling out of the new Victoria Station bound for London. The increased mobility and expanded horizons the railways afforded contributed to the general demise of the Pleasure Gardens, not least offering days

The Royal Victoria Gardens, 1844. Although it boasted many ornamental features, statues, urns, fountains, flower beds, trees and shrubs, and a long row of decorative alcoves, by the end of the decade these, and its other pleasures, were not enough to see it survive. The balconied pavilion appears to be the reception area to the adjoining circular Pantheon, the top and side of which project from behind it. The Full Programme of Events, all for the price of 6d is pictured opposite.

away at aspiring seaside towns with their fresh air, far from the fugs of the city. Although that said, in London, Cremorne Gardens in Fulham remained in business until 1877 and those called 'The Eagle' in City Road did not close until 1882.

But in Norwich, it was the end of the line. At the Victoria Gardens the railways saw a literal takeover as the Royal Albert Saloon, once able to furnish 'an extensive assortment of confectionery, ices, jellies &c...', became the station waiting room, and the Amphitheatre, the ticket office and luggage room. The *Norfolk Chronicle* reporting the station's inauguration, described with a mixed air of nostalgia, regret, and pride, the former gardens and their undoubted glory: 'The Norwich Ranelagh did not fall far short of its metropolitan prototype ... there was a time when they were the resort of our fashionable aristocracy; and the public breakfasts ... were amongst the most gay and pleasant assemblages, that it was ever our good fortune to encounter. They were attended by the first families of the county and city; and used to present an array of beauty, of grace, and of elegance, that few provincial towns could equal, and none could excel.'

ROYAL VICTORIA GARDENS
ST. STEPHEN'S GATES, NORWICH.

THIS PRESENT MONDAY,
THE FIFTH OF AUGUST, 1844.

MR. FRAMPTON
AND HIS CELEBRATED
JUVENILE BALLET COMPANY,
WITH
MISS BARNETT,
ARE RE-ENGAGED, (FOR THIS NIGHT ONLY).

MILITARY, BRASS, & CONCERT BANDS.

The Performances to commence with a New Ballet D'Action of Enchantment, introducing Two Tableaux, and arranged expressly for Mr. FRAMPTON'S celebrated Juvenile Ballet Company, (from the Adelphi Theatre, to be called

ONDINE!
OR, THE WATER SPIRIT.

The Music selected from the Popular French Ballet of the same name.—The Pantomime Action and Dances, &c., superintended by Mr. FRAMPTON.

PAS DE FASCINATION, BY MISS FRAMPTON & MASTER G. MASKELL.

PAS DE TROIS, BY MISS HARRIS, MISS MASKELL, & MASTER FORREST.

NEAPOLITAN TARANTELLA, BY ALL THE PEASANTRY.

THE SHADOW DANCE, BY MISS FRAMPTON.

GRAND OVERTURE.
AN IRISH DANCE, by Miss BARNETT.
Pas de Cinque a la Chinoise!!!
By Mr. FRAMPTON, Masters FORREST, MASKELL, FLAWS, & ANSLEY.
END OF THE FIRST PART.

A SET OF WALTZES BY THE BAND.
THE POLKA DANCE, by Miss Frampton and Master Forrest.
TARANTELLA, by Miss BARNETT and Mr. FRAMPTON.
PAS GROTESQUE, BY MR. G. MASKELL.
BAND.—MINUET.—*Mozart.*
HIGHLAND PAS DE DEUX, by Miss Harris & Master Flaws.
LA GITANA, BY MISS BARNETT.
BAND.—A SET OF WALTZES.
FLAG HORNPIPE, by Masters Forrest, Flaws, Maskell & Ansley.
NATIONAL ANTHEM.

SPLENDID
ILLUMINATIONS!!
The Amusements to conclude with a Brilliant Display of
FIRE-WORKS!!!

Performances commence at Eight.—Admission **6d.** each.

9

Botanic Connoisseur

Brian Ellis

> '... here is one of the finest botanical gardens of the country, containing an immensely interesting collection of trees and shrubs, and a vast collection of plants under glass, most of which Mr Mason has himself collected in the wild on his annual expeditions to various parts of the world.'

Leonard Maurice Mason, VMH (1912–1993), was one of the most distinguished gardeners of the last century. He developed not one, but two exceptional Norfolk gardens and arboreta, Talbot Manor, Fincham and Larchwood at nearby Beachamwell. His first garden at Talbot Manor was concurrent with the post-war development of gardens like the Valley Gardens at Windsor and the woodland garden at Knightshayes Court near Tiverton, Devon. Norfolk is not considered to be to the fore in its plant collections, but his collection of trees and shrubs defied this view and became one of the most notable in the country. He sought every kind of plant, and became renowned for his superb collections, the most spectacular under glass. Many of the specimens he brought back from his own plant-hunting expeditions abroad. He introduced and circulated a wide variety of plant material at home and overseas, and as an enthusiastic amateur exhibitor, achieved great success in his native county, at the spring and autumn Royal Horticultural Society (RHS) shows in London, and at Chelsea gaining many gold medals. His gardens were not famed for their layout or design, but for what he grew in them, which singled them out, and him, as being truly exceptional.

Maurice Mason (as he preferred to be known) grew up in the Tudor manor house of Fincham Hall and remembered being given a part of the garden to look after from the age of four – indeed his love of gardening must have been inherited, as both his mother and grandmother were enthusiastic amateur gardeners. From early childhood until the last days of his life he maintained this great interest in plants. His enthusiasms

Maurice Mason with his dog, Tilly, at Talbot Manor, 1960s.
'Maurice was as merry and giving as he was earnest and ambitious. It's no wonder plants grew so well for him.' Hugh Johnson.

Maurice Mason outside his house Talbot Manor, 1964. The garden's fame came from what was planted and contained in it, not from its layout or design, pleasing as it was.

ranged from the archetypal English garden plants, through the more unusual, to the rare and difficult to cultivate exotics. If a plant was new, unusual or presented a challenge to grow, then Maurice had to have it.

In 1932 at the age of twenty-one he acquired Talbot Manor at Fincham with 81 hectares (200 acres) of farmland. He became a highly successful farmer and businessman which allowed him to indulge in his passion for plants in all manner of ways. Although when he began there was no planting of particular note at Talbot Manor, he developed some 16 hectares (40 acres) into a wonderful garden which became the focus for

a remarkable collection of orchids (over 4,000 species at one time), exotics, trees, shrubs, and unusual hardy perennials. Remarkably he also went on to develop 48 hectares (120 acres) at Larchwood in nearby Beachamwell, transforming it into a huge and superb woodland garden.

Abundant planting in a section of the glasshouses at Talbot Manor.

Although Maurice Mason was interested in all plants, he was perhaps best known initially for his love of those species which needed to be grown under glass in this country. He preferred in his plant collecting trips to visit the lesser-known areas of the world, as there was then more chance of finding a new plant that could be brought back to his collection and introduced into cultivation. Of course, as he widened his interests to accommodate his expanding collection, the garden had to be enlarged. As he said, 'Gardens can grow, greenhouses don't.' From small beginnings – a greenhouse attached to the house, a small propagating house and a larger greenhouse – new glasshouses were added. Over the years, a complex of fourteen glasshouses and two polytunnels (for the propagation of hardy plants for his other garden at Larchwood) developed. These were mainly built by his own workmen, although the later aluminium glasshouses were purchased from Cambridge Glasshouses. His glasshouse collections could be separated into four divisions of plants: those which can be grown under the staging; those grown on it; those which can be hung above it; and those which are happiest trained up the sides of the house and perhaps on wires in the roof. He really did like to make full use of the space available. As his interests became more focused on shrubs and trees he developed a further area at Talbot Manor into an arboretum, with the assistance of Hillier Nurseries which he is reputed to have contacted and ordered three of everything. After this Harold Hillier sent him a specimen of all the new species that were raised there. This eastern extension of the garden has remained in the Mason family and has now come into maturity.

Maurice and his wife, Margaret, plant hunting in Madagascar in the late 1960s, one of three visits he made there. He was particularly interested in the island's succulents and orchids. The profits from his farm financed his annual two to three-month plant-hunting trips to tropical and subtropical regions of the world.

Maurice Mason did not like the cold and winter months in East Anglia, so the central heating was always set to high and log fires roared in the hearth. His gardeners learnt to use this to their advantage if they had not finished all their chores in the heated glasshouses when he had visitors. They would turn the heating down so that when the door was opened Maurice would say 'It's too cold we can't go in there.' Likewise the heating was always full blast in the car and Maurice smoked large cigars. On one visit Lady Priscilla Bacon opened the window to let heat and smoke out to be admonished with 'I think it would be prudent, Priscilla, to close the window as there is a draught.'

Beginning in the mid fifties, each year he took a break from his business interests to travel around the world searching for plants. In January, together with his wife Margaret, he would leave England for between four and six weeks to hunt for new plants in a warmer climate. Together they were to visit many tropical and sub-tropical countries such as Argentina, Australia, much of Africa, Borneo, Brazil, Colombia, Costa Rica, New Zealand, Peru, the Solomon Islands, and Venezuela. He also visited Papua New Guinea three times. First in his estimation, however, were Madagascar and the Mascarene Islands of Mauritius, Rodrigues and Réunion, the former having more endemic plants than anywhere else in the world. As the majority of them were new to him he enjoyed the challenge of trying to grow them to maturity when he returned to Talbot Manor.

Head gardener, Bob Sayer, with part of the collection of cacti and succulents. 1964.

Plants were collected in many ways. For instance, the judicious use of pidgin English would explain the purpose of their visit to a village headman, and this often resulted in the entire village population becoming involved in hunting for seeds or plants. A wide variety of means of travel had to be undertaken, including a ten-minute helicopter journey to 3,000 feet from Aropa, on the island of Bougainville, which meant a saving of at least two or three days' climbing.

The expeditions that he joined often had arrangements with a botanic garden in the host country which was given a proportion of those plants found. In this way his international circle of contacts steadily grew. He arrived back in Fincham with quantities of extra luggage in the form of seeds, cuttings and young plants in hessian bags. If he had worked with a botanist in the country of origin, these would be carefully labelled; otherwise, as the plants grew and flowered, samples would be sent for identification to Kew. All his acquisitions were meticulously noted in a series of ledgers which were later transferred to computer by his son Hugh. He used his expanding knowledge of the fine differences in native habitat of his plants to match their growing requirements in this country, and in this way was successful in keeping many that were new to cultivation – although he was not slow to admit that with some, he had little or no success at all.

He was a generous man, and, by propagating and distributing plants, helped to ensure their survival. Plants were exchanged with many like-minded enthusiasts and collectors both locally and around the world. There was nothing he liked better than giving fellow enthusiasts cuttings and plants. Christopher Lloyd got on well with him and said that when you went round the collections he would be asked 'You like?' and, if you expressed an interest in a plant, sure enough a few days later a parcel would arrive containing all those he had mentioned. John Morley recalls being invited to lunch with Lady Bacon to meet Maurice Mason. He was asked which plants he was interested in and said that his current interest was in the genus *Sambucus*, and quick as a flash a notebook and pencil appeared and he was asked which of them he grew. The next day a large box of cuttings and plants arrived for him. Each contact was given a number and John recalls that he was 247 and would sign his letters with the number which pleased and amused Maurice.

In fact, Maurice was quite upset when he was visited by Elizabeth Strangman who ran Washfield Nursery in Kent as she wouldn't accept any cuttings on her visit as the plants had not been watered the day before. A number on the label of his plants related to its provenance, and, by the time of his death in 1993, aged 81, he had plants from over 400 other gardens, including Windsor, Kew, Edinburgh Botanic Gardens, Harold Hillier, Lady Bacon at Raveningham Hall and other English collectors, as well as Lapostolle at Les Cèdres and Professor Rauh at Heidelberg University Botanic Garden (who shared his enthusiasm for bromeliads).

The drawback to such a collection (whether public or private) is the cost of maintenance, so when fuel prices soared in the 1980s the stove plants had to go. Predictably the Royal Horticultural Society at Wisley became the beneficiaries of the marvellous orchid collection. However, Maurice turned this to his advantage as it meant that the greenhouses were now freed up for plants that needed cooler conditions! In this way the greenhouses became home over time for large collections of orchids, bromeliads, *Hedychium*, citrus fruit, tender bulbs, *Tillandsia*, camellias, vireya rhododendrons, cacti, and succulents. The *Tillandsia* (air plants) were given a forty-foot greenhouse bench and were tied on to home-grown cherry branches with a small handful of osmunda fibre. The *Hedychium* alone occupied a forty-five by fifteen-foot house. When the seven acres of garden immediately surrounding Talbot Manor left the family's hands, the hardy camellias and rhododendrons from the glasshouses were lifted, propagated, and taken to the garden at Beachamwell. Last to leave were the cacti which were planted out in a hundred by thirty-foot house at Talbot Manor, rather than displayed in pots – this being one of the first examples of landscaping in a greenhouse. These and the Bromeliaceae have now been moved by the family to new quarters.

Maurice Mason was a regular supporter of the spring and autumn RHS shows, being awarded many medals over a period of some thirty-five years, as well as serving on a variety of RHS committees and on the council. In 1960 the Victoria Medal of Honour was conferred on him, '... an outstanding exhibitor of greenhouse plants and of trees and shrubs.' and in 1968 a gold Veitch Memorial Medal. H. E. Bates, writing in 1968,

Maurice with part of his *Tillandsia*, air plant collection. Part of the bromeliad family, *Tillandsia* is a genus with some 500 different species. They require no soil, instead extracting moisture from the air.

'Maurice was one of those rumbustious extroverts before whom shyer mortals cringe. "Are you salacious" was his opening gambit as one drew close to his willow garden. The question was usually addressed to the prettiest girl in the party. When he accosted my wife with this enquiry, she replied that she most certainly was and added that she was magnifica rather than fragilis.'
Charles Quest-Ritson, *Country Life*.

summed up the man and his passion: 'He is a man of fanatical horticultural dedication, something of a visionary, possessed with an insatiable thirst for plants and more plants, trees and more trees, much of it in defiance, perhaps, of the searing winds that pierce down from Spitzbergen and across the Wash: and that is right. Mason is also a very cheerful, very amusing, very forthright, very likeable, loquacious, tirelessly energetic man, both physically and mentally, possessed among other things of an astounding encyclopedic memory.'

It is fitting that amongst those plants named after him is the begonia which he brought back from Singapore in 1952 and introduced at the Ghent Floralies in 1955. *Begonia masoniana* won the award for the best new plant that year, but when he came to pick it up Maurice found that the Dutch nurserymen had stripped it of every available

Begonia masoniana – the 'Iron Cross' begonia, brought back from Singapore by Maurice Mason and introduced into cultivation in the UK in 1952. At first it was thought to be a hybrid but when it was recognised as a true species, it was named after him. Its origin could be from China or possibly India.

'*Begonias, which have a worldwide distribution in tropical areas, are a huge subject. I remember that Maurice Mason, with acres of garden near King's Lynn in Norfolk, devoted an entire greenhouse to them, most of the contents collected by himself, he and his wife Margaret being great travellers and used to hard conditions when need be. He was as generous a gardener as you will find and always sharing his plants.*'

Christopher Lloyd, from *Exotic Planting for Adventurous Gardeners*.

cutting and within a few years it was to be found everywhere, so becoming a pot plant of some commercial importance commonly known as the 'Iron Cross' begonia. Writing on begonias in the journal of the RHS nearly seventy years ago, he said 'A large part of the pleasure of exhibiting these plants at Chelsea is the fun of meeting amateurs who are interested in the same family and exchanging plants with them. In this way we have assembled a collection which is not inferior to that of any Botanic Garden in the country today, and in which no plant has been bought.'

It was proposed to him that he should take on the famed Monument site, the large central exhibit at the RHS Chelsea Flower Show. It is said that when it was suggested that it wouldn't be possible for a single, and indeed, amateur exhibitor to tackle this, his sights were set! A challenge exemplified by being asked at relatively short notice, as the exhibitor who was to have designed and planted the site had to unexpectedly withdraw. Derek Kemp, former head gardener, who was trained by Maurice Mason at Talbot Manor, recalls that in the autumn of 1979 birch was cut for the edging of the proposed display, the joints being pegged and jointed for easy construction. During the spring a replica of the site was built at Fincham so that at Chelsea in May 1980, all that was needed was for six to eight lorry-loads of plants to be transported down

Maurice Mason (left), HM the Queen, and Lord Aberconway, President of the Royal Horticultural Society at the Chelsea Flower Show in 1964 and again in 1980 (FACING PAGE), finding amusement in one of Maurices's bromeliads, part of the Mason exhibit at the Monument site, 1980.

to London. The staff rebuilt the stand between Thursday and Monday. The resulting cornucopia of agave, aroids, bromeliads, cacti, succulents, ferns, etc. etc. was well deserving of the Lawrence Medal, awarded for the best exhibit shown to the Society throughout the whole of 1980. One of the exhibits was a magnificent example of the New Guinea stag's horn fern *Platycerium wandae* (at one point he grew 12 of the 18 species of *Platycerium*) which was then given to Kew Gardens. He also received the Holford Medal for best amateur exhibit of the year a total of three times. His tastes changed, and the growing of hardy trees and shrubs gave him such pleasure that he increased the area of arboretum at Talbot Manor. At his last home, Larchwood, the design incorporated extra wide paths to give access by car, which meant that in his later years, although seriously disabled, he was still able to view all areas of the garden.

The trees at both Talbot Manor and Larchwood are now in their maturity, many of them are rare and interesting and have reached specimen size. There is not space here to catalogue the many remarkable trees in the collection, but a few deserve mention. The original planting included a magnificent *Acer pseudoplatanus* 'Brilliantissimum' with its

A selection of stove plants, from the Mason collection: crotons, *Sansevieria* and other tropical foliage, displayed at the Chelsea Flower Show in 1954 and 1956.

pink and cream spring foliage. There is a fine specimen of the Chinese fir, *Cunninghamia lanceolata* which with its thick, fibrous red-brown bark is closely related to the sequoia; the sharply pointed, lance-shaped leaves however, are more reminiscent of the monkey puzzle (*Araucaria araucana*). Of note too is an impressive Chinese wingnut, *Pterocarya stenoptera* with pendant, foot-long spikes of small, winged green fruit in summer; and an *Aesculus* x *neglecta* 'Erythroblastos', the sunrise horse chestnut which has red leaf stalks and leaves that unfold cream, turn bright pink, become yellow, and mature to green by midsummer. Sadly, although this last has received an Award of Garden Merit, it still remains little known and rarely planted. Indeed, much of the original planting that was developed with the help of Hillier Nursery features trees which are no longer in their catalogue. The extensive collection of genera in the gardens include maples, lilacs, dogwoods, rowans, euonymus, and bamboo.

John Simmons OBE VMH, former curator of living collections at Kew, knew Maurice Mason well and writes that, 'At the peak of his collecting, which was arguably in the early 1960s, Maurice Mason was successfully cultivating one of the largest collections of tender (greenhouse) plants in the British Isles. Within this many individual collections

His knowledge was readily imparted to visitors to Talbot Manor as here in part of the orchid collection.

Part of the maturing planting at Larchwood, 2019. Temperate trees and shrubs became such a passion for Maurice that Harold Hillier used to send him a specimen of every new species which was raised in his Winchester nursery.

were outstanding be it bromeliads, begonias, succulent plants (such as *Rhipsalis*) and orchids, which were his favourite group of plants. His collection of orchids eventually approached 4,000 specimens, and he declared this to be "unique in the United Kingdom, and just possibly in the world". He had a great knowledge of plants and concentrated on species rather than cultivated forms. Eventually his magnificent orchid collection, which contained many of his own collected plants from countries like New Guinea and Madagascar, was presented to the Royal Horticultural Society.'

In his later years he concentrated on his new arboretum at Larchwood which he had bought in 1947. During the war it had been used as an army dump and consequently was very untidy. First it had to be cleared (which took three years) and then planted – initially with the 'normal' forestry trees. Over time Maurice and Margaret, his wife, became more attracted to this area and built a small chalet there where they could lunch and inspect progress. Eventually this was expanded into the bungalow in which they would live. The forestry trees were gradually replaced by trees and shrubs which they had not grown at Fincham, or they particularly liked and he continued to expand the planting right up to his death, in fact ten days before he died he was visited by Lady Priscilla Bacon and his guests were told that he had planted his last three acres and had no room left.

Although the garden at Larchwood was so extensive, there was a maze of rides through it which enabled people to get within fifteen feet of any of the plants and, most light evenings, Maurice and his wife would drive round to see some particular planting

The contents of the Talbot Manor glasshouses were distinguished not only by the quantity of the species and varieties of plant they contained, but for their quality and the high standard of horticulture needed to maintain them.

that appealed to them. In later years, wheelchair bound, he was driven round the garden in his specially adapted car. The car, generally driven by Margaret, would proceed at a pace slower than walking speed which enabled many stops and opportunities to collect cuttings (as well as to get some fresh air and cool down) with the nurses walking behind. John Morley was 'promoted' to drive the car but went 'too fast' and was only allowed to carry on when he had mastered driving at such a slow speed. On one particular visit, the car was travelling so slowly that it overheated, and the engine burst into flames, Maurice having to be dragged clear by his nurses!

As with his tender collections, the plants at Larchwood were well grown and benefited from his own collecting, as for example from Bariloche in the Argentinian Andes. His plant collection was fully documented, and he had a full computerized

Maurice Mason with part of his cacti collection.

Maurice Mason's distinctive and appropriate headstone in Shingham churchyard. His wife Margaret is buried and commemorated here too. The verdigris is the natural weathered patina of the copper.

'Maurice Mason must have left more friends enriched both mentally and horticulturally than any other gardener of our times. To visit him in his two dendrological extravaganzas in Norfolk, to hear his throaty 'dear boy' greeting and to feel the hospitable warmth that he and his wife Margaret generated was as much as one could wish from any gardening friendship. Informality and hospitality masked but never hid the extraordinary scholarship the Masons shared and wanted to share with everybody.'

From *Hugh Johnson in the Garden: The Best Garden Diary of our Times.*

inventory compiled as well as an amazing botanical library with the full run of *Curtis's Botanical Magazine* from 1787, and many 'Herbals' and other early botanical books. As such his collections had great botanical value, and in the separate arboreta at Fincham and Beachamwell, he had one of the country's most significant collections of trees and shrubs. A private collector who, in range of species and cultivation standards, often exceeded those achieved by university and other state institutions.

As Larchwood was developed on an old woodland site it is not surprising that honey fungus could be a problem. Ever philosophical about such things, Maurice said that whenever something died, he promptly put another back in the hole from which it came and had yet to see the second plant killed. Another pest was rabbits which was countered by putting a net round the whole wood which virtually eliminated them. This was prompted after the heather garden, which was developed from three or four thousand cuttings given to him by Edinburgh Botanic Garden, was subjected to being chewed right down to the ground, resulting in very tight and compact growth. Pheasants could be another problem, especially in the wonderful extensive planting of *Lilium lankongense*, such that wire netting had to be used to cover the ground. Mass planting was one of the joys of Larchwood and huge areas of *Arisaema candidissimum* and *Paeonia emodi* were spectacular, as were the naturalised *Narcissus cyclamineus* and *N. bulbocodium*, seed of which had been planted in the grass near the house and seven years later began to flower, naturalise and produce hybrids, much to Maurice's delight.

In the 1960s an offer was made to transfer both gardens into the keeping of the University of East Anglia which, sadly, had to be later withdrawn. If this offer had been carried through the UEA would have had a botanical collection to rival that of any other in the country.

Inevitably when gardeners die the gardens move on. The garden of Talbot Manor lies between the High Street and Lynn Road in Fincham and is bisected by a public footpath. Sadly, this garden, including house, pool, workshop and bowling green is no longer in the possession of the family. Indeed, the workshop has also been converted into a home thus further dividing the original garden. Maurice Mason's son Hugh took the twenty-five acres of arboretum at Talbot Manor under his wing, replacing shrubs which were past their best. The main infrastructure of trees planted by his father between the fifties and seventies has reached magnificent proportions; the trees can be truly admired as representatives of their genera, just as Maurice Mason had planned. The original house at Larchwood was sold although 40 acres of 'Old Larchwood' was kept by his son.

The arboreta are a magnificent bequest to the horticultural life of East Anglia, from a remarkable Norfolk plantsman who would undoubtedly be pleased that a new generation is able to benefit from its use some seventy years after it was begun.

10

Hortus Episcopi

Graham Innes

On the north side of Norwich Cathedral lies a garden as old as the cathedral itself, the private demesne of the bishops of Norwich. Although it is one of the oldest gardens in England, surprisingly little is known about its history and development, as no account of it has ever been written. For approximately 700 years it extended to six and a half acres. Today the garden still extends to four acres, roughly corresponding to two thirds of the core medieval garden created by the end of Bishop Salmon's episcopate in 1325.

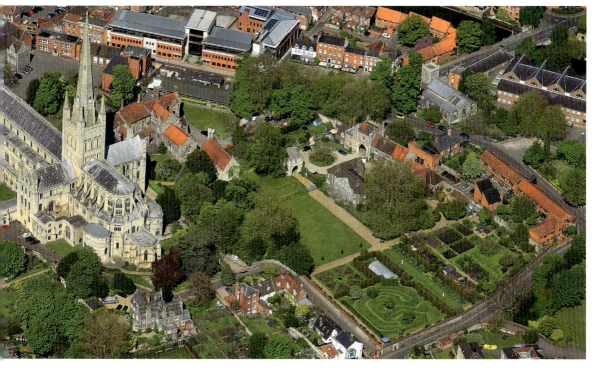

FACING PAGE The hybrid musk shrub rose, *Rosa* 'Penelope' in the Bishop's Garden, Norwich.
ABOVE To the north of Norwich Cathedral, hidden behind trees and a high wall is the largest private garden in the city – the Bishop's Garden.

In 1959 approximately two acres were ceded to the Norwich School along with the old Bishop's Palace itself and in 1972 about half an acre at the north-east corner, which had been acquired after the end of the fourteenth century, was sold to a housing association to provide flats for the elderly. Of great horticultural and arboricultural interest, the Bishop's Garden is remarkable above all for its incomparable setting in the shadow of the great Norman Cathedral of the Holy and Undivided Trinity. The cathedral is the main feature of the garden and dominates most views from it.

In 1096 Bishop Herbert de Losinga (bishop from 1091 to 1119) began to build Norwich Cathedral. By 1145 both the cathedral and the palace were completed, the latter built at a slight angle to the cathedral and joined to it on the north side. The land immediately round the palace became the first garden of the bishops. From this area we can still marvel at the wonderful patina of the original Norman stonework, especially on the north transept of the cathedral where it survives to a greater extent than anywhere else. Because this faces the Bishop's Palace it was more richly decorated than the south transept facing the monastic quarters. This view is only possible from the Bishop's Garden, and if the garden contained nothing else, this would make it a unique space.

However, the form of the garden today has been largely determined by the extensive building, demolition and rebuilding of the palace and its associated structures. The

Bishop Salmon's ruined porch, with beyond Bishop Reynolds' chapel, and gardeners at work. Drawn by David Hodgson and engraved in 1830.

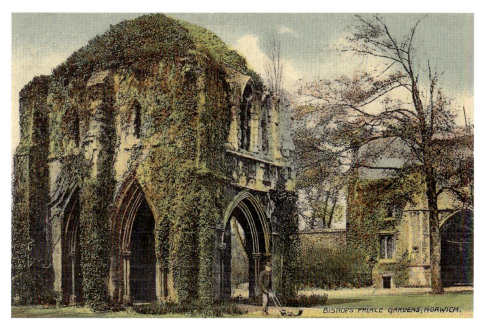

From a postcard of 1903. Bishop Salmon's porch and the south side of the fifteenth-century Alnwick Gate. A well-dressed gardener cuts the lawn.

upper terrace which adjoins the eastern arm of the cathedral, was once dominated by Bishop de Losinga's enormous 130-foot-long chapel dedicated to the Virgin Mary. The later modernisation of de Losinga's chapel by the great statesman-bishop John Salmon (1299–1325) included the insertion of larger Gothic windows. However, desecration by the Puritans during the Commonwealth (smashing the stained glass and, in particular, stripping off the lead from the roof) hastened the demise of St Mary's Chapel. After the Restoration, Bishop Reynolds (1661–76) demolished what was left of it, whilst saving some of the beautiful curvilinear windows with flowing tracery inserted by Bishop Salmon. These he reused in his much smaller Bishop's Chapel, which survives today as a delightful feature on the terrace (and, since 1970, the library of Norwich School).

In the early fourteenth century Bishop Salmon greatly increased the size of the garden by compulsorily purchasing additional land. He pushed Bishopgate eastward and northward, thereby extending the grounds to their present size. The walls that surround the garden today are substantially those built 700 years ago by Salmon to protect his enlarged demesne. Moreover, with the acquisition of this land he was also able to build an enormous hall, 120 ft long by 60 ft wide, across the upper terrace, at right angles to St Mary's Chapel. Again, it was Bishop Reynolds, after yet more Puritan excess (they had once again stripped the lead off the roof), who demolished the remains of this hall, with the exception of the very beautiful porch with its finely pointed open arches and room above. This survives as a major garden feature today, a genuine Gothic ruin. After walking through its arches one descends steps to the main axial garden walk. In 1662 Bishop Reynolds placed his new chapel over the opposite south, or dais, end of Bishop Salmon's great hall.

The last of the major medieval buildings to be built in the Bishop's Garden was Bishop Alnwick's Gate, started by Bishop Alnwick (1426–36) and completed by Bishop Lyhart (1446–72). The least well-known of the four medieval gateways (including the Water Gate today known as Pull's Ferry) around the Cathedral precincts, it used to be the main entrance to the old Bishop's Palace and now forms the main entrance to the modern Bishop's House, which was completed in 1959. Through the archway can be seen the 1959 walled forecourt which screens the garden from the outside world and at the same time successfully integrates Bishop Salmon's Porch in the centre of the wall with the new Bishop's House to the left. The gatehouse arch also frames an unexcelled view beyond the porch and above the wall of one of the finest of cathedral presbyteries. In summer partly obscured by a curtain of foliage, in autumn the falling leaves gradually reveal the beauty of the clerestory tracery. Viewed through the winter screen of branches, the enormous windows appear to float above the Romanesque walls below.

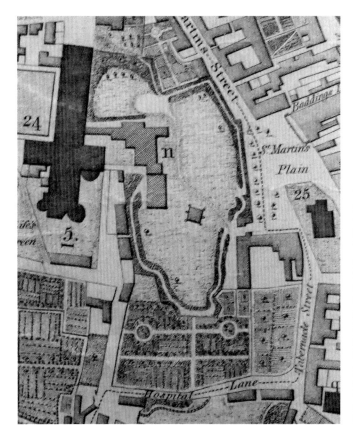

The garden as it appeared on Hochstetter's map of 1789. The extensive Bishop's Palace is marked 'n', and the informal garden stretches to the west front of the cathedral, at the top, with an outer circuit of trees and shrubs leading down to the formal layout at the bottom, to the east, bounded by Hospital Lane. A large part of this would have been the Kitchen Garden for the Palace, with an orchard planted to the right.

The Cathedral from the North-East and the Bishop's Garden, a print published in 1779, after a painting by Charles Catton the elder.

Although a very competent archaeological dig was conducted in 1859 on the upper terrace and a much more recent geophysical survey was carried out, maps of Norwich, in fact, provide the best accessible information we have for the garden over time. From Clere's map of 1696 onwards they provide increasingly reliable information up to the end of the nineteenth century. They show that the general form of the garden was laid down at least 300 years ago. The lower east end was the cultivated area, separated from the pleasure grounds nearer the palace by a wall running right across the garden. Although most of this wall has now disappeared, the two main areas still remain, variously subdivided and enriched by other features and planting.

Hochstetter's celebrated map of 1789 indicates that by the late eighteenth century a serpentine path wound its way round most of the upper pleasure grounds. Although this largely disappeared in the nineteenth century remodelling of the garden, the main gravel crosswalk shown still exists in the lower garden. Some time between 1830 and 1860 the cross-wall was breached, enabling the present main axial walk to be made. This runs eastwards from Bishop Salmon's Porch to the large blank arch at the centre of the Bishopgate wall.

The double herbaceous borders in 2020.

The major contribution of Bishop Pelham (1857–93) to today's Bishop's Garden was to link the lower garden visually with the upper, as part of his ambitious plan to refashion the palace grounds as well as the palace itself. This he did by demolishing most of the remainder of the cross-wall, except for the short ogival section still standing beyond the end of the Bishop's House. He then proceeded to plant the magnificent yew hedges that form the backdrop to the 160-foot-long double herbaceous border, the finest in a private garden in Norwich. At the same time as they lengthened the vista from Bishop Salmon's Porch, they bisected the lower garden and screened off what is now the Kitchen Garden to the north-east and the former orchard to the south-east.

Bishop Pelham's influence is also strongly felt in the upper west garden, where the old palace and the original demesne adjacent to it belongs nowadays to the Norwich

ABOVE A nineteenth-century reworking of a sketch by John Kirkpatrick of c.1720, showing the formal layout of gravel paths and grass around the Bishop's Palace; the earliest depiction of any part of the Bishop's Garden.

BELOW The north front of Bishop's Palace after its restoration, 1858–9, by Ewan Christian. Much rebuilt, the oldest sections of the building date from the eleventh century.

The Bishop's Garden. To the east, on the right of the picture, the garden is contained by a high wall running along Bishopgate. Inside this, protected by the wall, is much tender and sub-tropical planting. The Labyrinth is in the bottom right corner with the formal square Rose Garden to its left. Yew hedges on either side back the long double herbaceous border. Above these are working areas and the Kitchen Garden. The mid twentieth-century neo-Georgian Bishop's House looks out over a wide lawn backed by trees with the cathedral rising above them. To the right of the Bishop's House is one of the huge London plane trees, and behind the house Bishop Alnwick's Gate, the main entrance to the house and garden. Bishop Salmon's porch, partly obscured by a tulip tree, stands on its raised terrace next to the turning circle by the gate. Below it is Bishop Reynolds' chapel. To the left the sequence of adjoined buildings is the old Bishop's Palace, now part of Norwich School. The garden used to extend beyond the palace to the west front of the cathedral.

School. In an attempt to modernise the bishop's residence in the grand domestic Gothic style of the time, Ewan Christian (1814–95), architect to the Ecclesiastical Commissioners from 1851 until 1895, was employed around 1860 to undertake the remodelling of the old palace. After he had severed and demolished part of the unique connection in England between a Norman episcopal palace and its cathedral, he finally refaced the whole building in a grimly picturesque Gothic style, which only hints at its extraordinary underlying Norman structure. By 1885 Bishop Pelham's plans for both palace and garden had been realized and for the next 75 years little was to change.

However, a major reduction in the size of the historic Bishop's Garden took place in 1959, the same year that a new Bishop's House was completed. As the twentieth century progressed the palace had finally been considered too large, cold and draughty to be viable as the home of a modern bishop and his family. In November 1958, therefore, Bishop Herbert (1942–59) laid the foundation stone of the new Bishop's House. After his retirement the following year, both the palace and two acres of the upper west garden were transferred to Norwich School.

The section of garden transferred to Norwich School is never opened to the public, but it can at least be glimpsed through the fine but rather self-effacing wrought-iron gates to the left of the main entrance to the cathedral in the Upper Close. These were originally designed in the 1750s by Thomas Ivory for the Octagon Chapel in the Colegate and now became the main entrance to the old palace building. They open on to an area of great historic interest as it once formed the open-air Green, or Preaching Yard, of the cathedral until its destruction, once again, during the Commonwealth. However, overlooked by the dour west façade of the palace, this is now a somewhat gloomy area.

By way of contrast, east of the old palace, and overlooking the large lawn below the

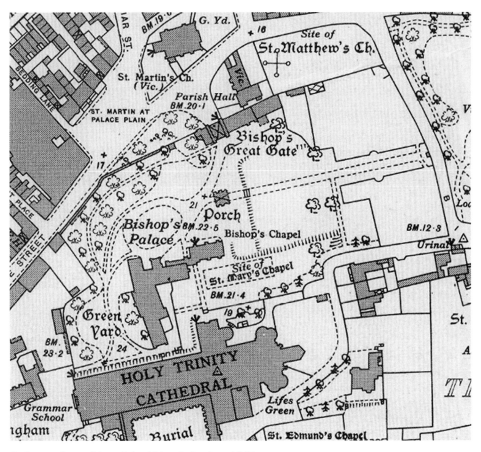

Ordnance Survey Map of the Bishop's Garden, 1947.

The view to the east from the main lawn in front of the Bishop's House. From the left: London plane, the herbaceous borders, yew hedging, the formal Rose Garden with the Labyrinth behind; sections of the ancient high flint walls surrounding the garden to the south and east, with the tower of the church of St Helen, Bishopgate, part of the Great Hospital. Tree-clad Mousehold Heath rises beyond.

upper terrace, is the new Bishop's House, a pleasant neo-Georgian structure designed by James Fletcher-Watson in 1958–59. The non-traditional purplish brick used, associated with most of Fletcher-Watson's Norfolk commissions, successfully blends with the flint-faced garden front. The new episcopal residence commands the best view of the cathedral and, indeed, from the upper terrace near the house there are fine views over the whole garden and eastwards, past the massive perimeter walls, to Mousehold Heath and the wooded slopes of Thorpe Hamlet.

In 1972 the last part of the medieval garden to be disposed of was sold to a housing association for development by architects Fielden and Mawson as accommodation for the elderly. Queen Elizabeth Court and its Victorian neighbour, the Vicarage of St Martin-at-Palace Plain, extend over the site of St Matthew-at-Palace to the left of Bishop Alnwick's Gate. Because of the loss of parishioners owing to the Black Death in 1349 the church was demolished in the late fourteenth century and the site enclosed

by a further wall outside Bishop Salmon's extant garden wall. This garden is shown on Hochstetter's map as probably an orchard next to what was then called Tabernacle Street. The small opening in Bishop Salmon's wall which formerly connected this enclosed area with the main garden was bricked up in 1972 but there are still four old apple trees and two pear trees, which pre-date 1972, in the small garden inside the housing scheme.

Back within today's garden proper a Holly Walk leading to the north transept has been planted more recently along the upper terrace, behind Bishop Reynolds' Chapel. Unlike the unfortunately sited Atlas cedar (*Cedrus atlantica*) nearby, this will in time enhance the superlative view of the cathedral and doubtless prove to be an attractive feature.

Immediately in front of the Bishop's House is the main lawn, a large sunken grassed area excavated in earlier times. The grass terraces round the lawn add interest to the topography and accentuate the gentle rise in the land from Bishopgate in the east to the upper west terrace where Bishop Salmon's Hall once stood. Two magnificent London planes (*Platanus* x *hispanica*) planted around 1850, one of which is the second largest in Norfolk, stand majestically either side of the main lawn. Several large trees on

ABOVE The cathedral from the north-east, across the main 'sunken' lawn bordered by terracing. Bishop Reynolds' chapel to the right. This can be compared with the Charles Catton view of 1779 on page 171.

BELOW A large tulip tree between Bishop Salmon's Porch, of the fourteenth century, and the seventeenth-century Bishop's Chapel.

The Labyrinth and wild-flower meadow with, at its centre, the 200-year-old pear tree, *Pyrus communis* 'Uvedale's St Germain'.

the main lawn which have been blown down over the years have not been replaced, however, to allow large outdoor diocesan and charitable events to take place there in the summer.

Elsewhere, many splendid trees still create much of the character of the garden. Also planted about the middle of the nineteenth century, possibly the largest tulip tree (*Liriodendron tulipifera*) in Norfolk rises up beside Bishop Salmon's Porch. Now in the school grounds, but best seen from the Bishop's Garden, is the finest purple beech (*Fagus sylvatica* f. *purpurea*) in the county.

Other smaller venerable trees include a mulberry in the Kitchen Garden, probably planted in the first quarter of the seventeenth century. In the centre of the former orchard stands an impressive 200-year-old pear tree (*Pyrus communis* 'Uvedale's St Germain'). It is surrounded by a wild-flower meadow planted in 2002 by Simon Gaches, head gardener from 1994 to 2019, who initiated a series of changes to the garden. The grass here is cut in the form of a labyrinth after the flowering. Seven beehives house the new residents in this area who have accompanied Bishop Graham and Mrs Usher on their translation to the see of Norwich in 2019.

ABOVE Part of the planting of hebes, purple elder and roses, inside the medieval garden walls.

BELOW The formal Rose Garden with pool and fountain at its centre set into a star-shaped circle of box, planted in 2001.

Among the many beautiful shrubs and wall-climbing plants nearby one curiosity is an exceptionally large and long-lived, white-flowered *Hebe brachysiphon*, planted from a sprig taken from Queen Victoria's wedding bouquet in 1840. The reason it came to Norwich was that Bishop Stanley was Queen Victoria's clerk of the closet from the time of her accession until his death in 1849.

A rose parterre was planted in the early 1900s in the enclave created in the south-west corner of the former orchard by an extension of one of the very long Pelham yew hedges that line the axial walk. It consists of eight sections divided by box planted in 2001 radiating from a small pond with simple jet and pergola, surrounded by what looks like a toddler-proof barrier of box planted in an original stellar pattern. The late Peter Beales donated the *Rosa* 'Norwich Cathedral' filling the triangular beds to commemorate 900 years since the foundation of the Norman cathedral. The north-facing bed alongside the adjacent south wall of the lower garden was replanted between 2016 and 2018 with a large range of hostas and scented old-fashioned varieties of David Austin roses.

Some of the more exotic planting sheltered by the suntrap of the west-facing wall.

Friendship with the late Will Giles, who created the Exotic Garden in Norwich, inspired Simon Gaches in 2007 to plant a striking Bamboo Walk or Bamboosery, and Fernery, next to the Kitchen Garden, along with such unusual plants as lancewood (*Pseudopanax*) and rice paper plant (*Tetrapanax*) with their bold and exotic-looking foliage and indigo (*Indigofera*) and Szechuan pepper (*Zanthoxylum*). In 2015 he started to create a raised boardwalk 'jungle' walk in the same 'tropical' style for summer interest along part of the Bishopgate wall. The microclimate here allows bananas, gingers, palms and other exotics to flourish. This was completed in 2017.

Other more recent developments have included a small brick and glass greenhouse in 2013 for the propagation and display of more tender plants. It overlooks the Kitchen Garden which provides organically grown fruit and vegetables for the Bishop's House.

In 2014 Simon Gaches initiated a five-year renovation of the long double herbaceous borders. Backed by the two extensive yew hedges that nowadays are loosely cloud-pruned, they once again constitute the garden's most spectacular horticultural feature. Today the head gardener, Sam Garland, one part-time assistant, and a team

The lower, eastern section of the garden. The Rose Garden is top left, below it is the Labyrinth, yew hedges and herbaceous borders are at the centre, and the Kitchen Garden and working area are to the right. The paths and hedges separating these areas were added in 2003. 'Tropical' borders run beside the flint wall, at the bottom, with rose borders planted either side of the gravelled Rose Walk, which runs parallel to the southern garden wall, on the left.

of volunteers do the work that occupied fifteen gardeners up to the First World War, and nine in the 1940s and 1950s. He continues to evolve the garden, particularly aware of Bishop Graham Usher's environmentally led approach to horticulture. The bishop has introduced beehives, and beds which can cope with drought are a new feature. Starting in 2002 the bishop's predecessor, Bishop Graham James, opened his garden regularly during the summer to aid local charities. The huge success of these openings has contributed many thousands of pounds for good causes, in 2018 alone over £27,000 was raised. The openings are now a permanent part of the life of the Bishop's Garden, for the first time in its history allowing regular public access to the largest private garden in the city.

TOP The Kitchen Garden. In addition to supplying the Bishop's House, the sale of plants raised here goes towards funding new projects in the garden.
OPPOSITE Bishop Graham's bees.
OVERLEAF The renovated herbaceous borders in 2020.

11

A Parterre by Two Ladies

Roger Last

In June 1930 *Country Life* published three articles on Blickling Hall. As one would expect they extolled the many virtues of the hall, its contents and its gardens. The writer was Christopher Hussey, who was to be the editor of *Country Life* from 1933–40, and a dominant force in the magazine. An architectural writer and garden historian, his views carried weight. It therefore must have been perceived as a hammer blow to Blickling's owner, the Marquess of Lothian, to have included some pointed adverse criticism. Hussey attacked the design of the Parterre. Attack is perhaps too dramatic a word – *Country Life* conducted itself, particularly when dealing with the aristocracy, with more decorum.

The Parterre is the principal garden space at Blickling. It runs the full length of the long east side of the hall, looked down on from the Long Gallery. It was undoubtedly Blickling's star turn. At least it had been. Hussey wrote, 'To the modern eye the patterned area is too small in scale. The lines of the design are lost in a multiplicity of dotted beds, beautifully filled, but without perceptible relation to each other or to the house. The broad avenue beyond is, in fact, more impressive.'

It was not much, but it was enough, and very clear – impeccable horticulture, but set in a muddled and inappropriate design. This was not said confidentially over a few drinks, but publicly for all, who mattered, to read. The death toll for the great Parterre had sounded.

Philip Kerr, the 11th Marquess of Lothian, may well have thumbed through his copy of *Country Life* with quiet satisfaction. It is quite probable that Christopher Hussey had viewed the Parterre with him and that both of them concluded that here was a design well past its sell-by date. It belonged to another age, the late Victorian, and to two progressive men of the 1930s, it was not an age they wished to prolong. Philip Kerr had succeeded to the Lothian title in 1929. His busy and high profile political and diplomatic career limited the time he could spend at Blickling. But he used it as often as he could as a refuge and for prestigious weekend social gatherings. When these

Norah Lindsay.

extended into the shooting season, those arriving on still autumnal afternoons found hovering above the hall a pall of black smoke, as every fireplace in the building was banked with coal to keep the company warm. It was not only an expensive house to run, but Philip Kerr was also faced with a property in need of major expenditure and with burdensome inheritance taxes. Reluctantly he sent the most valuable contents of the library to auction, (including the rare Anglo-Saxon *Homilies* dated 970). He also looked at ways of cutting costs. Where better to start than by reducing the massive gardening bill for the Parterre. The cost in manpower for edging the 'multiplicity of dotted beds', for feeding, watering, mulching, staking, deadheading, and renewing and in part bedding out annuals must have been out of all proportion to the relatively small area of ground covered. However, to pull out this gardening wonder at a place like Blickling was no easy matter, such could be the censure. But if *Country Life* had given the thumbs up, then that matter was made much easier, provided of course that what replaced it was appropriate and expertly handled. Fortunately for Blickling, waiting in the wings was Norah Lindsay.

Gertrude Jekyll, Norah Lindsay, Ellen Willmott, and Vita Sackville-West, are among the famous women gardeners of the last century who influenced their age and our own. Norah Lindsay (1873–1948) carried on the Edwardian tradition of garden making into the inter-war period, refining it with her own sense of style and gardening expertise. Born in Ireland, a granddaughter of the Earl of Mayo, she married Harry Lindsay, grandson of the Earl of Crawford. Her connections were invaluable throughout her gardening life. Indeed, she has been accused of being as interested in pursuing her social life as she was in gardens. So much time was spent socializing, particularly in the heady glittering world of 1930s high society, that she had little time to write the books which might have cemented her name in the canon of English garden

Philip Henry Kerr, 11th Marquess of Lothian, (1882–1940). Pencil drawing by Francis Amicia de Chadwick Biden Footner. He was a Liberal and as secretary to the Prime Minister Lloyd George played a prominent part in drafting the Treaty of Versailles at the end of the First World War. However, he believed Germany's treatment had been unjust and he was a leading advocate of Appeasement. He served as chancellor of the Duchy of Lancaster and under secretary of state for India, ending his career as British ambassador to the United States on the outbreak of the Second World War, and dying in Washington in 1940.

writers. Although with the ability and showing every sign of originality and promise, what garden writing she left is spartan in the extreme. Sadly too, the majority of her gardens have been lost.

A woman of strong views on design and planting, with unerring good taste, Norah seems to have drifted into garden design. Although not wealthy, she had money enough not to charge for her work. This was done for friends. One can imagine that her hosts, delighted to invite her for the weekend with her mix of wit, vivacity, eccentricity (James Lees-Milne called her 'stupid-clever') and her garden knowledge, might be hoping Norah would cast an eye over their garden and sort out that difficult area between the Long Border and the tennis court. But Norah had far greater gardening skills than that. Between the wars she became so in demand that her great friend Nancy Astor, glittering above the glitter at Cliveden, suggested that she simply must charge for her labours; so she did.

Norah Lindsay (left) with Sir Philip Sassoon. 1925.

Rich clients through the 1920s and 1930s kept her busy. Her most ambitious scheme was for Sir Philip Sassoon at Port Lympne, sitting above Romney Marsh in Kent. This was one of the great English gardens of the inter-war years. Designed by its owner and architect Philip Tilden, it was huge in scale with grand set pieces, including a magnificent classically inspired sweep of stairs linking a sequence of terraces, and a bathing pool with Deco overtones complete with fountains and theatrical viewing podiums, allowing wonderful panoramas over the marsh below. Norah Lindsay's extensive planting here included large double herbaceous borders stretching down the hillside.

It was in 1932 while staying with Sir Philip's sister, Sybil, Lady Cholmondeley, at Houghton Hall, (with the Kenneth Clarks there as well), that the party motored over to Blickling, and Norah first saw the great Parterre and the task ahead. She had already met Philip Kerr at the Astors' four years previously, and a friendship had grown between them. Norah declaring that she doted on him and found him 'more attractive every moment I am with him' – an attraction in particular to his intellect, and grasp of politics and world affairs. She had already given him a personal tour of the gardens at Cliveden and her work there. By 1932 Norah was overwhelmed with work as one rich client recommended her to another: Lord Berners at Faringdon, Ronald and Nancy Tree at Kelmarsh Hall and Ditchley Park, and Robert and Elsie Tritton at Godmersham Park. Over the years the client list had grown to over a hundred, and there was, as everyone knew, between 1930 and 1935, her work for the Prince of Wales at Fort Belvedere.

The Parterre as laid out and planted by Constance, Marchioness of Lothian. It was undoubtedly impressive, but the multiplicity of small beds, the variation of their shapes, and repartition resulted in a design which appears overloaded to contemporary tastes. Although herbaceous plants were incorporated, annual bedding-out plants are used in the smaller beds, labour intensive and if not controlled, multicoloured. Although the beds are not joined, there could be an influence here from strapwork, which was revived in the nineteenth century. The long gallery has an impressive Jacobean plaster strapwork ceiling. More occurs in the north-east turret bedroom. The Temple Walk beyond the Parterre is here narrowed and accentuated by plantings of trees and shrubs and columnar conifers either side.

So Philip Kerr was well aware of her design and planting capabilities. She agreed to add Blickling to her gardening portfolio at her now standard rate of £100 per year.

There is no record of what she thought of Blickling's Parterre. The sheer scale of the layout, the opulence of the planting and quality of the horticulture could not be dismissed. The design was then less than sixty years old, nothing in gardening terms, but light years in terms of the shift of taste and style since its inception. It had been conceived in the High Victorian era. It was being judged now from the viewpoint of the swinging thirties, with those in the know flirting with Modernism and Art Deco. Philip Kerr was already stripping away the layers of dark Victoriana from his house. Now it was the turn of his gardens.

Portrait of Constance, Marchioness of Lothian (1836–1901), by Sir John Leslie, 1866. Born Lady Constance Harriet Mahonesa Chetwynd-Talbot, in 1857 she married her cousin, to become the Marchioness of Lothian. A guest at Blickling remarked on her 'charm of manner and power of enjoyment of all the smallest things of beauty'. When she died, after presiding alone over the Blickling estate for three decades, she was buried in Jedburgh Abbey, near the Lothian family seat, Ferniehirst Castle, in the Scottish Borders.

The Parterre Norah Lindsay had been summoned to alter had been laid out from 1872 by Constance, Marchioness of Lothian. Her husband the 8th Marquess had employed Markham Nesfield, son of the influential High Victorian garden designer William Andrews Nesfield, and the architect Sir Matthew Digby Wyatt, to help redesign parts of the gardens at Blickling. Works were carried out on a major scale, yet it was not the Marquess who presided over these changes, but Constance. A sensitive and artistic woman, Constance is remembered for her kindness and gracious presence at Blickling. Her obituary in the *Eastern Daily Press* hailed her as 'one of the most genial and noble ladies the county has ever known'. 'Stately, unique, picturesque, great of mind, soul and person, beloved, revered and adored,' these were but some of the words ascribed to her. An 'In Memorial' in *The Spectator* quotes Mr Gladstone as saying that when 'he came to consider the great and good ladyhood of England, she stood first'. The eulogies were endlessly effusive. Constance being called an 'earth angel' and 'delightful, beautifully human, with a quick sense of humour, a heart full of pity and hands full of help'. Beneath the highly genteel and compassionate refinement she clearly had a practical and steelier side. She was to face thirty years of widowhood, and continued to live in, and preside over, the great house and estate until her death in 1901.

With her husband ill, with an unspecified disease he probably caught while travelling in India, it was Constance who looked over the plans and asked about the costs, and she who, in March 1870, ordered the work to begin 'with as much energy as possible'. She was no doubt mindful of her husband's condition, but nonetheless split the massive excavations about to take place into two parts to keep the dirt and unsightliness to a minimum. The area now filled by the Parterre had been grass, sloping down to the hall.

William Schomberg Robert Kerr, the 8th Marquess of Lothian, (1832–1870), by George Frederick Watts. He succeeded to the title aged nine. To the family he was known as 'Billy'. A distinguished scholar, he gained a Double First at Oxford. A collector of books and paintings, he championed contemporary artists, and wrote two books, one on the history, literature and art of Italy in the middle ages. Like his father, he met an early death through illness, aged 38. He died in Surrey and is buried in Jedburgh Abbey. His elaborate tomb chest with recumbent shrouded effigy with angels sculptured by George Frederick Watts in 1878 is in Blickling church.

ABOVE Blickling Hall from the north-east with the area below the east front laid to grass. From John Sell Cotman's *Excursions in the County of Norfolk*, 1818.

BELOW A sketch by Charles Marsham of Blickling's north and east fronts, 1844.

ABOVE AND FACING PAGE The Parterre as laid out by the Marchioness of Lothian.

Digby Wyatt had this excavated and the soil moved to back fill behind high ornamental walls. Made of local red brick, these were built on two sides, complete with alcoves and niches. Gravel walks were laid, and two substantial flights of stone steps constructed leading up to the higher ground with new walks above. This gave the east front a highly formal and sophisticated garden setting.

The Marquess never saw the completed transformation. He died in July 1870, at the early age of thirty-eight. It was left to Constance to drive the work forward and again to question the costs and hint at cuts. This she did in March 1871, with the works incomplete and the steps and much stonework not yet laid. Digby Wyatt was not inclined to cut anything and commented, 'I feel perfectly certain that if the whole now contemplated, including what is already done, shall be got through for a total cost of anything like £1050 it will be one of the cheapest jobs with which I was ever connected.'

Nesfield was asked what would be the cost 'of excavating and forming a sunk garden in the great central bed opposite the house', that is the newly created area of Parterre. His plans had shown this laid to grass. But this would not do for Constance. She loved flowers and determined that the Parterre should become a showcase for them. Perhaps, when it arrived, she was taken aback by Nesfield's estimate. Clearly confident however in her knowledge of plants, and of her design capabilities, or perhaps naively unaware of the pitfalls, she decided to undertake the task herself. So, it was Constance, and

her head gardener Septimus Lyon, rather than Nesfield, who was responsible for the all-important layout of the great Parterre.

The focal point at the Parterre's centre was a fountain. This had been bought by the 1st Duke of Buckingham in 1732 from the great sale of contents of Oxnead Hall. Dating from the early seventeenth century, it had formerly been sited near Lady's Cottage in the Great Wood at Blickling. Now it assumed pride of place in the centre of the grand design. Round the fountain Constance had planted eight columnar yews, and on either side, filling the east-west central axis which led eventually to the Doric Temple, were no less than twenty-six flower beds of varying size and shape. The complexity was made even more extreme by adding arches and trellis walks for climbing plants with two large circular wooden arbours, on the north-south axis, further augmented with eight scroll-shaped beds. To complete the corners of the design, four huge square herbaceous beds were laid out, each edged by more flower filled borders with additional topiary on each corner. There were astonishingly more than eighty beds in total, all of them set in grass walks of restless complexity. Clearly Constance thought big. She and Mr Lyon were determined, at least as far as the display of flowering plants was concerned, that Blickling had to have the best.

Constance filled her beds with herbaceous flowers, with phlox, Michaelmas daisies, monarda, helianthus, dahlias, and with roses. However, on closer inspection, despite some contemporary accounts to the contrary, here too were annual bedding plants,

ABOVE AND BELOW The Victorian Parterre as it remained until the 1930s.

whose garish colours might clash. The vogue for planting out massed tender exotics was not resisted either, for in went plants like cannas, which would find north Norfolk, particularly in the Victorian winter, very exotic. To our eyes the design seems over fussy in the extreme, as crammed full as a Victorian drawing room. But it reflected the taste of its time, which liked layered complexity often regardless of the visual turmoil of the result. Nevertheless, the new Parterre must have raised gasps of astonishment and delight when suddenly encountered from the Long Gallery.

The Parterre was further augmented by a large amount of ornamentation, plinths, urns, vases and sphinxes purchased in 1877. Contemporary opinion was unanimous. Constance had not only pulled it off, she had excelled. *Gardeners Chronicle* of 1894 describes the garden as 'a very charming example of the modern style of filling the beds, and we have little hesitation in saying that it is one of the best existing in which tender exotic plants are almost banished by hardy herbaceous perennials'. *The Gardening World* for 1887, which somewhat confusingly describes the planting style as being 'early English', was equally impressed. It was also impressed by the fact that Constance 'allows the public free access to the flower gardens, pleasure grounds, and the park every Tuesday during the months of July, August and September ... the plain iron gates ... are thrown wide open ... and the people walk about at will'. But it was left to *Country Life* and a compilation of its articles 'Gardens Old and New' in the 1900s, which opulently illustrated the very best gardens in the country, to set the seal on Constance's success.

'The judicious lady who carried out the work is an ardent admirer of hardy flowers, and her taste in the decorative use of them never wavered in the times when formal bedding was at its height. The result is that the garden is full of colour and fragrance, and that roses, pinks, carnations, lilies, bulbous flowers, and a host of other beautiful things, bloom in profusion. The design is bold and picturesque. Beds of simple character, disposed for broad effects, have been chosen, and the principal purpose has evidently been to give lavish effects of colour. The surrounding terraces are fine, and command most attractive and interesting views both within and without'. 'It is a happy circumstance

ABOVE LEFT Constance, Lady Lothian. c. 1885 and **(ABOVE RIGHT)** Norah Lindsay (left) with Madeline Whitbread, 1940.

Norah Lindsay's simplified Parterre at Blickling seen from the central window of the Long Gallery.

to be observed in relation to Blickling that the house and the gardens are in perfect accord.'

In less than thirty years came Christopher Hussey's censure 'the patterned area is too small in scale. The lines of the design are lost in a multiplicity of dotted beds, ... without perceptible relation to each other or to the house.' This in fact was the second time *Country Life* had poured scorn on the Parterre. Earlier H. Avary Tipping, garden writer and designer, and architectural editor of *Country Life*, had condemned the 'restlessness and confusion of the innumerable, many-shaped and differently treated beds that pullulate on the lawn'. So now it was over to Norah Lindsay.

On the face of it the two ladies were very different. There was Constance, stately, yet almost shrinking from public gaze, quietly dressed in plain black garb, her classically shaped head covered by an abbess-like veil or a large shady hat that partly obscured her features as she 'moved about her peerless garden'. And Norah, dressed in black and white with cherry red buttons and a flat hat 'like a pancake' down over one eye, a great and amusing talker and described as 'kittenish'. A waspish remark which failed to appreciate her charm, quick wit and consummate skills and instinctive flair as a garden designer. Undoubtedly the over-fussy Parterre design had to be simplified. But how? She could of course have had the entire eighty beds dug up and grassed over or have designed a new pared down layout of her own. But she did neither. Instead she retained the large key symmetrical elements of the design and gave them breathing room.

The Oxnead fountain was stripped of all its surrounding beds. And all the conifers, trellis, arbours and scrolled beds were removed. This left the fountain set in a clear broad cross of grass. In praising Norah Lindsay's work at Blickling many authorities to date have credited her with the introduction of the four large square herbaceous beds there today. She did not introduce these; they were already there. She retained them and their attendant outer 'L' beds. The multiplicity of topiary yews of varying sizes and shapes were reduced to sixteen, one at the corners of each of the four herbaceous beds. These have now been shaped into large distinctive 'acorns', a major feature of the Parterre. The area of grass between the beds was reduced and all of them replanted. Working in the tradition of Gertrude Jekyll these were colour graded, with blocks of blue, pink, white, and mauve near the house, and hot orange and yellows to the east of the fountain. She also retained the eight blocks of yew, shaped somewhat like grand pianos, but eliminated the unnecessary planting either side of these. Her plans called for more than 1,200 roses to be added to the Parterre garden, although it is doubtful if that many were actually planted.

The long Temple Walk was opened up. A broad swathe of planting, including many conifers, either side of the Walk was removed, and the narrow grass bands running its entire length were turned into wide lawns. In the areas bordering the Temple over 600 highly fashionable azaleas and rhododendrons were introduced. A new herbaceous border was added at the base of the south wall of the Parterre. In addition, any remaining

bedding schemes in the grassed-over moat were removed and the planting at the base of the walls augmented with a mix of shrubs, climbers, and perennials.

Norah Lindsay's cleverness lay in being able to see past the muddle and confusion of the Victorian design and to expertly select what must go and what should remain. Although the retained herbaceous planting still constituted twenty separate beds, to the eye there were four large square beds with a fountain at the centre, the whole design perfectly balanced and proportioned. Norah Lindsay was in her sixties when she carried out the redesign at Blickling. Hers was a pragmatic approach, a grand essay in garden sense and sensibility. She worked at Blickling between 1932 and 1939.

One of Norah's greatest friends was Lawrence Johnston, and she advised and worked with him on his famous and influential garden at Hidcote. In fact, so highly did Johnston rate her, that he wished to leave her the garden when he retired, for health reasons, to the south of France. Unfortunately, this was not to be. She died in 1948 from kidney cancer. Neither was she able to ensure the survival of her own Berkshire garden at Sutton Courtenay. She was forced to sell it and the new owner immediately had it redesigned. Such is the vulnerability of gardens, so often as much victims of fashion as

Today the large yew 'acorns' mark the corners of the four planting beds. Wide lawns either side of the central path to the temple, with the tree and shrub planting pushed back, open up the vista.

of time. But at Blickling she has fared better. Her design there is now eighty years old and remains the best surviving example of her work. Constance, Lady Lothian's great square herbaceous beds are there too, the Oxnead fountain, the steps, sphinxes and ornaments and the piano topiary.

Philip Kerr died in 1940, while still British Ambassador to the United States. Churchill described him as 'the greatest Ambassador to the United States we ever had'. Blickling, the house, its gardens and its lands Kerr left to the National Trust, the first country house of major importance, with a large estate to maintain it, to be handed over to the Trust. The stability this has brought has ensured that the great Parterre remains unchanged, a fusion of two styles and of two divergent ages.

In the ongoing debate about which styles should hold sway in our historic gardens, there is room to question the historic appropriateness of the Blickling Parterre. In common with the rest of the garden it fails to make reference to the hall's highly

distinctive Jacobean architecture. Indeed, there are not gardens in a Jacobean style anywhere at Blickling. Originally the hall's architect Robert Lyminge, designed and placed a banqueting house where the Parterre is now, with a very different garden around it. But any notion of the recreation of this is beyond the pale, as the Parterre is now the accepted grand centrepiece of Blickling's garden, a much admired and enjoyed stylistic synthesis dominated by the creativity of two remarkable ladies.

ABOVE Memorial, in Blickling church, white marble relief to Constance, Marchioness of Lothian by Arthur George Walker, c.1904. Constance on her bier attended by angels. In the background is a representation of part of the garden at Blickling.

12

The War Memorial Gardens, Norwich

Lesley Kant Cunneen

The 2018 centennial commemorations of the First World War focused renewed attention on the many and varied commemorative monuments, gardens and landscapes across the country. However, the Norwich War Memorial Gardens were not originally intended as such, but as an ornamental terrace, bridging the reconstructed marketplace with the new City Hall. Although their construction took place in 1938, just prior to the outbreak of the Second World War, their story begins twenty years earlier.

After the First World War the scale of casualties was so great that it was decided not to attempt to bring home the war dead. Previously they had been buried in mass graves where they had fallen. The Imperial War Graves Commission (IWGC) had been established in 1917, largely at the compassionate instigation of Major General Sir Fabian Ware, who was determined to ensure appropriate and dignified burial: the bodies were re-interred in new cemeteries overseas, in simple graves, without discrimination in rank or provenance. An outpouring of communal grief galvanised public bodies and institutions to create memorials across the country. In some cases, these were practical, such as parks and hospitals. Living memorials were also encouraged: single trees and avenues were planted along roadsides, as promoted by the government's *Roads of Remembrance as War Memorials* pamphlet. A somewhat bizarre initiative, 'Tanks for Towns', was established by the War Office. Tanks, battered in enemy action, were distributed to those towns which had raised significant funds for war bonds. Norwich was one of 254 urban recipients and the tank proudly took its place in Chapelfield Gardens.

Norwich alone lost 3,544 people to the war and the tank did not appease its citizens, who sought a more conventional memorial. The City Corporation was slow to respond to public clamour. Finally, in 1926, the Lord Mayor, C. R. Bignold, seized the initiative and launched a public appeal for a more fitting monument, appropriating an existing hospital subscription to include the proposed memorial. Donations flowed speedily from

The newly restored War Memorial Gardens in 2011. The Art Deco gardens, in their urban context, were never intended for mass planting. Instead, their formal hard landscaping places repeated seating, lamp posts, and containers to the fore.

all sectors of the Norwich populace. The foremost architect, Sir Edwin Lutyens, by the 1920s at the height of his fame, was commissioned to design the memorial. Lutyens had extensive experience in such work: he had earlier played a major role in planning the cemeteries of the IWGC, as well as individual monuments, such as the Cenotaph in Whitehall. At the time of his Norwich commission, he was completing his vast layout and monumental architectural designs for New Delhi. In his most important memorials he incorporated a Stone of Remembrance which became a Lutyens signature piece. Lutyens worked at speed: September 1927 saw the War Memorial being winched into place on the east wall of the medieval Guildhall. The historic location was selected by Lutyens himself, to considerable public disquiet over his choice, because of the building's age and importance and concern about damage.

Lutyens' cenotaph, crafted from Portland stone, is classical in style: the wall acts as a catafalque, supporting a wreath-topped sarcophagus, with gilded bronze flambeaux raised on pedestals at each end of the wall (with the unique capacity to emit flames on commemoration days) and elaborate gilded fixtures for ceremonial standards. The city coat of arms surmounted by a crown and supported by two guardian angels is centrally placed. The Stone of Remembrance lies below. 'Our Glorious Dead' is inscribed on the wall and 'Their Name Liveth for Evermore' on the stone. The names of the war dead were documented on parchment scrolls and interred within the tomb. The work is imposing and traditional. It was unveiled on 9 October 1927 by General Sir Ian Hamilton and local ex-serviceman Bertie Withers, whose name had been drawn at random from applicants hoping to share the honour. As a complement to the cenotaph, Lutyens was asked to create a further memorial in which the names of the fallen would be visible. The resulting free-standing

Architect of the Memorial Sir Edwin Lutyens (1869–1944). Regarded by many as the greatest British architect since Wren, he was knighted in 1918 for his work on New Delhi. This photograph was taken when he was 55, in 1924.

oak case, entitled the Roll of Honour, encloses sixteen, single and double oak panels on which the names of the war dead are painted. It was originally intended to be housed in the proposed new City Hall, but the delay in the Hall's construction resulted in its temporary removal to the Castle Keep, where it languished until its restoration in 2016. Eighty years after its completion the Roll of Honour, the only one of its kind, was eventually installed in the foyer of the City Hall.

With the Lutyens War Memorial in place, the populace was silenced for a time but gradually concerns about accessibility surfaced: the site was cramped and sloping and did not lend itself to ceremonial services. A solution eventually emerged. In 1932 the

The Lutyens War Memorial in its original position in 1934, somewhat diminished beneath the Guildhall and on an awkward sloping site.

City Corporation was engaged in a controversial proposal to build a new city hall and reconstruct the marketplace. The eminent architect, Robert Atkinson, the President of the Architectural Association, oversaw the project and provided the specification for a national competition that drew 143 entries. Atkinson had hoped to be entrusted with the final commission and his detailed ground plan reveals a raised terrace at the head of the market square, with space for a large sculpture. C. H. James and S. Rowland Pierce were the successful entrants, but the City found it hard to raise the necessary finances. Construction of the project eventually began in 1937.

Architects Charles James (left) and Stephen Pierce on site during the construction of Norwich City Hall. They designed both the City Hall and the War Memorial Gardens in front of it.

The War Memorial Gardens, Norwich

ABOVE Norwich, 1935, the buildings fronting the marketplace demolished to make way for the City Hall and the War Memorial Gardens.

BELOW 5 June 1938. With the City Hall completed the construction of the elevated gardens moved forward at speed with first the erection of the undercroft. There was a deadline to meet with a Royal opening scheduled for October.

September 1938, the gardens nearing completion. To the right is an entrance to the undercroft, the other to the left, the space to be used for storage. The newly paved marketplace in the foreground.

The emergent building bore little resemblance to any municipal architecture in the city: it boasted distinctive brickwork, classical pillars, a Stockholm-style asymmetric clock tower and an impressive sweep of steps leading up to imposing bronze entrance doors, guarded by two, highly distinctive, Art Deco bronze lions. It dominated the city centre. The design was celebrated in architectural circles and a special edition of *The Architectural Review* was devoted to the innovative building. The Norwich population was more sceptical: the use of sand-coloured bricks earned its affectionate nickname 'the marmalade factory' and residents grumbled that their rates were rising in line with the tower.

In the successful plan, the raised terrace, seen so clearly in Atkinson's outline, becomes an ornamental garden. The site is effectively a sheltered roof garden, to the east of St Peter's Street, across the road from the City Hall: a narrow strip of land running north-south and raised on a deck above an undercroft and the market. There was no indication that it might become a garden of remembrance and it was clearly intended as an accompaniment to the busy market square and an attractive vista for the occupants of City Hall. The possibility of moving the Lutyens monument to the terrace was first raised in 1935, although the final decision was much later, and the negotiations proved difficult. The veterans approached the transfer with caution, only agreeing after a canvas mock-up had been placed *in situ*. Once installed, the Memorial became the dominant feature, upstage centre in the new gardens. James and Pierce had considerable misgivings about the positioning of the Memorial: they argued that it obstructed the view of the City Hall's imposing facade from the market square.

The term 'Ornamental Gardens' used in the council's contemporaneous documents, confirms that the gardens were originally perceived as an aesthetic entity: a stylish pleasure garden rather than the Memorial Garden it became once the Lutyens monument was introduced. How far the final landscape was influenced by this marriage of convenience is difficult to assess; the gardens had to reconcile two significant but different players, the arresting and eclectic City Hall and the Lutyens Memorial. The result is a garden very much of its period. A modernist and elegant space using York and Clipsham stone in the hard landscaping and bronze accents in the decorative features; these resonate with the bronze of the flambeaux on the tomb and the doors of the City Hall. The design owes much to Art Deco in its rhythmic use of tall pillars with bronze bell-lamps which front the Memorial and echo the concept of the eternal flame; simple circular urns and rectangular planting beds; a finely conceived stone wall which curves to mirror the urns; two stately flag standards, which are embellished by bronze Egyptian-style figures signifying 'Peace and Plenty'; and sweeping and graceful flights of steps which accommodate beautifully the difficult slope of the site. The railings on the market-side wall are an understated but effective safety feature. Seating was omitted from the original plan but appeared at the opening ceremony, simple in design, facing the tomb to enable quiet reflection. The position of Lutyens' monument confirms it as the focal point of the gardens but the decorative features of the landscape confirm its link with the City Hall.

ABOVE George VI and Queen Elizabeth, with the Lord Mayor, Charles Watling, and his wife, walking through the War Memorial Gardens, immediately after the official opening.

OVERLEAF The crowded marketplace, still free of its stalls, on the official opening day in October 1938 of both the City Hall and the War Memorial Gardens. The gardens are seen running along the bottom of the picture.

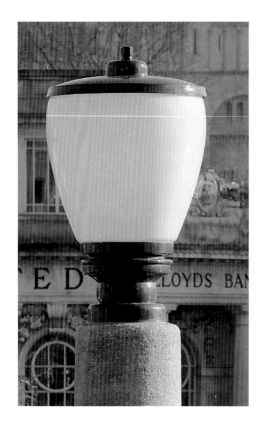

The designers, architects rather than landscapers, made no mention of a planting scheme. At short notice the responsibility for the maintenance, but no budget, was transferred from the Markets Committee to a reluctant Parks Committee and the planting entrusted to Captain Sandys-Winsch, the gifted Norwich Parks' Superintendent, and the designer of many of the Norwich parks. On completion of the gardens, he filled the urns with chrysanthemums as a temporary measure (it was autumn) and stated that these would be replaced by salvias before the grand royal opening ceremony of the City Hall and terraced gardens by George VI and Queen Elizabeth on 29 October 1938. Undoubtedly the salvias would have been the red bedding variety, which was a staple of municipal planting at

ABOVE One of the eight bronze bell-lamps.

BELOW The newly opened City Hall, and the War Memorial Gardens busy with visitors, in November 1938. With a fine open space in front of them, the linear structure of the gardens is clear before being hidden behind the reinstated market stalls.

An early colour picture of the gardens in pristine condition with salvias in the circular planters.

the time; the splash of scarlet providing a symbolic touch at the wreath-laying by the king. The Captain announced that berberis and varieties of cypress would be used in the permanent scheme. Photographs of the opening ceremony, the largest gathering in Norwich's history, reveal floriferous beds and urns planted with military precision, with miniature cypresses, like soldiers, standing to attention at the head of each bed. The horticultural bill was a hefty £304 (approximately £20,000 today). Generous planting continued throughout the fifties and early sixties but in later photographs is sparse. It is probably the original cypresses that can be seen by the seventies to have outgrown their situation: they straddle the dividing wall between the market and the terrace and obscure the fine curves of the interior wall.

Concerns about the upkeep of the gardens quickly surfaced. Dogs at the time were often left to wander freely and proved to be prime culprits, preoccupying the Parks Committee for some years. Complaints about litter became increasingly vociferous and there were frequent letters to the press expressing distress at the lack of respect for the Memorial and all it represented. A large curved central bed, which mirrored the curved railings of the market-side wall, had disappeared by the forties and was replaced by further seating. Waste bins had not featured in the plans, nor in early photographs, but by the

LEFT AND ABOVE The bases of the two flagstaffs, with bronze sculptural reliefs by James Woodford. The figures, in an Assyrian style, are enriched with animals, flowers and foliage, suggesting agricultural abundance. Their date, XCXXXVIII, encircles the top. Woodford also designed the series of bronze roundels on the City Hall doors.

ABOVE LEFT Hardly the day for reading, but at least quiet after the rain. The gardens are themselves littered with litter bins and inappropriate and neglected conifers. 2007.

ABOVE RIGHT With the gardens neglected and in decay, it clearly made no difference to many if they used the litter bins or not; bins which frequently were not emptied. 2007.

sixties their installation had done nothing to counter the litter problem. The addition of seats and bins obscured the clean lines of the design and cluttered the terrace. Vandalism probably accounted for overturned urns and early damage to the bell lights – one irrevocably; water penetration caused cracks in the concrete deck. Nor were the veterans satisfied for long. Initially overjoyed by their new prominent position, as they grew older concerns about accessibility resurfaced. Steps posed a problem for the elderly or infirm and when veterans from the Second World War joined the services in the late forties, and it became evident that there was insufficient space to accommodate the processions. By the fifties, the term 'Ornamental Gardens' was no longer in use, replaced by 'The Garden of Remembrance'. In the sixties changing attitudes to war were publicly voiced, with robust exchanges in council meetings about the hypocrisy of remembrance services. Petitions to turn around the Memorial so that it faced the City Hall and allow St Peter's Street to be used for remembrance services finally met with political acceptance in 1982, with the parsimonious caveat that funding had to be to be borne by the veterans. Before the gardens could be altered irrevocably, the site was listed as a Grade II monument by English Heritage. And the gardens acquired their third and current title: 'The War Memorial Gardens'.

The rear of the resited Lutyens Memorial and Paul de Monchaux's *Breath*. Either side new steps and a curving ramp lead to St Peter's Street. 2019.

Over the ensuing twenty years the gardens degenerated further, albeit in common with many municipal parks across the country. The horticultural neglect and general wear and tear, coupled with vandalism, vagrancy, skateboarding youths and litter, meant the site became an embarrassing eyesore, particularly given their cynosure position. Finally, in 2004 the gardens were closed to the public on the grounds of public safety: the undercroft (at the time a convenient storage area for the market traders) had been damaged by iron erosion from the reinforced concrete used in the garden's construction. For a further four years the future of the gardens lay in doubt. In the meantime, a besieged City Council attempted to stem a tide of public criticism over their neglect. The veterans, who had never abandoned their campaign for the Memorial to be repositioned, achieved success in principle by 2006. In September 2007, mounting public concern generated a spate of critical letters in the *Eastern Daily Press*, which also ran a series of censorious editorials. These were augmented by the former MP and war correspondent Martin Bell, who branded the condition of the Memorial a disgrace and 'the worst he had seen outside Iraq'. These indictments at last provoked a pledge that restoration work would start in 2008 at a cost of £4,000,000 but a further year passed before the council announced that a final budget of £2,600,000 had been negotiated.

The papers presented to the city's Planning Committee in early 2009 make reassuring reading with an impressively researched historical backcloth and detailed

Edwin Lutyens 1927 War Memorial on its third site, facing St Peter's Street and the City Hall.

recommendations for all aspects of the restoration works; commendably it was proposed to upgrade some materials to reflect the original design intention. Disability access was a key feature which had some inevitable but necessary implications for the integrity of the restoration. The garden deck and the marketplace wall were raised by 15 centimetres with changes to the steps to accommodate this. The recommendations proposed a new contemporary sculpture to inhabit the void left by the repositioning of the Lutyens Memorial. *Breath*, an abstract patinated bronze by Paul de Monchaux, was the eventual choice, designed to reflect the furtherance of peace and to provide a link with the Lutyens monument. At the request of the veterans, a connection with the former Memorial and the gardens was created by opening the wall to St Peter's Street and providing a new access ramp and steps. The piercing of the wall is the only discordant note in the scheme and undermines the intimacy and rhythm of the space. As a gesture of atonement, a small committee chaired by the Lord Lieutenant was established to keep a watching brief on all municipal war memorials in the city. On Armistice Day, 11 November 2010, a resplendently glistening War Memorial,

Paul de Monchaux's *Breath*.

successfully restored and relocated to face the City Hall, was unveiled for public view.

The gardens were officially reopened in March 2011 and there was considerable public acclaim at their transformation. The new planting plan made clear that there was no intention to reprise the original that relied extensively on bedding-out: it was described as restrained and formal, with a strong reliance on topiary box in the urns and perennials such as hellebores, sisyrinchiums, grasses and alliums in the raised beds, edged with lavender and box cubes; white vinca providing an evocative carpet below *Breath*. The choice was intended to complement the hard landscaping and decorative features, as well as provide for easier maintenance. However, eight years later, the selection (apart from the box) has not proved totally successful. The vinca turned out to be blue, the soft planting in the raised beds provides little resistance to their habitual use for seating and the terrace has become a popular picnic venue, given the increased access to take-away food in the busy market stalls below. The Monchaux sculpture has not yet endeared itself to the public. The relocation of the Lutyens Memorial appears to have accelerated the public's casual, and occasionally uninhibited, use of the terrace; it is rarely used as a reflective space for remembrance and Armistice services now take place in St Peter's Street. The landscape historian John Dixon Hunt has long argued that the survival of gardens is highly dependent on the public's use and that gardens necessarily adapt and change over time. In the case of the War Memorial Gardens perhaps it is time to accept the inevitability of public usage and allow it to revert to its original title: 'The Ornamental Gardens'.

With their central position overlooking and adjoining the marketplace, the gardens have proved a popular stopping-off place.

13

Lakes in Norfolk Landscaped Parks

Tom Williamson

We often associate lakes with the 'naturalistic' landscape parks created by Lancelot 'Capability' Brown and his contemporaries in the second half of the eighteenth century, with their broad sweeps of turf irregularly scattered with trees, their clumps and encircling belts. But lakes were by no means an indispensable element of such landscapes, in Norfolk or elsewhere, and most examples did not in fact contain one. Perhaps more importantly, like other elements of Brown's style lakes had earlier origins and did not just appear as part of his familiar stylistic package.

If for the sake of argument we define a lake as a body of water with an area of over two hectares (c. six acres), and a maximum width of more than thirty metres, then there were perhaps no more than fifteen in the county by c.1800, and most country houses made do with more diminutive water features. Particularly common were slightly widened streams or rivers, often referred to in contemporary documents as 'broad waters'. These were a common feature of smaller landed properties, such as Pickenham, Bayfield, Lexham, Walsingham Abbey, Riddlesworth and Rackheath, but could also be found even in some of the larger parks, such as Costessey. In a typical eighteenth-century combination of 'beauty and utility' a number of examples also functioned as mill ponds, supplying a head of water for estate water mills, as at Shotesham, Hilborough, and Bolwick Hall in Marsham.

FACING PAGE The lake at Wolterton Hall, 2020.
RIGHT Bolwick Hall, Marsham.

Other mansions were graced by what were, in effect, ponds rather than true lakes, including Felbrigg and West Tofts. In a few cases these were created by adapting existing moats, thus creating a body of water which lay uncomfortably close to the windows of the mansion. At Gawdy, for example, a map of 1734 shows that the hall was still surrounded by a moat; but by 1789, when a second estate map was produced, this had been altered to form a serpentine body of water, ranged roughly north-south, immediately to the west of the house. Many eighteenth-century country houses thus had ornamental water features but large lakes, placed in the middle distance, were comparatively rare.

Norfolk arguably had fewer lakes than many other counties, although as Wendy Bishop has demonstrated – in an important thesis completed at the University of East Anglia since the original version of this article was published – they were nowhere ubiquitous features of eighteenth-century parks. The reasons were largely cost, and the fact that they could only be created in certain environmental circumstances. The creation of parkland lakes did not, for the most part, involve large amounts of excavation, for they were made primarily by damming a stream or river and ponding back the water behind it. Nor (in spite of what is often suggested) did their construction usually involve 'puddling' the area they occupied with rammed clay. As Bishop has again demonstrated, only the retaining dam was usually treated in this way. Nevertheless,

BELOW The 20-acre lake at Raynham Hall, looking south along its length, although the true extent of this is hidden by the merging trees in the distance. The water extends beyond them (**BOTTOM**) in line with the main axis to the west front of the hall.

The lake at Hoveton Hall.

constructing dams and altering watercourses were expensive undertakings, so that the lake at Raynham, for example, cost over £1,100 in the 1720s. Most lakes were thus to be found in the grounds of the wealthiest members of society, although even they could only have one if the terrain was amenable. Norfolk being a topographically challenged county, many parks occupied fairly level ground, and where watercourses existed, they often had shallow valleys and wide floodplains, expensive to span with a dam. Elsewhere, in the west and north of the county especially, the ground was porous and any water retained by a dam would soon drain away. The park around Houghton Hall mainly occupies an area of sand, overlying chalk, but to the west of the house there is a narrow deposit of boulder clay which provided the raw material for the bricks employed in the internal walls of the hall, built in the 1720s, as well as for the walls of the Kitchen Garden and for the various ha-has around the gardens. A series of maps, including those published as engravings in Colen Campbell's *Vitruvius*

Britannicus of 1722 and Isaac Ware's *Plans and Elevations of Houghton* in 1735, show a lake here. There was clearly a plan to create one by linking and filling the various clay pits, but this was never successful, and visitors repeatedly criticised the park for its lack of water. Some landowners went to considerable efforts to overcome the limitations imposed by the 'genius of the place'. At Westwick Park, for example, it was said in 1779 that: 'It was long thought impracticable to obtain an ornamental Piece of Water for the further Improvement of the Scene, on Account of the elevated Situation of the Place, and the nature of the Soil: but the Difficulty is at last fully surmounted; Mr Petre [John Berney Petre II, the owner] having been able, by an ingenious Application of two Archimaedian Screws, to raise a sufficient Supply from a large Reservoir below to the Summit of the Hill.' The screws were powered by a windmill, and a channel three miles long delivered the water to the lake.

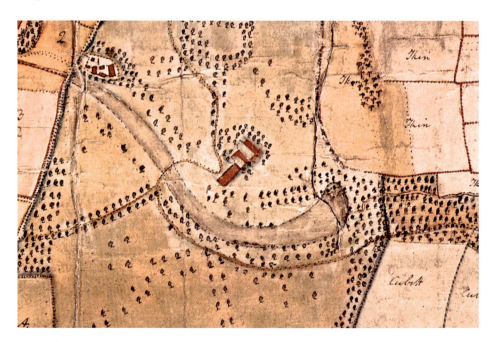

FACING PAGE, BOTTOM The serpentine lake at Beeston St Lawrence, designed by Nathaniel Richmond, as shown on an undated late eighteenth-century estate map.
BELOW Beeston Hall and its lake, 1779. Drawn by Humphry Repton.
ABOVE The lake today.

All this said, the county contains some fine examples of lakes which were formed when parks were created, or modified, in the second half of the eighteenth century. The lake in the park at Hoveton Hall was in existence by 1794, and was perhaps created not long before, as it appears to have been designed to complement a new house (the present hall), built on the rising ground to the north in c.1810. The lake – of classic serpentine form – at Beeston St Lawrence was created in the 1770s, perhaps by expanding an existing 'broad water', by the prominent designer Nathaniel Richmond. That at Ditchingham, created by damming the Broome Beck and magnificently backed

ABOVE The lake at Ditchingham, one of the most impressive eighteenth-century examples in the county.

by woodland, was probably formed soon after 1764, when a map was surveyed showing the old walled gardens around the hall, but including annotations giving the relative heights of various points in the surrounding area. It was certainly in existence by 1778, when John Butcher published an engraving of the park. There is a persistent rumour that both park and lake were designed by Lancelot 'Capability' Brown and a number of people claim to have seen, in the past, a map or plan signed by him: this cannot now be traced, however, and Brown's involvement here is unlikely, although it must be admitted that this is a quintessential Brownian composition. Brown himself worked on few parks in the county: leaving aside a possible role at Buckenham Tofts, he seems to have been responsible only for Kimberley, Langley, and Melton Constable. At Langley his proposed lake, on the relatively level ground to the north of the hall, does not appear to have been created; while at Melton Constable he was likewise thwarted by topography, the lie of the land ensuring that the lake has an outline reminiscent of a squashed octopus and is located at a considerable distance from the hall. At Kimberley, however, the ensemble of house, sloping lawn and irregular lake is far more successful, although the lake was not entirely new. It was created by adapting and extending an existing, semi-geometric body of water which had been created earlier in the century.

Kimberley is an important reminder of the fact that large water bodies were a feature of designed landscapes long before the advent of Brown and 'naturalistic' parklands in the 1760s. Indeed, most of the larger lakes in Norfolk's parks originated in the first half of the eighteenth century, mirroring a national trend again highlighted

by Bishop. The lake at Raynham, for instance, was first constructed in the early 1720s; that at Holkham was formed between 1725 and 1731; while that at Wolterton was created, probably to designs by Charles Bridgeman, in the late 1720s. The two lakes in Gunton park were in existence by 1754, and were probably constructed around 1740, when the mansion itself was rebuilt to designs by Matthew Brettingham.

TOP AND ABOVE Kimberley Hall and its lake to the south-west.

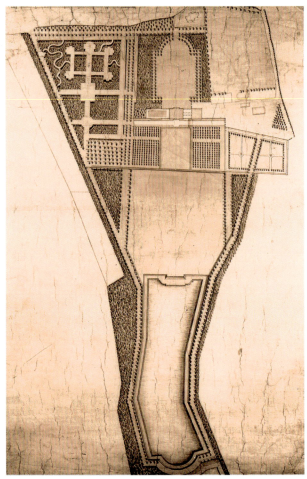

PREVIOUS PAGE The lakes at Gunton Park, linked by a canal.

RIGHT Charles Bridgeman's design for the gardens at Wolterton, late 1720s. Like several lakes in Norfolk parks, the lake here, at the bottom of the plan, originally formed part of a geometric landscape design.

BELOW The southern end of the lake at Raynham Hall was created for Charles Townshend, 2nd Viscount (1674–1738) on swampy ground next to the River Wensum in 1724, at the cost of £1,100. Rectangular, five times longer than it is wide, it is fed by springs. Today it is considerably silted, but still impressive. Sketch in graphite and grey and brown wash by John Sell Cotman, c.1818.

That at Kimberley was in place before 1739, while the present lake at Blickling developed from a substantial (c.12 acres) body of water which was already in existence within the park when mapped by James Corbridge in 1729. There are also grounds for believing that the lake at North Elmham was created in the late 1740s, when the park itself appears to have been laid out. While the Blickling lake in its first incarnation may have functioned as a large fishpond, those at Holkham, Raynham, Wolterton and Kimberley, while perhaps likewise fulfilling a similar purpose, formed elements of large, geometric, 'formal' landscapes, even if their size ensured that their precise form was determined by the natural topography, so that one or more of their sides exhibited a curving form. In short, the easy assumption that lakes formed a part of the 'naturalistic' Capability Brown 'package' is wrong, and it remains uncertain why their numbers should have increased so markedly in the first half of the eighteenth century, although we might perhaps associate this development with the general increase in the scale of landscape design occurring at this time. The first lakes, that is, were simply large versions of the canals and basins which had graced earlier, smaller formal grounds.

These early lakes were soon altered, often in stages, as tastes changed towards more serpentine and irregular forms of landscape design in the middle and later decades of the century: Brown's modifications of the lake at Kimberley were one stage in a complex development. In 1739 Francis Blomefield described how the small (14-acre) lake here was 'now extended into a noble lake of about 28 acres, which seems to environ a large wood or carr on its west side; rendering its appearance to the house much more grand and delightful; the rivulet that ran into it is now made a serpentine river, laid out in a neat manner, and is the boundary of the park, on the west and north sides, being about a mile in length; the declivity of the hill, on the northern part, is a fine lawn, with the serpentine river at the bottom of it, which is seen at one view from the house, which was built by the present Sir John Wodehouse, who hath much augmented its beauty and pleasantness, by the addition of these beautiful waters'. At Holkham there were similar changes. The southern end of the lake was made more irregular in shape, an island created, and the lake connected to the basin to the south of the house by a 'serpentine river' between 1739 and 1741, under the direction of the great William Kent himself. As the full-blown naturalistic style of Brown took hold, other lakes were similarly altered. At Blickling the great pond in the park was probably expanded in two stages: in the 1740s, by the First Earl; and in the 1760s, by his son the Second Earl, who commented in a letter to his wife in 1762 how 'The bottom of my water is almost covered and the surface increases not quite so fast as the hour hand on a watch'. It was extended both to the north, where it was retained by a dam more than six metres in height, and also to the south-east, where it was merged with the western half of the former Wilderness Pond within the gardens beside the house. As a result, the lake came much closer to the house than today, almost up to

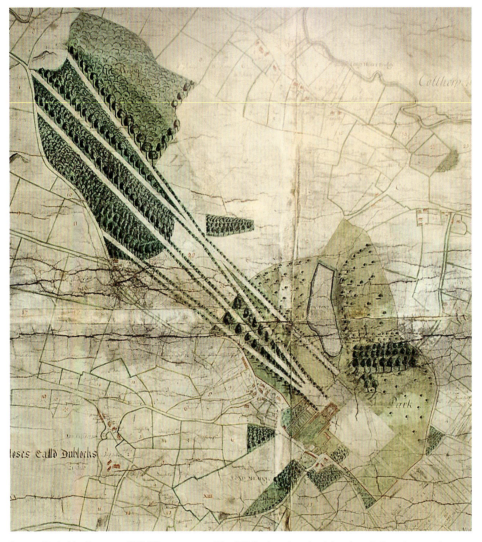

James Corbridge's map of Blickling, surveyed in 1729, showing the lake already in existence in the park.

the windows of the north front, suggesting that this section must have been carefully 'puddled' with clay, to prevent water from seeping into the nearby cellars.

This pattern of repeated modification continued throughout the later eighteenth and into the nineteenth century: most parkland lakes have 'histories', rather than single dates of creation. That at Holkham, as modified in c.1740, remained too stiff and formal for later taste. In 1784 its southern end was provided with a stylish 'twist' by the designer William Emes. This was mirrored by a similar twist to the north when the lake was extended in 1811 under the direction of Emes' former pupil and associate, John Webb. A new island was created at the same time, and in general the later eighteenth and

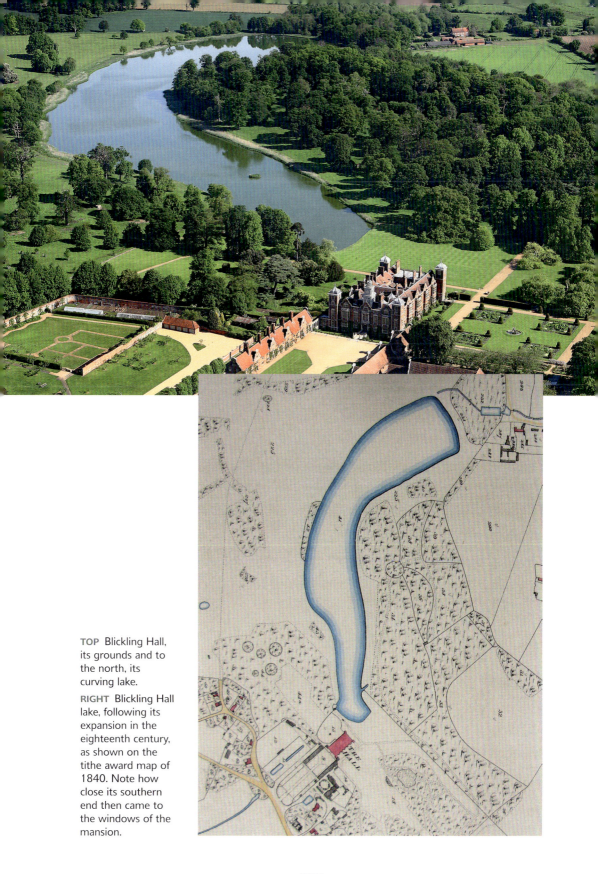

TOP Blickling Hall, its grounds and to the north, its curving lake.

RIGHT Blickling Hall lake, following its expansion in the eighteenth century, as shown on the tithe award map of 1840. Note how close its southern end then came to the windows of the mansion.

ABOVE AND FACING PAGE The lake at Holkham Hall.

early nineteenth century saw a fashion for breaking up the lake surface with increasing numbers of islands, often planted with some care. The designer John Hare suggested adding three to Brown's existing island at Kimberley in 1786, while at Ditchingham a second island was added in the 1820s or 1830s: in 1841 Grigor reported that this 'was studded chiefly with the poplar tribe which, in the distance (their true position) afford, by their spiral forms, a striking contrast to the round and globular contours of the forest trees' (the other was planted with shrubs, including large amounts of ornamental dogwood). This enthusiasm for islands reflected, to a large extent, the Picturesque penchant for busy variety, and at Wolterton William Sawrey Gilpin, who made many changes to the grounds in the 1820s, produced a number of designs for the lake, several of which would involve the creation of one or more islands as well as the creation of a more irregular shoreline, in one case ornamented with boulders.

Lakes continued to proliferate, and continued to be altered and adapted, right through the nineteenth century, notable new examples including those at Didlington, Narford, Heydon, Hillington, Ketteringham, Lynford, and Gunthorpe. Some were still

ABOVE Wolterton Hall and its lake to the south.
FACING PAGE TOP One of William Sawrey Gilpin's designs for improving the lake at Wolterton: 1820s.
FACING PAGE BELOW The design as executed. The view today from the hall.
BELOW Part of the Wolterton lake with its island, looking north.

Lakes in Norfolk Landscaped Parks

ABOVE The huge lake at Narford Hall is one of the most impressive in Norfolk, extending to 54 acres.
LEFT The tranquil beauty of the lake at Sennowe Park.

being created at the start of the twentieth century, as at Sennowe in c.1909. That created by the Buxton family at Shadwell Park in the 1850s is a particularly striking example of such later lakes. Formed by damming the river Thet with a substantial cascade, and covering some 34 acres (14 hectares), it was part of a wider programme of landscaping which was undertaken when the mansion here was remodelled and extended in 'Gothic' style to designs by S. S. Teulon. It is suitably romantic and picturesque in character, with no less than eight irregularly shaped islands. As represented on early Ordnance Survey maps it displays a feature more widely shared, by lakes of all periods. The parishes of

ABOVE Part of the curving lake at Shadwell Park, Brettenham, with its well-wooded islands.
BELOW Loudon's lake at Stradsett Hall.

Rushworth and Brettenham were divided by the river, the serpentine course of which was preserved by the line of the parish boundary, picking its way across the surface of the lake.

Wherever possible, owners were advised – by Humphry Repton, amongst others – to place their lakes to the south of the house, so that the sun glistened on the surface of the water. While Norfolk landowners often achieved this aim – as at Wolterton, Kimberley or North Elmham – they sometimes failed, as at Holkham and, in particular, Blickling. This was a combined consequence of the character of the local topography and the general reluctance of owners – which has never been fully explained – to relocate great houses on new sites, even when they were being systematically rebuilt. At Hoveton the lake was made to accompany a hall built in a new location to the north of the shallow valley which it occupied, but this was one of the rare exceptions. Stradsett would have been another. The lake here, designed by John Claudius Loudon, lies to the north of the hall but the owner, Thomas Bagge, originally planned to rebuild the hall on a new site, still further to the north, and was thwarted by lack of money.

We should be wary of seeing lakes simply as pretty adornments to the view. The earliest examples, as at Blickling and perhaps Gunton, were primarily intended as 'great waters' or fish ponds; indeed, the remains of small 'stews' or holding ponds, where fish were initially kept prior to consumption, survive beside the lakes at the latter site. Such practices continued later than we might expect – similar ponds exist immediately below the dam at the north end of the lake at Holkham, presumably dating to the time of its construction in 1811. But by this stage lakes were mainly used for recreational fishing, and for rowing or sailing. Repton's Red Book for Holkham of 1789, which was entirely concerned with the creation of an extensive pleasure ground around the lake, includes a design by the architect Samuel Wyatt for a 'fishing lodge' which was to double as a boat house. The text describes how the boat which was sailed on the lake was specially ornamented on 'public days'. Boathouses were normally of wood and even those constructed relatively recently have generally left scant remains, but amongst the exceptions we should note the remarkable underground example, probably dating to the early twentieth century, beneath the Italianate terrace to the west of the hall at Didlington. Also, at Didlington, and of similar date, are the remains of an underground pumping room, containing the machinery which served to regulate the levels of the lakes, a reminder that however 'natural' lakes might appear they were actually works of engineering. Even eighteenth-century lakes involved not only considerable earth movement – with particularly massive dams at Beeston St Lawrence and Blickling – but also the provision of such things as bypass channels, to protect lakes from floods and surges which could damage their dams and fill them with silt. That at Kimberley is carried across a stream running into the lake on a low aqueduct. At Bayfield in the early twentieth century the lake was expanded, partly lined with tiles and provided with a bypass channel which runs for part of its course in an underground tunnel.

Many lakes were provided with silt traps, for in Norfolk especially the slow-moving character of watercourses ensures that silting is a perennial problem: some examples are now less than a metre deep beneath their placid surface. Parkland lakes are indeed artificial impositions: without constant attention they would eventually disappear from our landscape.

TOP AND LEFT
The long sinuous lake at Bayfield Hall was created by damming the River Glaven which flows through it.

FACING PAGE
Lakes continue to be made, such as this one to the north of Raveningham Hall, created in 2000.

14

Art and Industry

Roger Last

'He is dirty & filthy in his habits ... thinks that he is surrounded by imaginary beings whom he calls devils ... is exceedingly noisy and incoherent.' This was a sad end to the life of a man whom the aldermen and councillors of Norwich declared was 'the most eminent of architects ... one of the ablest men that Norfolk ever produced'. Thomas Jeckyll was confined to two padded cells in the Bethel Hospital in Norwich. Mentally deranged for the last five years of his life – at the end he was unable to walk without assistance having been weakened by powerful drugs designed to sedate him. He died on 30 August 1881 and his reputation, already on the decline, died with him.

Thomas Jeckyll (pronounced 'Jeckle') was born in Wymondham in 1827. He was to become both a successful architect and a renowned designer. As a designer he

FACING PAGE Thomas Jeckyll's Pavilion displayed at the Philadelphia Centennial International Exhibition in 1876. The exhibition commemorated the signing of the Declaration of Independence and was the first world trade fair to be held in the USA. Thirty-seven countries contributed exhibits and the exhibition attracted ten million visitors. Made by the Norwich firm of Barnard, Bishop and Barnards, who saw this as an opportunity to showcase their manufacturing skills, the highly singular Pavilion was constructed of both cast and wrought iron, and gave Thomas Jeckyll his greatest design opportunity and challenge to date. The Pavilion was described as 'intended for use upon Lawn, or Ornamental Grounds'.

RIGHT Thomas Jeckyll c.1860s.

moved to the fore of a world he co-habited with James McNeill Whistler, George du Maurier, Frederick Sandys, and Dante Gabriel Rossetti. Jeckyll was a pivotal figure in the emergence of the Aesthetic Movement whose adherents placed aesthetics to the fore in artistic endeavour above social, moral or political themes, for them beauty came before message. Jeckyll was also to the forefront in promoting from the late 1850s an interest in the art of Japan. His inventive designs of the 1860s and 1870s are rich with Japanese-inspired motifs.

The finest Jeckyll ornamental designs were the result of commissions from the Norwich firm of Barnard, Bishop and Barnards, who were to build a national, and indeed international reputation for the quality of their workmanship in cast and wrought iron. The two most outstanding of these collaborations brought both their designer and manufacturer international plaudits, and both of these acclaimed commissions found their way into Norfolk gardens.

Towards the end of 1826 Charles Barnard set up in business, aged twenty-two. An enterprising and inventive young man he soon designed a self-rolling mangle, an early lawnmower and a new type of slow-combustion stove, all manufactured in his own foundry. His most celebrated invention would seem to reach prosaic extremes, yet it is it something Norfolk is proud to claim the credit for – hexagonal mesh wire netting. As a farmer's son from a large agricultural county, he knew only too well the damage caused by rabbits and vermin. His highly useful wire netting was a great success. First, the netting was woven manually. In 1844 he designed a machine to make it, and later it was also galvanized. John Bishop joined him as a partner in 1846, and in 1859, Barnard's sons. The firm thus became Barnard, Bishop and Barnards. They produced a wide range of cast- and wrought-iron goods for farm, house and garden. They installed the heating system in Norwich Cathedral and in 1860 even produced a cast-iron frame lighthouse which was shipped to the coast of Brazil. Their ever-expanding works were in Coslany in Norwich, opposite Bullard's brewery, and stretched down the side of the River Wensum. Their rivals in the city were Boulton and Paul, operating

Charles Barnard, c.1850.
Portrait by Frederick Sandys.

The Norfolk Iron Works, the extensive factories of Barnard, Bishop and Barnards by the River Wensum in Coslany, Norwich.

out of their Rose Lane works. Whereas Boulton and Paul concentrated to a large extent on the manufacture of conservatories and utilitarian products, Barnards, while still turning out wire netting and run-of-the-mill items, concentrated on producing ironwork of superior quality.

In 1859 Barnards embarked on producing a huge and elaborate set of park gates. These had not been commissioned, they were purely speculative. The firm, however, was fully aware of the great showcase for manufacturing that the Great Exhibition of 1851 had been. They had exhibited an ornate decorative door hinge there, but nothing on a grand scale. In 1862 there was to be another International Exhibition in London. What was needed was a large showpiece exhibit, something with which to capture the public's imagination. It was a big gamble, and an expensive one, but success could

Jeckyll's original design for the Barnards' gates.

The Barnards' gates on display at the International Exhibition, London, 1862. This was staged in South Kensington, fitted round part of the Horticultural Society of London's garden, the site now occupied by the Natural History Museum. At the time cast-iron products accounted for a large share of the market and skilled British wrought ironwork was in decline, French and Prussian work being considered superior. This was an opportunity to prove both the quality of indigenous design and wrought-iron workmanship. The original upper central section of the design has a knight's helmet and coronet, and central shield with supporters.

make the firm's reputation. They were clearly confident of the skills of their workforce and prepared to test them to the limit. Before a start could be made, they needed an imaginative design.

Thomas Jeckyll had set up an architectural office in Norwich in 1853, and one in London followed in 1857. By this time, he had a quantity of successful architectural work to his credit. In the 1850s he had been consulted on the restoration of over twenty churches, carrying out extensive work. He was also busy designing houses. He was responsible for the restoration and remodelling of Elsing Hall in 1852–53. Jeckyll also worked on the interiors and their fittings of both churches and houses, designing metalwork, furniture and fireplaces. He carried out commissions for some important Norfolk families, among them the Lombes, Boileaus, Gurneys, Birkbecks and Buxtons. Of the designers in Norwich, Jeckyll was the obvious choice for Barnards to turn to. In fact, he had collaborated with them as early as 1850, on the design of a particular iron window frame, and at about the same time, he had designed an entrance gate for

Norwich Lodge at Ketteringham Hall, which is believed to have been made by Barnards.

The new gates Jeckyll designed for Barnards were on a huge scale, twenty-five feet high and forty feet wide. They were also highly elaborate. Who was leading who in this enterprise, it is impossible to say, but it was probably Barnards, who clearly thought big and were eager for a technical and artistic challenge. Jeckyll certainly gave them one. The four, square piers, needed to take the immense weight of the structure, were to be in strong cast iron, the detailed decoration of the gates themselves and the flanking side framework, in wrought iron. Jeckyll called for hand-hammered flowers and foliage, twisted spiral colonnettes, griffins supporting emblazoned coats of arms, interlaced hawthorn branches, vine branches, oak stems, convolvulus, ivy and other climbing plants. It was a tour de force of ironwork and took Barnards a full three years to complete.

When exhibited at the International Exhibition in London of 1862, the gates caused a sensation. *The Times* called them 'the most elaborate perfection of wrought-iron workmanship', declaring that 'nothing finer had been produced in this country'. The naturalistic design of the gates, running counter to the current taste for Gothic, also won praise. *The Times* thought them superior to George Gilbert Scott's and Francis Skidmore's elaborate screen for Hereford Cathedral, now in the Victoria and Albert Museum. Indeed, the gates have been credited with kindling the revival of decorative wrought-iron work in this country. They certainly made Barnards' reputation, and Thomas Jeckyll's. Whistler referred to Jeckyll's 'exquisite sense of beauty and great knowledge'. The designer became dubbed 'Jekyll (*sic*) of the Gates'.

There was more good news to come. Circumstances came together brilliantly; the success of the gates, and in 1863 the marriage of Edward, Prince of Wales, and his fortunate purchase of a large property in Norfolk. What better wedding gift could the delighted people of Norfolk give their future King for having decided to live (from time to time) among them, than these now celebrated home-grown gates, and where better to display them than as entrance gates to the Prince's new home at Sandringham. They were duly purchased by public subscription, although Barnards would have been delighted enough with the cachet bestowed on the firm, regardless of the money.

FACING PAGE, ABOVE AND BELOW The delicate and imaginative detailing of the gates.

ABOVE The Norwich Gates in their original position, c.1910. The short avenue of ancient limes which had run from the gates to the house was uprooted by a violent storm in 1908 and removed, opening up a clear view from the gates to the house.

BELOW The Norwich Gates, as they were now to be called, at Sandringham, May 1864, shortly after their erection. The gates are 25 ft (7.5 m) high and 40 ft (12 m) wide. Titles of the Prince of Wales are represented on the heraldic shields held by the four griffins. The inset panels on the gate pillars bear the coats of arms of various Norfolk towns. The shield and helmet have been removed awaiting the more appropriate royal attributes. Neither in place is the continuation of the ornamental railings either side of the gates.

J. J. Colman was among the deputation which went to Sandringham to present the gates to the Prince in April 1863, who said in his reply, 'Connected intimately as I am now with Norfolk, I regard with pride so beautiful a specimen of Norwich Workmanship and Art.' The gates, now named after the city in which they were made, are undoubtedly the finest nineteenth-century entrance gates in the country, and among the finest from any period. There was a little local dissent. The Revd Benjamin Armstrong of Dereham, who clearly regretting the ostracism of Gothic, found the gates too decorative for his taste, and thought they 'looked odd, transformed to this wild scene'. They were erected at the end of a short but ancient lime avenue directly in line with the house and closer to it than their position today.

LEFT The Norwich Gates at Sandringham House, seen from inside the grounds; The Avenue, beyond. The weight of the gates is taken by piers, girders, and frames in cast iron, leaving the gates themselves to display in finely crafted wrought iron, exuberant ornamentation with sprays of varying foliage.

After this joint success, Jeckyll and Barnards collaboration continued. Another fine pair of gates was to come in 1867, ornamental wrought-iron terrace or garden entrance gates, first exhibited at the Exposition Universelle, in Paris. They were thirteen feet wide and seven feet high, and forty workmen took three months to complete them. The design is assured and inventive, moving on from the Norwich Gates in terms of sophistication, incorporating Japanese-inspired motifs. They were also exhibited at the Weltausstellung in Vienna in 1873, where they won a medal. They are now known as the Four Seasons or Vienna Gates, and are displayed in the Museum of Applied Arts, Vienna.

TOP The area above the centre of the gates was redesigned when presented to the Prince of Wales. The heraldic badge of the Prince, white ostrich feathers, crown and motto 'Ich Dien', replaced the shield with supporters, and a crown supplanted the knight's helmet. The whole is set in a wealth of sprays of hawthorn, rose and holly, the holly forming perpendicular growths.
ABOVE Jeckyll also designed curved flanking railings for the gates with combined emblems of rose, thistle and shamrock.

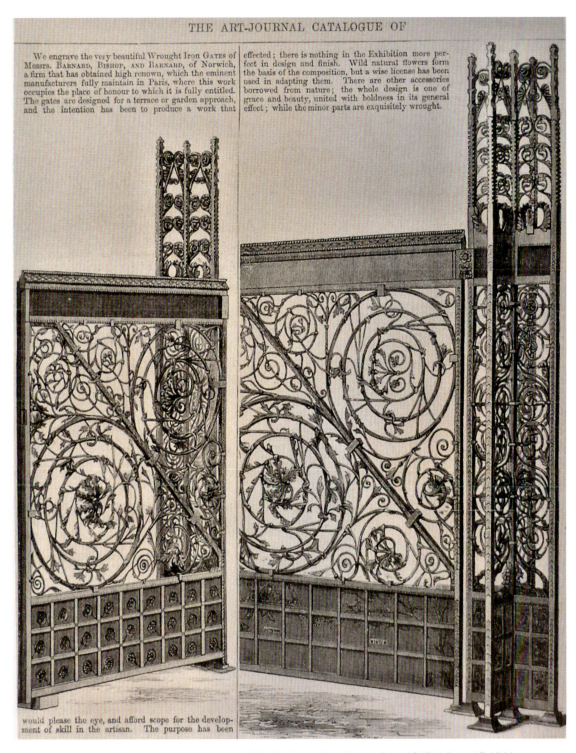

The Four Seasons or Vienna Gates from *The Art Journal* catalogue of the 1867 Universal Exhibition.

ABOVE Compared with their Sandringham predecessors, the gates advanced considerably in the Aesthetic modernity of their form, while still allowing the display of Jeckyll's gift for flowing design and fine detailing.

RIGHT A self-portrait of Thomas Jeckyll, c.1857, with his left arm in a sling.

Jeckyll also designed carriage gates for the Gurneys at Sprowston Hall, incorporating Japanese-inspired wave patterns. There followed the highly successful, in terms of design and manufacturing, series of fire or stove fronts, devised for Barnards' innovative slow-combustion stoves. These too were influenced by Japan in their decorative design. They are highly imaginative and show Jeckyll's skill at its best. It is on them above all that Thomas Jeckyll's reputation as a designer rests.

Oriental inspiration was to dictate the basic form of Jeckyll's last great collaboration with Barnards, one of the most extraordinary garden structures ever devised, a 'Pagoda', which for seventy years formed the centrepiece of a Norwich public garden. Again, the commission was for an international exhibition, the Centennial Exposition in Philadelphia of 1876. What Jeckyll designed was a garden pavilion in cast and wrought iron, loosely following the form of a Chinese or Japanese temple, but with an upper storey, which allowed the word 'pagoda' to be applied to it. Pagoda it was not but the name stuck. Initially the Pavilion was to be used as an exhibition stand for a range of Barnards' products. Its life after that was to be as an ornamental garden structure. It was folly-like in its apparent lack of practical use, either as an exhibit stand or garden shelter,

Thomas Jeckyll's Pavilion on display at the Exposition Universelle, Paris, in 1878.

although it did provide some shelter and views from its upper storey. Its ornamental credentials however were impeccable. Barnards wanted another showcase for their mastery of decorative ironwork, and here Jeckyll was at the height of his powers. He was also on the verge of his mental breakdown, perhaps in part caused by overwork. The structure was opulent with inventive detail, and, whatever one made of its form, the quality of its detail was beyond reproach. Later generations were to fall out not only with its form, but the quantity of its detail, and of that there seemed to be no end.

Weighing in at forty tons, costing £2,000 to construct (roughly £250,000 today), and shipped off from Limerick to Philadelphia in fifty-four containers, the Pavilion fully met with the hoped-for success. *The Art Journal* declared that its cast- and wrought-iron work was 'one of the greatest triumphs of the art'. Neither the inventiveness of its design nor the quality of the workmanship could be faulted. What was faulted, however, was that parts of the structure, its sunflowers, were painted, in 'lemon chrome paint'. The American literary periodical *Scribner's Monthly* found the building's 'imposing character shaken by its absurd coloring – its prevailing tint being bright yellow'.

This did not prove to be a fatal flaw, for the Pavilion went on to more international acclaim in Paris and Vienna. It had gone to America unfinished; Paris saw the missing stairs, ceiling and roof panels completed, and the Pagoda/Pavilion was clearly rebranded as a garden pavilion, complete with especially designed chairs and loungers. In Paris it won more medals and praise.

On its return to its native city, again, as with the Norwich Gates, good fortune abounded. The Pavilion was bought by Norwich Corporation for a nominal sum of £250, with a further £250 charged for carriage, foundation work and for repainting. The erection of the building probably cost double what the city paid for it, but Barnards were rewarded in that their celebrated creation was to be erected in a prominent public place for all to admire in the city of its manufacture. In 1880, it was erected in Chapelfield Gardens, where it became the centrepiece of the newly restored and laid out gardens. A spacious and ornamental garden, in the 'Old English style' had been laid out under the direction of Mr R. Elphinstone, from what had been 'well-nigh wilderness hedged around with primitive wooden railings'. So reported the *Eastern Daily Press*, in a long and detailed account of the restored gardens opening, which was attended by thousands of enthusiastic citizens on a bright November day. From the top floor of the extraordinary Pavilion the band of the 6th Inniskillen Dragoons played the National Anthem, while below, civic dignitaries quite rightly congratulated each other on these important and public-spirited civic improvements. The Mayoral party and guests then duly retired to the nearby Drill Hall for extensive refreshments. It is poignant to reflect that while these celebrations were going on, only a stone's throw away, in the Bethel Hospital, Thomas Jeckyll was confined in his padded cell with his imaginary demons.

The long account of the proceedings in the *Eastern Daily Press* mentions the designer by name, but perhaps finding his current state a delicate matter, does not say a word

ABOVE From c.1889, Thomas Jeckyll's newly erected Pavilion in Chapelfield Gardens in Norwich. Around it are his sunflower railings and his ornamental cast-iron 'chairs', designed in 1878, garden benches with Japaneseque-designed backs.

OVERLEAF The Pavilion in Chapelfield Gardens, Norwich. 1890s.

more about him. It does however describe the design of his Pavilion in detail. It was thirty-three feet long, eighteen wide and nearly forty feet high. From photographs we know what it looked like, but what cannot fully be appreciated is the wealth of detail incorporated into its design. Just the spandrels of the brackets alone which supported the verandah offer a glimpse. These were rich with bas-reliefs – apple blossom with flying birds, whitethorn with pheasants, Scots pine with jays, sunflowers, chrysanthemums, narcissus. Round the entire building was a railing four and a half feet high, comprising seventy-two panels, each one presenting a large wrought-iron sunflower with six leaves hanging from its stem. It was a triumph of the art of the metalworker, a tour de force of design, the most bizarre structure, garden or otherwise, Norwich has ever seen, or is likely to.

As auspicious as were the circumstances surrounding the preservation of the Norwich Gates, the circumstances surrounding the fate of the Pavilion were equally

inauspicious. The twentieth-century reaction against High Victorian Art saw it stripped of its sunflower railings. Twelve of these sunflowers found their way into Heigham Park, as entrance gates to the tennis court in the newly laid out Sandys-Winsch park. What, may be asked, happened to the remaining sixty?

Worse was to come. Wartime neglect and reported damage in the Norwich blitz – in fact it was only superficial – left the Pavilion, so the city council stated, in an unsound condition. The immediate post-war mood of adopting a brave new world and severing

TOP A hand-coloured postcard from the 1900s appears to show the Pavilion painted green and terracotta.

ABOVE The Pavilion in Chapelfield Gardens in 1934, stripped of its sunflower railings, but otherwise in good condition.

links with a troublesome past was dominant. In 1945 the city produced the most radical plans for its rebuilding and modernization, with wholesale demolition of much its medieval and other heritage to be replaced by blocks of uniform contemporary buildings with networks of wide new roads. Even a huge viaduct seventy feet high was to plunge from Bracondale across the river towards Thorpe Road. In this heady atmosphere of off-loading the past to embrace a Utopian future, to commit money for the repair and maintenance of that anachronistic, ugly structure in Chapelfield Gardens was an anathema to the city councillors. The city architect suggested it be replaced with a brick shelter. The council voted for its demolition. In 1949 the Pavilion was demolished, and sold for scrap, realizing £98. What a contrast to the attitude of

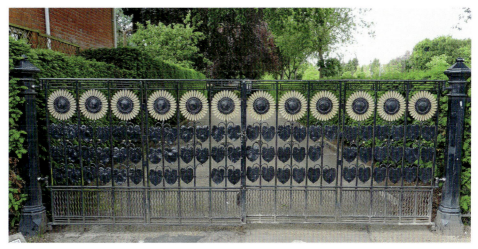

The Heigham Park gates in 1956 (BELOW) and 2012 (ABOVE). The only remaining fragments of Jeckyll's Pavilion.

A rare colour photograph of the Pavilion, here painted green, from 1935.

the civic fathers seventy years before, when the cost of keeping this 'very fine piece of Norwich workmanship' was met by public subscription, and the Pavilion became the proud centrepiece of expensively restored gardens.

In the architecturally callous 1960s there was still no love lost for the vanished Pavilion. Although Nikolaus Pevsner was elected the chairman of the Victorian Society in 1964, championing what was then highly unfashionable Victorian architecture, he did have his limits. Earlier he had charged some architecture of that age as being a 'fancy dress ball' of historical styles, and able to slip into 'profound artistic dishonesty'. His ambivalence is clear when he mentioned the Pavilion in the Norfolk volumes of *The Buildings of England* (1962). Presumably, he remembered the structure from his earlier visits to the city. '... there stood in Chapel Field one of the most gorgeous Victorian cast-iron monstrosities in England, the PAGODA, ... and not looking in the least like a pagoda, nor indeed like anything else.'

Norwich undoubtedly lost a minor masterpiece when the Jeckyll Pavilion came down. However outlandish the concept, the detailing and craftsmanship excelled. Today, this Victorian extravaganza, with its riot of stylized ornament and motifs, surrounded by its fence of iconic sunflowers, would be on any tourist's route, a flamboyant symbol of the city where it was made. Fortunately, the other great Jeckyll and Barnards' work, the Norwich Gates, are still resplendent at Sandringham, perhaps not given the attention they deserve, but a fitting formal entrance to this royal house and garden.

Under the aegis of George V, in 1914, to gain more privacy, part of the perimeter road round the gardens was realigned, and the Norwich Gates were resited further north and away from the house, yet still in line with its north front. However, particularly when the private car became more affordable, the privacy issue remained. From the gates the public were able to look directly at the house entrance and its comings and goings. That is until the major landscape transformations by Sir Geoffrey Jellicoe in the late 1940s, which eventually concealed the mansion from view.

15

The Holkham Fountain

Christine Hiskey

The fountain at Holkham Hall, the ancestral seat of the Earls of Leicester on the north Norfolk coast, is unique in the county for size and magnificence. It is the focal point of a Victorian transformation of the grounds on the south side of the eighteenth-century hall. 'It seems as if a fairy wand had waved over the well-remembered scene,' commented *The Gardeners' Chronicle* of 16 October 1858: 'Persons who visited Holkham twenty years since, although they may have heard rumours of change, will yet be not a little surprised when they enter the park through the triumphal arch ... There stands that hall – the same, yet changed ... Terrace upon terrace rises, broad and noble as are the walks – sloping banks of velvety green intervene, while on the broader verdant surface small beds of flowers ... give the surface a gay beauty ... In front is a magnificent fountain, the centre representing St. George in the act of striking the dragon, from whose open, upturned jaws spouts a continuous flood. Beneath are dolphins which play upon the centre, and around the whole is a basin of well-proportioned dimensions into which the jets of water fall, to replenish the fountains, sparkling in the light.'

The terraces and fountain, although built 100 years after the hall, unintentionally echoed an earlier formality. In the 1720s their site had been the first part of the park to be created by Thomas Coke, later 1st Earl of Leicester. In a scheme of great vision and confidence, some ten years before he began building the hall, he imposed a formal design on the ancient landscape of fields and sheep walk that lay south of his family's old manor house. The latter was to remain as his home until 1756, when the new hall, although unfinished, was ready for occupation, so the new gardens and landscaping were intended to give pleasure to his family and guests throughout the long years of building as well as in the future. In the immediate vicinity of the manor house, he took advantage of the fact that its gardens on the south sloped down to the road that ran east-west through old Holkham Town. He closed the road, cleared cottages where necessary (rehousing their occupants in the other existing village at Holkham Staithe) and planted lawns running down to the natural hollow. Here he created a

The highest jet is reserved for the dragon on the
St George and the Dragon fountain at Holkham Hall.

The *St George and the Dragon* fountain was first run in the autumn of 1856. Edward Adveno Brooke's depiction shows it in its first summer, in 1857, the same year his coloured lithograph was published.

large formal basin, bordered by wide gravelled walks and flanked by two ornamental pavilions: a perfect scene for leisurely walks, a little gentle boating and pauses for rest or refreshment. Where the ground rose again beyond his formal gardens and basin, teams of labourers toiled for months to transform arable land into a 'great lawn', stretching up the slope towards the hill where he would erect the Obelisk, in line with the centre of the proposed hall. To the west, the basin was linked by a 'serpentine river' to the lake that Coke was creating from old fish ponds and a natural stream.

TOP The south front of the hall in 1816, with the parkland running up to its base. Forty years later this was certainly not to be to Victorian taste.

ABOVE The fountain forms the focal point of William Nesfield's ambitious terraces.

The 2nd Earl of Leicester, Thomas William Coke, (1822–1909) by George Richmond, c.1850. Painted at the time he embarked on major landscaping to the south and west of the hall, which included the Nesfield terraces and the *St George and the Dragon* fountain.

William Andrews Nesfield (1793–1881), the most prestigious garden designer of the mid nineteenth century. Contemporary with his designs for the Holkham fountain and terraces, in the 1850s, he designed the *Atlas* fountain at Castle Howard, 1853, and shortly after a not dissimilar but much larger fountain than his Holkham tour de force, the *Perseus and Andromeda* fountain, complete with huge serpent, at Witley Court in Worcestershire.

This early designed landscape lasted little more than sixty years. Around the end of the eighteenth century, Thomas William Coke, the celebrated agriculturist, great-nephew of the builder of the hall and later 1st Earl of Leicester of the 2nd creation, replaced it with a more naturalistic landscape, in tune with the fashions of the time. The basin and the serpentine river were filled in and the formal walks and pavilions removed, leaving 'a long green slope which gradually descended into the richly turfed undulation' of the parkland. This designed landscape also lasted about sixty years.

The next generation followed mid nineteenth-century fashion as it turned again to symmetrical formality. It is this phase which survives at Holkham today. Its instigator, the 2nd Earl, was T. W. Coke's son, born in 1822 when his father was 68. He inherited Holkham at the age of twenty and married shortly afterwards. For some years he concentrated on improvements and refurbishment inside the hall but in 1849 his attention turned to the exterior. Here the earliest project was to be seven years of major landscaping and construction work to the south and west of the hall. Gradually the long slopes that had once led down to the village street and subsequently to Thomas Coke's formal basin were carved into broad rectangular terraces. At the centre of their southern edge, a semi-circular terrace projected into the parkland to provide a striking setting for the focal point, a massive fountain.

The Holkham Fountain

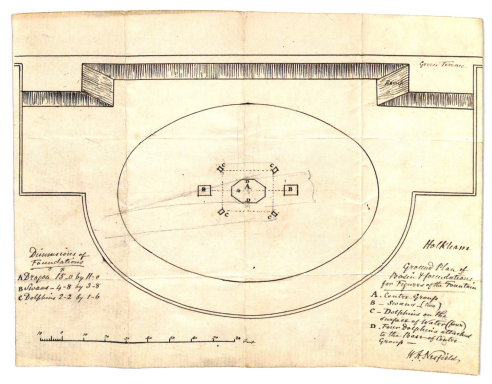

ABOVE *Ground Plan of Basin and Foundations, for the Figures of the Fountain.* Drawn and designed by W. A. Nesfield. A: Centre Group. B: Swans (two). C: Dolphins on the surface of the water (four). D: Four Dolphins attached to the Base of the Centre Group.

BELOW 'This is a drawing of the Swans which I designed for the Sculptor.' Sketch by Nesfield of the proposed Swan flank jets. On the left, the female on her nest.

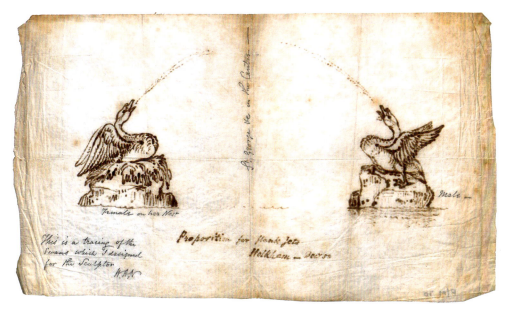

The architect S. S. Teulon (1812–73) had submitted designs for the terraces in the 1840s, when he had been involved in designing park lodges, but he had fallen out of favour at Holkham and it was the leading landscape architect, W. A. Nesfield (1793–1881), whose designs were adopted and constructed between 1851 and 1854, working in cooperation with the country-house architect, William Burn (1789–1870), who was busy at the same period on major additions to practical areas of the hall, and the Norwich masons, Watson's, who had recently built the monument in the park and repaired stonework on the hall.

FACING PAGE One of the flanking swan jets.
ABOVE The seven parts of the completed sculpture.

The designs incorporated manicured lawns, elaborate parterres and gravelled walks linked by wide shallow steps, interspersed with stone vases and tazza. The terrace walls were finished with stone balustrades and the eastern end of the terraces terminated at a stone pavilion, the latter built by a Manchester building firm, Bramall and Buxton, who were also engaged on major building work near the hall. It is likely that the fountain was always to be the focal point of the scheme. A report and estimate in May 1853 for a new water supply to the house and gardens – an essential part of all the additions and alterations – has not survived, but it included calculations of the water supply for the proposed fountain, and the Holkham agent emphasized that Lord Leicester's priority was 'to have all the pipes laid and every part of the work performed this summer which will be required to complete the terraces'.

It was, however, another three years before the fountain appeared. The sculptor was Charles Raymond Smith (c.1799–1888) who was perhaps introduced to Holkham by Nesfield: the latter was responsible for approving Smith's account for the vases for the terraces and he appears to have had some part in designing the fountain, certainly the flank jets. Nevertheless, Smith was a well-established sculptor in both stone and bronze. Born in 1799, the son of a monumental mason, his chief work is said to have been a series of heroic figures for Mamhead Park, Devon, which remained there until they were sold in the 1980s, and his most famous, an effigy of Grace Darling in Bamburgh churchyard, Northumberland. His life-size figures of Michelangelo and Raphael for Bowood, Wiltshire, now stand by the entrance to the walled garden there. He exhibited several times at the Royal Academy and at the Great Exhibition of 1851. No evidence has been found to show exactly when he received the Holkham commission, or how long it took him, but he was paid £115.15.0. in January 1856, £300 on account in April 1856, and a further £936.2.10 in the following January, all for the fountain, in addition to £541 for 'sculptures to the terrace'. It was obviously a large commission

and probably his major work in the mid 1850s.

The fountain depicts St George and the dragon. It was called the 'St. George fountain' in the estate records, *The Gardeners' Chronicle* of 1858 and a new guide book to Holkham published in 1861. At some time during the mid-twentieth century, however, perhaps when such sources of information in the archives and library were not so readily available as today, it was said to represent Perseus and Andromeda, which doubtless seemed more in keeping with the architecture of the hall and its classical paintings, and that title persists today. Carved in stone (apart from St George's sword,

which has the green sheen of bronze) it shows St George poised at the summit of a massive rock, his sword swung back ready to strike the dragon, which apparently, he has taken by surprise from behind. The dragon is arching its head back towards St George, so that its open jaws are breathing fire – or rather, water – in a vertical stream; its massive claws are raised in the air as it tries to reach backwards, and it preserves its balance with its scaly wings outspread, its body curling round the rock where St George appears to be standing on its tail. Almost unnoticed below this high drama, the king's daughter half kneels on a lower ledge, straining back to escape or perhaps to see what is happening above.

The sculpture is a massive piece of work. The foundation for the central piece is shown on plans as measuring 16 by 11 feet (4.9m x 3.35m) and the pipes supplying the three main jets rise 18 feet (nearly 5m) to the dragon's mouth. At the base of the dragon are four dolphins, rather ferocious in appearance with jets from mouth and nostrils, and two shell jets. The sculpture stands in a basin approximately 111 feet long by 82 wide (34m x 25m) holding 156,000 gallons. Around it, in the basin, two large swans and four extra dolphins produce six more jets. Below, in passages for maintenance access, the water was supplied in 15- and 12-inch pipes (38cm and

ABOVE Beneath the terraces, accessed from the parkland, a tunnel runs to the fountain's centre carrying the pipes and allowing access.

LEFT Side tunnels carrying the water to the swan flanking jets. The vertical piping feeds the main sculptural group directly above. Each pipe carries its original lead identification label.

BELOW AND FACING PAGE Set on a ridge of higher ground to the south-east of Kent's Obelisk, the Fountain Reservoir. Ninety feet across at the base, it has a brick bottom and retaining wall twenty-eight inches high. Both were lined with cement. From the rim of the wall the bank, set with flints in mortar and lined with cement, stretches back twenty-three feet to an upper rim. Set in a recess in the reservoir's floor, the pipes brought water pumped up from the hall, and took a gravity-fed supply direct to the fountain. Although the reservoir was sited in open ground, away from trees, it still needed an annual emptying and cleaning to stop debris building up.

30cm), and then to the smaller jets in 7-inch pipes. The larger pipes alone cost about £730 and the others £200.

While the sculptor was creating the fountain, great technological changes were taking place at Holkham. The work on the terraces was not the only construction activity for, starting a year or so later but again lasting several years, a sustained building campaign was transforming the area east of the hall with great new ranges of domestic buildings (laundry, brewhouse, game larder, engine house, and stables). The stables and coach houses now house the gift shop, restaurant, offices and exhibition; the laundry forms part of a new events venue known as the Lady Elizabeth Wing. A massive conservatory was built to complete the separation of these utilitarian buildings from the new pleasure grounds, the terraces, to the south of the hall, emphasizing the social distinctions and desire for privacy which were so typical of the Victorian age.

A major component of the 2nd Earl's extensive improvements, indoors and out, was a new water supply system. This proved to be a difficult and expensive project, involving two new systems within the space of ten years, largely because of the demands of the new fountain. For the past hundred years, the water supply for the hall had been raised by a horse-drawn engine from a well near the south-east wing of the hall. The new system, designed and constructed in the early 1850s by a leading London firm of water engineers, Easton and Amos, replaced the horse with a steam pumping engine, installed in one of the new buildings to the east of the hall, and drew water from the lake. Hundreds of yards of pipes were laid from the lake, west of the hall, under the north lawn to a well next to the engine and onwards up to a reservoir which was excavated about a mile south of the hall. Digging the reservoir, which was to be 136

feet in diameter at the top, 90 feet at the bottom and 8 feet deep (41.5m by 27m by 2.4m) started in April 1854. The agent soon reported that it had hit a solid bed of chalk, doubling the expected cost. No record has been found of the cost or the number of men doing the massive amount of digging but it was apparently done by the estate rather than by contractors. To save some of the expense of carting, the estate engineer suggested using an 8-inch layer of crushed chalk, 'which would set as hard as any concrete', and reducing the top layer of clay 'puddle' to 10 inches. This was not entirely successful: fourteen years later it was proposed to clean out the reservoir and re-build the bottom and sides in brick.

The reservoir was ready to receive water by the middle of September 1854. From the reservoir the water fed by gravity through a system of valves back to the house, the firecocks round the house, the fountain and terraces, pleasure gardens, kitchen gardens, and stables. The water pressure had to be sufficiently strong, not only to rise to the top of the fountain but, even more importantly, for the jets from the firecocks round the hall to reach over its highest roofs. The engineer, James Easton, had extensive experience in constructing water supplies, including that for the Trafalgar Square fountain (subsequently extended to public buildings and Buckingham Palace), many

ABOVE Looking down on the pumps that supplied water from the artesian well to the reservoir from 1868 to 2004.

towns and numerous country houses, but the fountain at Holkham effectively defeated him. The new system took two years to install, at a cost of £2,730. Part of it was in operation by October 1854, but a serious problem arose in the following May, when the engineer belatedly realized that the supply would be insufficient for the proposed fountain. He proposed an additional 12 inch (30cm) pipe but the agent immediately voiced doubts whether 'in taking this additional supply for the fountain we shall be in a position to return it to the reservoir in sufficient quantities'. The original scheme had envisaged a supply to the fountain of 400 gallons (1,818 litres) per minute but with the house and gardens using a minimum of 20,000 gallons (91,000 litres) per day, the reservoir would be exhausted if the fountain ran for six hours on three consecutive days. With the engine pumping 125 gallons per minute, the agent calculated, it would take 66 hours just to replenish the reservoir. By comparison, disposing of this massive supply to the fountain appears to have been relatively straightforward: around this time it was proposed that the overflow would be taken by a 9 inch pipe running under the south lawn into a cesspool and from there into the lake. Further details (particularly as to how the overflow was controlled) are lacking but it is probable that this provision continued until the modernisation of the system in 2015 enabled the water to be re-circulated within the fountain basin.

Shell jets and dolphins spouting water from their mouths and nostrils circle the base of the main sculpture, which also take the full force of the water dropping from above.

In July 1856, fourteen months after the Earl had reluctantly agreed to the engineer's proposal for a larger supply pipe, the fountain was sent by ship to Wells-next-the-Sea and on by carts to Holkham, to be plumbed in at the beginning of October. The difficulties of running the fountain for any length of time were soon compounded by the unreliability of the water from the lake, as regards both quality and quantity, to supply the hall. It was decided that the only solution was to sink a deep artesian well, sited close to the existing steam pumping engine. Work began in November 1864, but it took more than three years of demanding specialist work, during which Easton and Amos were dismissed and replaced by another firm, to reach a reliable supply by borehole at a depth of 700 feet. The well shaft was deepened and lined, the borehole was piped, and the pumps were at last refitted in 1868. Up to 540 gallons (2,455 litres) a minute could be pumped to the reservoir and it was anticipated that it would rarely be necessary to run the pumping engine on more than three days a week. Even so, the fountain could be run only for limited periods.

The basin surrounding the fountain was itself a source of pleasure, for early family films show young members of the family swimming there and tobogganing into it down a wooden slide. In the late twentieth century, the fountain was usually played for forty-five minutes on the afternoons when the house was open to the public. For each hour that the fountain ran, four hours of pumping was needed to replenish the reservoir. It was a matter of fine judgement to balance the supply to the reservoir with the consumption of water at the fountain and the demands of the gardens: one

LEFT Part of the electrically operated pumping system installed in 2016 in its new subterranean pump house.

BELOW The fountain basin is emptied each year to be cleaned and to allow for repairs to stonework and general maintenance.

of the staff at the hall would check the level of water in the reservoir every day in the spring and summer in order to decide (by eye and by experience) how long the engine should pump.

The steam pumping engine was replaced in 1912 by an electric engine and in 2004, although the original pumps remained in place, their work was taken over by a submersible electric pump. In about 1960 the hall itself was connected to the mains supply. In all other respects, the water system installed in the 1860s worked into the 21st century.

Looking south from the hall on a late October afternoon. Kent's Obelisk in the distance.

In 2009, however, the long runs of pipe below the south lawn from the reservoir to the fountain began to fail and the stonework of the basin required repair; for some years the basin stood empty. In autumn 2015 work started on a restoration programme to return the fountain to working order. The seven-month project, costing over £200,000, was carried out by a Suffolk-based firm, Miles Water Engineering Ltd. A new underground pump room was constructed to house pumping and filtration equipment, circulating water from the bowl of the fountain through the twenty-five water jets. Repairs to the various sculptures were carried out by stonework specialists, Messenger Conservation Ltd of Stamford in Lincolnshire. By April 2016 the fountain was back in full operation, capable of being run for longer periods of time, and controlled, no longer by observation at the reservoir and the turning of external stopcocks, but from within the Hall.

The Holkham fountain, as a sculpture, deserves more than the passing mention given to it in the few published descriptions of the work of Charles Raymond Smith. Less obviously, but remarkably, it prompted a major technological achievement which operated for 150 years, a reminder of the various types of expertise that lay hidden behind many such features. In its setting in the landscape, it introduces a contrasting dramatic element into the axis through the upright form of the eighteenth-century Obelisk to the south and the monument (completed only six years before the fountain) to the north. When playing, the fountain and jets are a mesmerising focal point within the wider views, whether seen from the windows of the state rooms or looking from a distance in the park towards the hall. It is unlikely that those involved in creating this part of the Victorian landscape were aware of Thomas Coke's original scheme, but their terraces and fountain proved to be appropriate successors to complement his hall.

FACING PAGE Nesfield's extensive parterres to the south and west of the hall, with his fountain as the culminating feature.

The Holkham Fountain

16

Carrow and the Colmans

Graham Innes

Hidden behind a long flint wall and an almost impenetrable barrier of trees and shrubs in the Bracondale district of Norwich, lie the grounds of Carrow House and Carrow Abbey, one of the most extraordinary and least known areas of the city. In 1856 Carrow House became the home for more than forty years of Jeremiah James Colman (1830–1898), the principal owner of what became the famous Mustard, Starch, Blue and Corn Flour Manufactory, later J. & J. Colman Ltd. He set up his factories by the River Wensum at the base of the elevated site and purchased the historic Carrow Abbey next door in 1877 as an annex for Carrow House.

The grounds of these two large properties, although reduced in size and considerably built over since the nineteenth century to accommodate factory expansion, together still extend to approximately fifteen acres. Carrow House, at the top of the site, makes up about four acres of the total. What may loosely be termed Carrow Abbey comprises the remainder, including several later factory-related structures.

Carrow House

The connection of the Colman family with the area had started in 1850 when Colman's decided to move its expanding business from the watermill at Stoke Holy Cross south of Norwich. They were able to purchase land from the Norfolk Railway Company close to the River Wensum and railway in Carrow. This site had the advantage of excellent water and rail connections with Great Yarmouth and, after 1851, with London. The first industrial building to be completed on the Carrow site was the Mustard Mill in 1854. Following his father's death in the same year, Jeremiah at the age of twenty-four became in sole charge of the manufacturing side of the business in Norwich.

Jeremiah James Colman, 1830–1898, by Sir Herbert von Herkomer, 1899.
Mustard manufacturer, philanthropist, antiquarian, collector, Liberal MP for Norwich, 1871–1895, Sheriff of Norwich, 1862, Mayor, 1867, Deputy Lieutenant of Norfolk, 1880; by 1893 Jeremiah Colman employed more than 2,000 people. A devout Christian, he was recognized for the social and humanitarian care of his employees.

LEFT Drawing of Jeremiah Colman in the 1860s.

BELOW The grounds of Carrow House and Carrow Abbey. Top left is a section of the River Wensum with factory buildings running beside it. Bottom right, the roundabout outside County Hall. Bottom left, the southern end of King Street. Above this is Carrow House, with a contemporary building attached. Above this, in the trees, is a bridge which crosses the access road which divides the site. In the centre of the picture are the three joined sections of Carrow Abbey, with, to its left, the large modern works canteen. Above this are the remaining eastern gardens and grounds of the Abbey.

FACING PAGE The east front of Carrow House in the 1870s, with its grass terraces leading down to fashionable circular and crescent-shaped beds for bedding-out, nineteen in total. High on the roof is a balustrade which allowed for spectacular views over the city below and into the Yare valley to the east.

In 1855 Colman bought a large three-bay Victorian villa standing at that time on a sharp bend in King Street leading uphill to the junction with Bracondale. This building stood in just over two acres of grounds and still constitutes the core of Carrow House today. The garden and various buildings associated with the adjoining malt house backed on to the developing factory to the north. After his marriage to Caroline Cozens-Hardy of Letheringsett Hall in 1856, the Colmans moved into Carrow House. It was very unusual by this date for a manufacturer to be living adjacent to his factory but there were many advantages for the Colmans, not least the proximity of Carrow to Norwich's main railway station at Thorpe. This enabled Jeremiah to reconcile his close family life with attendance at business meetings at Colman's sales office in London and his later career as a Liberal MP at Westminster.

In 1860–61 they became temporary tenants of the nearby Abbey to enable them and their architect Thomas Jekyll to extend Carrow House to the north in an Italianate style. Apart from providing much needed extra room, the extension helped to shore up the existing house on its precipitous site. Both Jeremiah and his new wife were keenly involved in the development of the building and grounds at Carrow House. Caroline especially had an active interest in and extensive knowledge of the botany of both wild and cultivated plants. In addition, she inherited her father's fondness for landscape gardening following the extensive tree planting and other improvements carried out by his uncle William Hardy to the gardens and estate at Letheringsett outside Holt.

ABOVE AND BELOW Prior to 1885 King Street ran directly in front of the western side of Carrow House. Note the two factory chimneys and works beyond the garden to the right. After the road was realigned, the same approach became a secluded and private entry to both house and garden.

The east front of Carrow House c.1890. Tiered grass terraces lead down the sloping site, with the planting simplified and maturing tree and shrub growth. In the distance, to the far right, is the top of the Black Tower of the medieval city walls.

Entrance to the garden from Carrow House was through a door in the basement at the rear from where the lawn sloped in stages down to the main lawn below. This at first featured a large circular floral design consisting of a central polygon surrounded by teardrop paisley pattern flower beds cut into the grass. However, Caroline's dislike of ribbon borders, the artificiality of patterned bedding-out and formality in general, eventually led to the abandonment of this style of horticulture. Meanwhile she encouraged the perimeter planting of trees and shrubs to screen the growing factory to the north, a feature which still characterizes Carrow today. The vinery, mentioned in the 1855 sale particulars, was soon replaced by a very tall and long lean-to glasshouse with central Conservatory, which backed on to and partially obscured the factory behind.

In 1877 Jeremiah Colman bought Carrow Abbey along with the rest of the Martineau family estate in Bracondale. This led to the closure of Abbey Lane to the south of Carrow House and the eventual extension of the garden on this side. In 1885 the sharp bend on King Street was realigned with the result that the front of the house was set further back from the road. It could now be screened from the passing traffic by many fine trees and shrubs including a magnificent Hungarian oak, *Quercus frainetto*, considered by many to be the most handsome of all the oaks.

Colman family group taken at Carrow with the Gladstones, 19 May 1890.

Seated, left to right: Mrs Henry Gladstone, Jeremiah Colman, Mrs Catherine Gladstone, William Gladstone (then Leader of the Opposition, before his fourth and final premiership), Caroline Colman with Florence Colman in front, Russell Colman. Standing, right to left: Ethel Colman, Prof. James Stuart, Laura Colman, Alan Colman, Helen Colman, Henry Gladstone.

Jeremiah was a close friend of Gladstone, who offered him a baronetcy. This he declined saying: '… anything I can do to promote the principles I have always supported … I am glad to do, but I much prefer that it should be without the reward or rank a title is supposed to give.' Jeremiah and Gladstone died within four months of each other in 1898. Caroline Colman said of Gladstone: 'He is altogether the most delightful guest than any hostess can entertain. He is so courteous and considerate, and so grateful for the least kindness shown him …'

Further from the house and beyond the end of the original garden purchased, lay a meadow on the north side of the lane from the Abbey which formed part of fourteen acres initially rented from the Martineaus prior to their purchase in 1877. It seems to have been developed as the kitchen and children's gardens for Carrow House. However, the factory's need for more land led to the loss of these gardens and a much-loved sandpit in the early 1900s and their replacement by the large new Kitchen Garden to the east of the Abbey. The pressure imposed by the contiguity of house and Abbey to an ever-expanding factory was to become a recurring theme throughout much of the factory-related existence of both Carrow House and Abbey.

At Carrow House there were further late nineteenth-century additions which had an impact on the gardens. In 1895 the architect Edward Boardman was engaged to extend the house southwards. At the same time, a large and ornate Boulton and Paul Conservatory or winter garden was added. Illustrated in the 1898 Boulton and Paul catalogue, this originally connected to the house by a glazed passageway incorporating a

TOP AND ABOVE The Boulton and Paul Conservatory from the mid 1890s – which was top of the range in its superior attention to detail and ornamentation – as it appeared after its restoration in 2005.

small dome. It is a fine example of a late nineteenth-century timber and cast-iron framed Conservatory. It has a long rectangular plan with semi-hexagonal ends and a short central transept. The garden entrance is from a doorway to the right of the transept and opens directly on to steps leading down into what was shortly to be developed as

TOP The Boardman children at study in the palmed Carrow House Conservatory, with ceramic fountain to the right, c.1911.

ABOVE In the Fountain Garden, the 'umbrello' seat. 1909.

the Fountain Garden. Although not the largest in Boulton and Paul's range, its superior quality is indicated by the generous use of stained glass, the weather vane, finials, and decorative cresting along its ridge, glazed clerestory and, most expensive of all, sheets of curved glass extensively used in its roof instead of much cheaper straight sections. The south end contained a ceramic fountain made by Doulton of Lambeth, removed to the Plantation Garden, Norwich, probably some time after 1922.

In 1896 the Colmans' youngest daughter Florence married Edward T. Boardman from the second generation of the Boardman firm of Norwich architects, and Edwardian family photographs taken by Florence Boardman show the Conservatory planted with palms and ferns and other tender climbing plants. As late as 1979 an edition of the Colman's quarterly house magazine, *Carrow News*, refers to the site's well-kept gardens with 'the Conservatory, the Carrow gardener's showpiece'.

After the death of Caroline Colman in 1895, followed three years later by her husband Jeremiah in 1898, the Abbey ceased to be an annex of Carrow House. It was then doubled in size by their architect son-in-law Edward T. Boardman in order to provide a home for the Colmans' eldest daughter, Laura, and her husband, Prof. James Stuart, who became a director of Colman's at Carrow until his death in 1913.

Meanwhile two unmarried sisters, Ethel and Helen, continued to live at Carrow House after the death of their parents. In 1908 they initiated the last major garden development at Carrow House when their brother-in-law Edward T. Boardman created

The Fountain Garden, Carrow House. 1907.

the Fountain Garden, a fan-shaped sunken plat in the Arts and Crafts style. This was in the odd angle produced at the end of the house between the Conservatory and the 1895 extension. A number of stone balls and finely carved dressings distinguish the low rendered walls which surround the beds once filled with bright annuals. A simple jet fountain in a circular lily pond, with the date 1908 set round its edge in knapped flint, is the elegant focal point of the garden. The most extraordinary feature of this area, however, is a curved seat that looked out over the garden and the King Street Meadow beyond. It is still furnished with a curious maypole-like wooden 'umbrello' seat which used to support a sunshade in the summer months.

In 1922 on the death of their eldest sister Laura, the two sisters vacated Carrow House and moved down the hill to live in the Abbey. Carrow House then became used purely for company purposes and garden developments inevitably slowed down and became largely reactive to the needs of the factory. In the mid twenties ancillary factory facilities, which necessitated

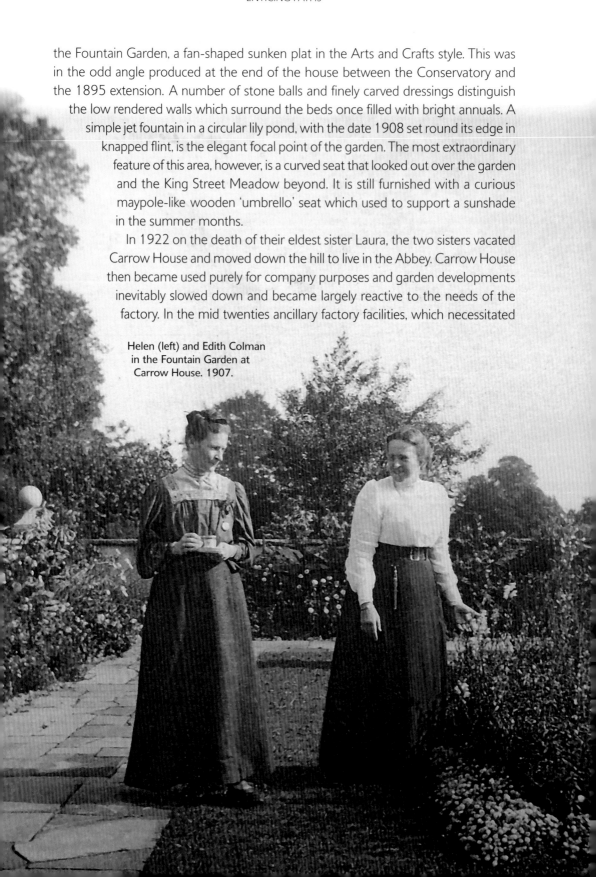

Helen (left) and Edith Colman in the Fountain Garden at Carrow House. 1907.

the demolition of the very large lean-to vinery and Conservatory abutting the factory to the north, began to make their appearance in the original garden at the back of Carrow House. The first of these was the provision of a Staff Luncheon Club, followed by the somewhat smaller first aid or Ambulance Room in 1926. These were sited beside the lawns and flower beds in the long hollow behind the house 'in the most agreeable of surroundings' according to Dr S. H. Edgar. Both facilities were designed by Boulton and Paul of Norwich from their hugely popular range of bespoke timber-framed buildings.

In 1938 J. & J. Colman merged with Reckitt and Sons of Hull to become Reckitt & Colman Ltd. The declaration of war the following year led to the creation of one of the least-known features at Carrow, the ARP, or Air Raid Precautions, shelters. Five parallel tunnels 100 feet long were bored into the steep wooded chalk cliff below Carrow House, meeting a transverse connecting tunnel at their far ends. These could accommodate up to 1,000 people and were much used during the early years of the war. Four still survive, two beneath the trees and remaining grounds of Carrow House.

As the second half of the twentieth century progressed, however, the grounds came under increasing pressure from the inexorable growth of the factory to the north. In 1959 a large modern office block extension was added on to the 1860 addition to Carrow House. Designed by the in-house architect's department, it has three floors at the front and five at the back to accommodate the steep fall in the land towards the factory and River Wensum to the north. There were further drastic changes in 1986–7 which were to prove to be the largest and last of significance made by Reckitt & Colman affecting the factory, with major consequences for Carrow House and Abbey and their grounds. Project Apollo was the name given to the £26 million Carrow site redevelopment, which had three major linked components: a new production unit for Robinsons drinks; an inner road system replacing the old narrow exit on to King Street opposite the bottom of Carrow Hill, with a new factory exit on to the Bracondale roundabout at County Hall that could be more easily negotiated by the latest juggernauts; and increased warehousing space. The results for Carrow House were twofold: most of the remaining lawn and trees at the back disappeared under the yard of the new drinks factory; and a new approach road was built from Bracondale. The visual disruption caused by this was mitigated to some extent by much of it being

The 1987 access road. Although sunk in a cutting, it severed the grounds, the only direct link between Carrow House and Carrow Abbey being by the footbridge.

sunk in a cutting through the last section of the Bracondale slope before reaching the factory yard. Today it forms most of the boundary between Carrow House and Abbey. On the Carrow House side, an ornamental garden of brick walls, paths, pergola and an octagonal paved area was created, leading to a pedestrian bridge built over the new road to link the now severed grounds.

In 1995 Reckitt & Colman sold off its food holdings to Unilever along with the Abbey and associated buildings. The soft drinks business including the Robinsons brand was acquired separately by Britvic. Carrow House was sold off to Norfolk County Council the following year. The original largely Victorian house was used as the home of the Norfolk Museums Service Costume and Textile Study Centre until 2018 when it became the coroner's court, while the attached 1959 office block provided extra accommodation for Social Services.

The Conservatory was restored in 2004–5 and once again made accessible from the house as well as up the flight of steps from the Fountain Garden. It has never been replanted, however. The two acres of ornamental grounds originally purchased in 1855 along with Carrow House have been largely reduced by factory expansion to a tarmac path which clings to the top of the precipitous tree-covered slope overlooking the drinks factory yard. However, they have since been augmented by approximately four acres of land formerly linked to the Abbey which subsequently became the Conservatory and the Fountain Garden, the 1980s landscaped path leading to the pedestrian bridge over the access road, and the tree-girt King Street Meadow, since 1986 a car park entered from the new factory approach road.

Carrow Abbey

For almost 120 years after the purchase of Carrow Abbey in 1877 the grounds of both Carrow House and Abbey were to all intents and purposes maintained as one integrated entity. However, the recorded history of Carrow stretches back over 850 years. Although popularly called an Abbey, in 1146 a Priory was built for a Benedictine order of nuns on the gently rising slope that lay between the marshy ground close to the River Wensum and the heights of Bracondale. The chancel, tower and transepts were constructed in the prevailing Norman style, the later nave, in Early English Gothic. At 195 feet in length, it was the largest religious building in the city after the cathedral. Despite its size, the permanent population of the Priory was not great, usually about a dozen nuns.

The last major architectural addition to the Priory came much later, around 1514, when the penultimate prioress, Isabel Wygun, built a magnificent new Prioress' House,

Carrow Abbey rising up behind a planting of conifers on its elevation above the River Wensum. The banks of the river became the site of the Colman's Mustard Factory. Early nineteenth-century engraving by James Stark.

consisting mainly of a large Guest Room or Strangers' Hall, the Prioress' Parlour, a staircase and an upstairs bedroom. Because it could be used as a secular building, it is the only significant part of the Priory to survive the Dissolution of the Monasteries after 1536. It forms a wonderful backdrop to much of the Abbey grounds and makes up about half of the building known today as Carrow Abbey.

Of the Priory church and conventual buildings, only the stumps remain of the ruins to the north and east of the house. Following a visit by the British Archaeological Association in 1879, Jeremiah Colman directed that the scanty archaeological remains be systematically excavated, disclosing the plan of the church, cloister and nunnery buildings. These much-reduced fragments became part of the ornamental layout of the garden created by head gardener Henry Jones with the active involvement of Caroline Colman in particular. A curving path led past the ruins, through newly planted shrubbery, to the large four-acre pasture Carrow Lawn or Meadow beyond. Somewhat diminished today by the loss of more land to the north over the years, such as for the imposing eighty-five feet high bank of concrete mustard silos erected in 1952, this part of the garden is now maintained as a wild-flower area. A succession of naturalized

ABOVE John Thirtle's early nineteenth-century watercolour of Carrow Abbey from the north-east. Here the building is not romanticized but depicted as it was, roofed and intact, but seemingly in an unrestored condition. The foreground projecting extension did not survive subsequent restorations.

FACING PAGE John Crome squeezes every inch of drama out of his depiction of Carrow Abbey, 1805. Seemingly in part roofless and ivy clad, it appears as more Gothic ruin than domestic dwelling.

ABOVE Bluebells in the Carrow Abbey grounds, less than a mile from the centre of Norwich. 2018.

BELOW The Ordnance Survey map of 1928 shows King Street cut through Bracondale Grove, extending the grounds to the west of Carrow House, with a tree belt to add further privacy. The Conservatory, added in the 1890s, is on the southern end of the house. To the far right are the rectangular plots of the large Kitchen Garden.

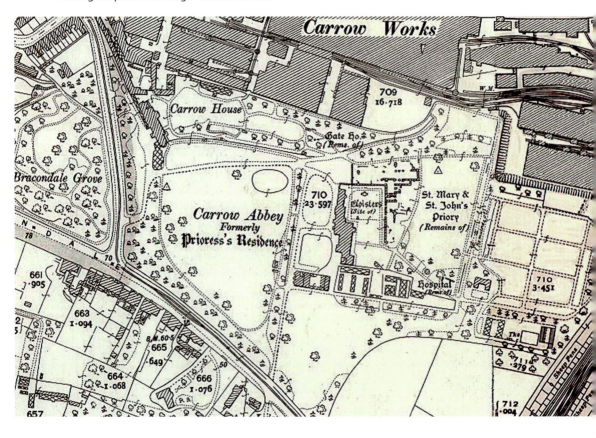

snowdrops and daffodils in spring is followed in May by the fresh foliage of some of the finest of the Carrow collection of deciduous trees.

Further east, beyond the Abbey Meadow, a new Kitchen Garden was created from land running up to the Great Eastern Railway line and by 1881 the initial developmental phase of the Abbey gardens was complete. This consisted of six rectangular plots whose paths lined with espaliered fruit trees made a spectacular show of blossom in the spring. The usual Carrow expedient of generous tree planting eventually screened off signs of the expanding factory to the north.

In 1885, Jeremiah commissioned Edward Boardman Senior to begin the restoration of the Abbey House. After Jeremiah's death in 1898, his daughter Laura and son-in-law, James Stuart, Professor Emeritus of Mechanism and Applied Mechanics (between 1875 and 1890) at Cambridge University, and a director of Colman's, had the house extended southwards, doubling its size. The work was carried out in 1899–1900 by Edward Boardman and his son, Edward Thomas, who was by now married to the Colmans' youngest daughter, Florence. The picturesque result is surprisingly successful, the old and new portions knitting well together.

The Stuarts were responsible for introducing the many Arts and Crafts features into the garden. Beyond the Abbey's main entrance on the west side, Edward T. Boardman designed a sunken oval Rose Garden laid out with regular-shaped beds, steps, low walls, seats, and an Italian well-head as its central feature. In the Cloister Garden to the east

The restored west front of Carrow Abbey, c.1890.

ABOVE Part of the east front of the Abbey, c.1890. The building dates from 1514. The area laid to lawn was once the Priory cloisters.

FACING PAGE BELOW The substantial south extension to Carrow Abbey, completed in 1900, with the garden meandering through the remains of the Priory church. 1907.

FACING PAGE TOP The Carrow Abbey buildings and Priory remains today.

of the house, a tall stone pier records the association of James and Laura Stuart with the site and carries their initials and the date 1903. It is decorated with Arts and Crafts motifs of climbing roses, pomegranates, and a vine scroll. The stone pillar at Carrow originally stood at the head of a shallow pool aligned with the centre of the path along the north side of the Cloister Garden, which could be used by the Stuarts' nephews and niece in the summer. The pool was later filled in and the pillar alone moved to its present position because of its proximity to a new Works Dining Room built in 1968.

However, probably the main contribution of the Stuarts to the grounds at Carrow is the exceptional range of trees and shrubs that they planted with the assistance of their Head Gardener, Henry Jones, continuing the tradition started by Caroline and Jeremiah Colman. In 1924, after fifty-nine years of service to the Colman family, he produced a remarkable list of more than 200 varieties of trees and shrubs, many of them rare or of great interest and beauty. A supplementary list describes the main characteristics and whereabouts of the most select of these. These include the magnificent weeping

Carrow and the Colmans

beech, *Fagus sylvatica* 'Pendula', near the scanty remains of the chancel and the south transept of the Priory church. A 'vast and majestic tree', it is believed to be the second largest of its type in the United Kingdom. On the lawn at the south-east corner of the Priory ruins, a fine specimen of the fern- or cut-leafed beech, *Fagus sylvatica* 'Aspleniifolia', was so admired during a visit by the renowned statesman, political colleague, and late-Victorian Liberal prime minister W. E. Gladstone that the Colmans subsequently dispatched a dozen trees to his Flintshire estate at Hawarden. Just beyond the fern-leafed beech, in 1896, the then Duke of York and future King George V planted the weeping lime, *Tilia dasystyla* subsp. *caucasica*, in 1924.

After James Stuart died in 1913 his widow, Laura, continued to live in the Abbey until her death in 1921. In the next year it became the home of her sisters, the Misses Ethel (Lord Mayor of Norwich, 1923–4) and Helen Colman, who cherished the house and its beautiful setting. Helen died in 1947 and her sister Ethel, the following year, finally severing the direct Colman family domestic link with Carrow after more than ninety years. In 1950 the house was leased to the Norfolk branch of the Red Cross, who used it as their county headquarters until, finally, in 1968, it reverted to Reckitt & Colman. In recent years the Abbey has been used as a conference centre. Today the gardens in the immediate vicinity of the

LEFT The elaborately carved stone pier commissioned by the Stuarts in the Cloister Garden of Carrow Abbey.

FACING PAGE TOP The Rose Garden at Carrow Abbey, 1907.

FACING PAGE BELOW The pillar in its original position. The pool was a garden feature much appreciated by the Boardman children, 1910.

TOP AND ABOVE The imposing weeping beech (*Fagus sylvatica* 'Pendula') near the Priory ruins.
OVERLEAF The Carrow Abbey mural.

Abbey mostly consist of mown lawn with flower and shrub beds next to the house. From the south end of the house a serpentine path leads to the south end of the Abbey Meadow through a wide shrubbery belt sheltering a decayed, rustic thatched summerhouse with wood block floor and plaited reed walls.

In the same area a patch of the rarely found medicinal herb *Aristolochia clematitis* or birthwort survives among the abbey ruins. An extract might have been administered by the nuns as a painkiller for the benefit of local women during childbirth. It is celebrated in a remarkable Arts and Crafts mural painted above the musicians' gallery in the Great Hall in 1906 and restored more recently by Unilever. The Carrow mural portrays nature in the form of flowers and trees, birds and butterflies, for example, many of which, like the lords-and-ladies, *Arum maculatum*, and birthwort depicted, must have been found in the garden. Also, near the Priory ruins at the south-east corner of the Cloister Garden is a large summerhouse used for eating in the summer, formerly called 'The Reeden'. Thatched and with overhanging eaves, it is open at the front and glazed each side by three large Crittall-style metal-framed windows. It seems to have been put up by the Misses Colman after they moved into the Abbey in 1922.

ABOVE Detail from the mural.

LEFT Birthwort, *Aristolochia clematitis*.

FACING PAGE Helen and Edith Colman take tea in The Reeden, c.1930.

The first of two major post Second World War encroachments into the Abbey grounds were the large and now defunct Research Laboratories built at the foot of the King Street Meadow in 1962–3. However, the largest and most dramatic modern incursion into the grounds came with the building in 1968 of an enormous Works Dining Room attached to the Abbey's north end and built over the site of the nave of the Priory church. More than anywhere else at Carrow this could be seen as a diametrical clash between Abbey and gardens from a pre-industrial era and the factory from the post-industrial present. However, in 1948 the Abbey grounds became a de facto adjunct to the factory when the family residential link with Carrow was broken. The new Dining Room was to be the greatest investment in employee welfare ever made at Carrow. It was designed by Colman's in-house architectural department in the style of International Modernism developed for relatively low-rise buildings of one or two stories. The *Evening News* of Norwich wrote in 1968, although the old and new buildings 'might in theory clash strongly with each other ... in practice they set(ting) off

each other's particular qualities ... against the background reminiscent of a mellowed country house garden'.

There were further drastic operational changes in 1986–7 which were to prove to be the last of significance in the complex history of Carrow House and Abbey and their grounds. The third and final phase of the massive Project Apollo was that the old Abbey Kitchen Garden beyond the Abbey Meadow to the east was built over by additional warehousing but was still screened from the Abbey by the trees of the Meadow including two survivors of the original row of senescent red horse chestnuts, *Aesculus* x *carnea*.

In 2018 Britvic announced that it was going to move its production elsewhere. Shortly after Unilever made a similar announcement, and by September 2019 all manufacturing had ceased, with the whole site up for sale, probably for conversion to housing and business development. In 2021 Norfolk County Council sold Carrow House to Norwich City Council. The property is to be refurbished for temporary office space until the master plan for the whole area is determined.

In the face of the almost ceaseless activity and growth of the factory from its inception in the 1850s till final shutdown in 2019, the survival of the two contrasting houses and their protean gardens is remarkable. However, it is by the discreet siting of mainly welfare- and research-related activities in the gardens that the demands of the factory have, to a surprising extent, been reconciled with Carrow's atmosphere of rural tranquillity. Although the juxtaposition of the ancillary industrial buildings with their sylvan setting might be described as bizarre, far from wrecking the Arcadian beauty of the site, this amalgam has produced a uniquely memorable spirit of place.

ABOVE Typical in its 1960s style and lack of sensitivity, the Works Dining Room, attached to the north end of the Abbey and standing over the nave of the Priory church.

FACING PAGE Carrow Abbey in 2020. The Works Dining Room is on its left. Diagonally to the right of that the remains of the Priory church, the weeping beech, and the remaining meadow and trees. The industrial buildings (top right) cover the site of the Kitchen Gardens.

It provides a singular example of the Roman poet Martial's concept of *rus in urbe* or 'country in the town'.

On a site much of which had once been bare and exposed, the legacy of meadows and wonderful tree planting surrounding them is now in its maturity. The names most closely associated with this legacy are those of Caroline Colman, Prof. the Rt Hon James Stuart, Edward T. Boardman for the two Arts and Crafts gardens and features, and Henry Jones, who outlasted them all as the Head Gardener for all but six of his sixty-two years of service, at the time of his death in 1927.

As Ethel Colman wrote in 1927 in her obituary for Mr Jones in the *Carrow Works Magazine*: 'The garden in which Henry Jones worked has always been bordered on one side by Carrow Works. The boundary has been pressed back further and further to the South, as additional portions of the old garden were needed for extensions of Carrow Works ... Such encroachments on the old garden necessitated many changes, and these were loyally and skilfully carried out by the Head Gardener.' This remained true almost to the end of the manufacturing life of the factory so that it can probably be asserted today that no other large gardens in Norfolk have undergone so much change in the past 160 years as those of Carrow House and Carrow Abbey, once again in a state of flux in their transition from a proprietorial family past to a post-corporate future.

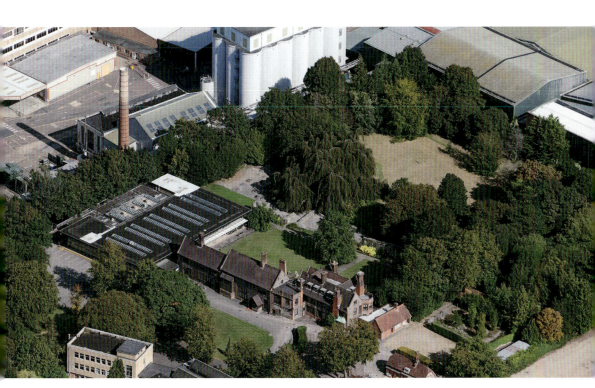

17

The Renaissance of Gunton Park
Elise Percifull

Gunton has been owned by the Harbord family since 1676. In 1742 it passed to Sir William Harbord who commissioned Matthew Brettingham the Elder to build a new Palladian mansion on, or close to, the site of an earlier house. An undated plan of c.1730, attributed by the Bodleian library (where it is held) to Charles Bridgeman, shows an area of ornamental woodland north of the house, known as the Grove, whilst a further estate map of 1754 gives an indication of the layout of a park at this time, extending to more than 150 hectares and including two lakes. In 1769 Robert Adam

FACING PAGE Sheep grazing the restored pastures of Gunton Park.

ABOVE The Hall was designed by Matthew Brettingham the Elder in c.1742. The south front's colonnade and its projecting pavilions are thought to be the 1820s work of William Wilkins. The true scale of the building is revealed by its east front, as seen in this 1870 lithograph, being nearly three times as extensive as the south front. Samuel Wyatt added to the east front and designed the Service Wing, the Brew House and Stable Block beyond, in fact doubling the length of the range of buildings seen here.

ABOVE St Andrew's church, designed by Robert Adam, is the architect's only building in Norfolk. It is sited facing the east front of the Hall. With its columned portico, it is in the style of a classical temple, and in perfect accord with many classically inspired garden structures of the period.

BELOW The elegant bridge of 1812 was built to carry the drive from Hanworth Lodge over the canal linking the two lakes.

was commissioned to replace the medieval church of Gunton, which sat beside the Hall, with a chapel designed to resemble a garden temple. Sir William Harbord died in 1770 and was succeeded by Sir Harbord Harbord, later 1st Lord Suffield. From c.1774 onwards he employed Samuel Wyatt to make alterations and additions to the Hall and to add the main Hanworth Lodge, while at the same time the park was extended to the west of the lakes. In 1812 a new bridge was added over the watercourse linking the two lakes (possibly as a result of advice received from Humphry Repton), while in 1824 a water-powered Sawmill, intended as a picturesque embellishment to the park as well as a practical building, was constructed below the retaining dam on the southernmost lake.

Between 1797 and 1835 the park was extended to the south and east and a continuous belt of perimeter trees was planted, encompassing an extensive area of farmland to the north, called North Park. In 1810 Sir Harbord's eldest son, William Assheton Harbord succeeded to the title and whilst he only used Gunton as a shooting box, he did employ Humphry Repton to offer suggestions for improvements. However, William's younger brother Edward, who succeeded him in 1821, took a greater interest in the estate, completing the building of Gunton Tower (also known as the Observatory) in 1830 and commissioning William Sawrey Gilpin to design the East Park in order to provide the Tower with an appropriately grand parkland view. The estate fortunes declined under Edward Vernon Harbord (1835–53) but revived under Charles, 5th Lord Suffield (1853–1912) during which time the gardens were developed to national

ABOVE The picturesque water-powered Sawmill with its hipped thatched roof was built in 1824, to saw timber felled on the estate. It takes its waters from the Hagon Beck which flows through Gunton's two lakes. The tail waters eventually run into the River Bure. The mill is unique in Norfolk and rare in Britain and a remarkable survivor. It ceased working in the 1950s and was threatened with demolition until being restored by the Norfolk Industrial Archaeological Society and the Norfolk Windmills Trust, 1979–1988.

RIGHT The 120-foot Observation Tower of 1830. Built for Edward Harbord, constructed of gault brick, the upper storey of the Tower is glazed on each face. From the roundels in the roof it is possible to see the sea. Strangely, for such a prominent and expensive structure, the architect is unknown.

The derelict Hall in 1980 and the parkland round it, even up to the balustraded boundary wall of the Hall's formal south terrace, is under the plough.

acclaim with the guidance of the Head Gardener William Allen, within a balustraded design by William Teulon (1870). At its peak in the mid nineteenth century the estate covered c.17,000 acres and ranked with the greatest estates in Norfolk. However, in 1882 much of the Hall was gutted by fire and in 1895 a substantial amount of the park and plantation timber was destroyed in a storm. The decline escalated in the twentieth century as a large part of the park was put under the plough and in 1979, on the death of Doris Harbord, the remaining estate was sold into divided ownership.

Thus it was that Kit and Sally Martin came to Gunton. Kit Martin had been involved in country-house rescues in the past, and he and his wife purchased the burnt and neglected Hall in 1980, together with a small area of gardens, wooded pleasure grounds, and a little strip of park to the south. Their vision was to create a 'village' by restoring the Hall, outbuildings, stables and offices into a series of twenty houses and cottages, each with an upper and lower floor and their own area of garden. While each individual property was to be sold freehold, right from the start the decision was taken

The Avenue looking north to the restored Hall, with oaks planted in 1902 to extend the surviving remains of an eighteenth-century avenue. Additional planting was added in the 1980s; up until then all of the grassland here was ploughed and growing cereal crops.

to set up a management regime, which through covenants would retain control over the external appearance of the buildings and gardens, in order to protect the historic character and setting of the Hall. This decision has proved a key element in the success of the project, which won the Graham Allen Conservation Award in 1985. But when it came to the wider landscape, Kit Martin had little idea of the scale of the battle he was taking on, or that things would get much worse before they got better.

His philosophy on country-house conversions had always been that the wider landscape of gardens, pleasure grounds, walled kitchen gardens, woodlands, walks and parkland, should be maintained, revived and restored along with the buildings. At Gunton this was to prove perhaps the greatest challenge of all and one which has taken from 1980 to the present day to see realized. It has taken not just Kit Martin's vision, but the energy, resources and determination of other like-minded individuals who, over the years, have come to live at Gunton and been caught up in its spell. But the beginning of the 'fight for Gunton Park', as Marcus Binney called it in a *Country Life* article in 1986, was to prove far more difficult than anyone could have imagined.

When the Hall was sold, a large area of parkland was divided up into six lots before being purchased by the farming tenants. The perimeter shelter belts had been resold by the Forestry Commission in 14 lots, while the then Lord Suffield's son, Charles Harbord-Hamond, inherited Dairy Farm and its setting. Before the sale took place, North Norfolk District Council had taken the commendable step of designating the park as a conservation area, and so it might have been reasonable to believe that what survived of the historic landscape would be protected and conserved. But this was not the case – almost as soon as they obtained ownership of their lots, the farmers began to fell trees and plough up the remaining areas of parkland grass. At the beginning of the 1980s conservation area designation was not as well developed as it is today, and the Council found themselves in a difficult position. With no national policy guidance from the Department of the Environment on tree felling or planting to draw on, they felt unable to object to what was happening at Gunton in case they were seen to be preventing reasonable farming operations. The result was an escalation in the number of old park trees being felled, much to the growing dismay of both Kit Martin and the increasing number of new families living in the Hall.

By 1983 Kit and Sally Martin had purchased a key area of parkland to the south of the hall and had begun replanting. They also took the decision to demand that the Council use its conservation area designation to prevent further tree losses, but they did not

The southern lake, the Sawmill Pond.

react, and some 80 old trees were subsequently felled. In the principal areas more than half the old park trees were felled during this period, but eventually the issues raised at Gunton came to the attention of Norfolk County Council who, together with the district council, took another progressive step. They commissioned a historical account of the development of the park (undertaken by garden designer George Carter, based at the University of East Anglia at the time) with the purpose of preparing guidance on its future conservation and restoration. Even while the strategy was being prepared, further felling took place, leading Kit and the residents to instruct a solicitor to write to the Council, pointing out their duty, under the 1971 Town and Country Planning Act, to preserve and enhance any designated conservation area. At last, this produced the result many people had been looking for – the district council acted decisively, placing individual Tree Preservation Orders on all the remaining parkland trees.

Things were finally starting to look up, and 1987 proved to be a real turning point. A joint county and district council policy document was published, making a clear commitment to the conservation area and ensuring that no more felling of parkland

ABOVE The disused Observation Tower with the ploughed parkland round it, 1981.

BELOW After Ivor Braka's restoration of the tower and the restoration of the parkland. To the left, one of the replanted Gilpin clumps.

trees in the park landscape could take place. The other major event at Gunton in 1987 was one which, to begin with, just looked like another disaster. The great storm that swept across parts of the UK in October 1987 followed a route in which the few surviving trees at Gunton were caught up in its path. It must have been devastating for the residents to wake up the following morning, seeing so many of their much loved and fought-for trees brought down by storm-force winds. Yet, out of this destruction came yet another enlightened step – the setting up, by the (then) Countryside Commission, of Task Force Trees, a scheme offering grant support to produce plans providing guidance on the replanting of storm-damaged historic parklands. Gunton was to be one of the first into the scheme, despite the land remaining in divided ownership, and it was to prove the start of a very dynamic relationship which would set the tone for the future.

In 1986 Gunton Tower had been purchased by art dealer Ivor Braka, who had come across it while staying with a friend living in the Hall. The existing owner of the Tower had joined them for dinner and mentioned his desire to sell. Having read Marcus Binney's *Country Life* article on 'The Fight for Gunton Park', Ivor Braka became not only the new owner of the Tower, but a passionate supporter of Kit Martin's vision for the parkland. Together they began to take every opportunity to buy back the land, and together they entered the Task Force Trees scheme (an unusual situation at the time), which helped pay for landscape adviser John Phibbs to complete a landscape survey and provide guidance on where to replant trees. They were joined in this venture by Charles Harbord-Hamond and as a result of the enthusiasm and determination of these three, the revival of the Gunton landscape began to take shape. The landowners were able to start working with the support of the authorities for the first time and when the Countryside Commission launched its Countryside Stewardship scheme, Gunton was one of the first to enter, allowing all the principal landowners to move forward together towards the same end.

Left to right: The three principal instigators of the Gunton restoration: Ivor Braka, Kit Martin and Charles Harbord-Hamond (1953–2016).

While Kit Martin, Ivor Braka and Charles Harbord-Hamond were the principal forces behind the restoration, over the ensuing 30 years more and more residents have joined in as the desire to see the designed landscape returned to its former glory has snowballed. A unique kind of 'partnership' of like-minded people has contributed to the success. For example, the Sawmill on the banks of the south lake was restored by the Norfolk Windmill Trust, and the Robert Adam church has been rescued by the Redundant Churches Fund, now the Churches Conservation Trust. The north lake has been purchased by the artist Gerard Stamp, who has built a fine Arts and Crafts inspired boathouse on its shore, which he uses as a studio. The woodlands, once owned by the Forestry Commission and little managed, have now been brought into more sympathetic ownership and their historic character is being restored. Owners

The team behind the restoration of Gunton Park, 2007.

Front row from left: Kit Martin, Ivor Braka, Sally Martin, Charles Harbord-Hamond.

Back row from left: Amy Martin (in trap, highland ponies bred on estate), Pippa Sims (horses), Judy Lynes (Mr Braka's housekeeper), Steph Birch (restoration of historic orchard), Mick Thurston (forestry), Nigel Dixon (park cattle), Chris Lakey (sheep), James Ellis (founder of Gunton deer herd), Philip Almey (cattle), David Weaver (Defra), James Squier and Simon Evans (estate management), Brian Ducker (joiner for restoration of park buildings), Ian Roberts (master builder for restoration), Nick Gear (blacksmith for park railings), Barre Funnell (Norfolk Windmills Trust for the Sawmill), David Thurston (forestry), Kate Weaver (Churches Conservation Trust for Gunton church), David Richardson (water bailiff), Keith Ward (groundsman) and David MacLintoch (tree planting).

TOP The northern lake, the thirty-acre Great Water.

ABOVE The Boathouse Studio overlooks Great Water. With its mix of brick, oak frame and Norfolk reed, the building is in perfect harmony with its setting. It was completed in 2004, and architects Purcell Miller Tritton closely followed an original concept by Kit Martin, with additional input from Gerard Stamp. It won a Heritage Award from the RIBA.

FACING PAGE Gerard Stamp in his studio, 2019.

ABOVE The restored parkland.

BELOW The herd of deer, now numbering around 750, was established in 1991 and is a mix of red, fallow and sika deer.

of parts of the Hall and its grounds are all keen to ensure that they manage their land in historically appropriate ways and the nineteenth-century wooded pleasure grounds have been sympathetically rejuvenated. Views have been reopened between the Hall and the parkland, crossing ownership boundaries but embracing a common cause. The more the existing residents achieve, the more it seems that new residents with a similar will to contribute, are attracted to Gunton and thus the success continues to grow.

Between them, Kit Martin and Ivor Braka have slowly regained ownership of most of the park and it is all now back under grass. Ten years ago, the final parcel of arable land, with nine surviving parkland trees on it, was purchased by Ivor Braka. It sits on high ground to the south-east of the Hall in a prominent location, and its restoration was a fitting 'final piece' in the jigsaw: the land was reseeded with parkland grass, clumps replanted and fenced using a style common to the rest of the park, part of a Bridgeman era avenue was restored, ponds were recreated, individual trees replanted, and the line of the original Repton drive was restored. In relaying the drive, a view of the Hall was reopened, and made possible by the collaboration of the owner of that part of the Hall landscape, who felled some self-set trees on his land in order to make the view work. The total area of parkland, well in excess of 1,000 acres, has been recreated and more trees planted than in any previous period of Gunton Park's history.

Kit Martin's determination to restore both the landscape itself, and its relationship to the Hall, and to persuade others to join or support him, led to Gunton Park being chosen as the recipient of the *Country Life* Genius of the Place Award in 2007. While

the award was given jointly to Kit Martin and Ivor Braka, the accolade is all the more remarkable because it was achieved through the collaborative work of so many owners, individuals and craftsmen, seeing off tough competition from such sites as Rycote Park in Oxfordshire. In fact, all the other finalists were properties in single ownership, where large budgets and personal visions had driven their restoration. In accepting the award, Kit Martin paid tribute to his fellow 'adventurers' at Gunton – to 'friends and neighbours, agents and agencies, stockmen and builders, blacksmiths who remade miles of park railings, those who helped put nearly a mile of electrical cables underground', and also to James Ellis the deer-keeper who reintroduced fallow and red deer to the park, creating a herd which is now one of its most impressive elements. Today Gunton deer are widely known and respected, and the herd has been able to supply some of the great deer parks in the country with new stock – including Harewood in Yorkshire and the Royal parks at Richmond.

When he arrived at Gunton Kit Martin cannot have imagined what lay before him, but his extraordinary vision, together with Ivor Braka's single-minded mission to restore the landscape and ecology of the park has, perhaps uniquely, carried many people with them in a growing wave of energy and enthusiasm. They have come up with inspiring and unusual solutions to difficult problems and the result is that the park is once again a perfect setting for the listed Gunton Hall and its associated listed buildings throughout the landscape. Norfolk is indeed lucky that is can, once again, count Gunton Park amongst the greatest designed landscapes in the county.

TOP The parkland from the Observation Tower.
FACING PAGE Into the open parkland through the Observation Tower arch.

18

Didlington's Golden Age

Roger Last

Those sitting back in their cinema seats in the Britain of July 1950 waiting for the main feature to begin, would first be harangued, with its unique mix of urgency and authority, by British Pathé News. 'Their Homes, Our Heritage' ran the headline, and on to the screen flashed Didlington Hall, shot in April that year at the time of the great sale. For Didlington, a victim of requisition during the Second World War and mistreatment at the hands of the 7th Armoured Division, and further assailed by high taxation and costs, 'hope comes too late', the commentary declared and indeed for 'treasures like this marble fireplace from the Vatican taking their chance at auction

ABOVE The south front of Didlington Hall. c.1888. The hall, which had twelve reception rooms, forty-six bedrooms, and seven bathrooms, was extended and remodelled twice in the nineteenth century.
FACING PAGE The classical colonnade of Didlington's Swimming Pool.

Didlington Hall from the south (**ABOVE**) and the north-west, (**FACING PAGE**) May 1830.

alongside the more useful bath'. Increasing numbers of important country houses, keeling under financial pressure, much of it government imposed, were sold off or demolished. Didlington, one of the greatest houses in the county, once full of rich and indeed fabulous collections, was stripped bare. A final sale in 1952 saw the selling off of the mundane and the functional – the joists, window frames, copper piping. What remained was razed to the ground.

Just before the outbreak of the First World War it would have been inconceivable and bewildering to those luxuriating in the opulent vastness of the house, strolling through its beautiful grounds or boating on its lakes, to know that within thirty-eight years everything would have gone. Nearly everything; the stable block being retained with its elegant curved façade and high lantern and clock, along with some of the hard landscaping and structures in the garden. The park went under the plough. The gardens went back to nature.

There had been an earlier disaster for Didlington. In 1906 the owner, Lord Amherst, was informed that his much trusted and liked family solicitor, Charles Cheston, over a protracted period had embezzled, and then lost through reckless stock dealings, a

large part of his fortune, over a quarter of a million pounds (over £30 million in today's prices) in addition to the loss of estate and trust funds amounting to £60,000 (over £7 million). The repercussions of these defalcations were catastrophic. Cheston poisoned himself, although not before writing his own obituary notice, playing a game of bridge and saying goodnight to his wife. William Amherst had to embark on a series of sales including that of his beloved and important collection of books. His extensive library was famous, among the incunabula were such rare volumes as a Gutenberg Bible of 1455, seventeen books printed by Caxton including bibles from the 1470s, and there was a first folio of Shakespeare. All the artworks in the house, including major collections of porcelain, tapestries, and sculpture, went to sale too. The last sale took place in 1909 a few months after William Tyssen-Amherst, aged 73, had died from apoplexy, a death hastened by the severe stress of the sales and various legal actions taken against him stemming from Cheston's fraud. The fraud also resulted in Britain losing irreplaceable treasures to the United States, and in 1910, the Amhersts were forced to put the house up for sale. Fortunately for Didlington, the new owner, a banker, Colonel Herbert Francis Smith, had the money and drive to see that the estate remained intact, for a few years longer.

The original house, built by the Wilsons in the seventeenth century, was enlarged in

ABOVE The Rose Garden.

FACING PAGE William Amhurst Tyssen-Amherst, Lord Amherst of Hackney, (1835–1909) in 1855, aged twenty. He was then an undergraduate at Christ Church, Oxford, but in December that year his father died, and he inherited the Didlington and London estates.

the late eighteenth century and given a new north front in the early nineteenth. In the early 1850s it was sold to William George Tyssen-Amherst who added an Italianate observation and water tower and remodelled the south and west fronts adding wide angular bay windows, with more emphasis on internal convenience than exterior aesthetics. Before the building works were finished, in 1855 he died, and the estate passed to his twenty-year-old son, William Amhurst Tyssen-Amherst (1835–1909), later Lord Amherst of Hackney. He completed the works his father had begun and it was under him over the next fifty years that the house and its contents, the grounds and gardens reached their magnificent peak.

The estate was more than 7,000 acres, seven miles across, with an approach avenue of limes, two and a half miles in length; there were lesser avenues too. The first of these was planted in 1689. There were 1,000 acres of woodland and a park of 700 acres. The huge house stood on a raised terrace fronting the upper of two lakes, the water 60 acres in extent, with islands, a trout stream – the River Wissey – and

ABOVE The garden to the east of the house.
FACING PAGE Some of the exotic tree planting, including a Wellingtonia.

the gardens boasting most of the elements of design and layout an enthusiastic and wealthy Victorian landowner would think essential. Naturally a fine Rose Garden, the roses displayed in what now would be seen as an excess of small beds, dotted with columnar yews. After 1885 and the building by Richard Norman Shaw of a long and architecturally considered garden wall, an immense south-facing herbaceous border was planted in front of it, approaching 500 yards in length and 20 feet wide. It, like all things at Didlington, was immaculately maintained. The Tyssen-Amhersts were an erudite and cultured family with wide and varied interests, and every pursuit was undertaken with diligence and scholarship. Their gardens were not just the expected adjunct to a great house, their interest in them, in the landscape and botany was genuine and keenly pursued. There were extensive plantings of flowers in areas to the south of the house and a fine collection of exotic trees, a Fernery, a Green Garden, planted with bamboo and other 'tropical' plants, a maze of yew and that essential element of later Victorian gardens, a Rockery, its plants all carefully labelled. There were innumerable woodland walks and within the lakes, which supported a collection of water lilies of various colours, were eight small islands and five large ones. A variety of boats and punts ferried the family and visitors alike around the extensive waters, and visitors were 'charmed to notice that the garden was of "the old-fashioned type"', which meant it was not overrun with stridently coloured acres of fashionable bedding-out.

To the north, beyond the church and well out of sight, was the Kitchen Garden, entered by the original gate to the Manor House of Hackney at Shacklewell. The Amhersts still held land there and collected considerable rents. The Didlington range of glasshouses, on a scale commensurate with everything on the estate, approached 260 feet in length. The long lean-to section was backed by a heated wall and an extensive boiler system. At the centre stood a tall square glasshouse, housing larger palms, ferns and exotics, and supporting a glazed octagonal lantern.

FACING PAGE The hall across the upper lake c.1880.

BELOW *The Lady of the Lake*, one of many boats, with Birdcage Island behind.

ABOVE The main glasshouse. c.1880.
FACING PAGE Part of the interior of the glasshouse with palms, tree ferns and tender acacia.
RIGHT *Amherstia nobilis.*

A high, freestanding glasshouse projected forward completing the three-wing plan. Here were vineries, peach house, palm house, nectarine house, and a pineapple house. The greenhouses and gardens were worked by twelve men, with extra help brought in when needed.

A reporter from the *Norfolk Chronicle* visited in November 1885, having obtained permission to write a piece on the estate and its owner, then MP for south-west Norfolk. He remarked on the 'large area of glass filled with choice and rare plants and our particular attention is directed to the *Amherstia nobilis*, a plant which requires a temperature of not less than 75 degrees, and which there are but two other specimens in England ... *Amherstia nobilis* is a small tropical tree, also called The Pride of Burma and the Orchid Tree which was discovered in 1827 and named after Lady Sarah Amherst, wife of the Governor General of Bengal'. The reporter continued: 'The Hall, which is an old-fashioned house in the Italianate style of architecture, is beautifully situated in a finely-wooded park, which is some 1500 acres in extent and contains a magnificent stretch of water, dotted over with picturesque little islands. On the border of the lake, on rising ground stands a round tower in brick called 'The Castle Cave', from which charming views are obtained of the fine avenues of limes, which are a conspicuous feature of the scenery. This lake has a history attached to it which reflects lasting honour on the squire, for it has been twenty-five years in the making, and originated from Mr. Amherst's desire to employ the labourers when out of work, during the winter season, when every other source of labour failed, and which has been regularly done.' The lake in question is the southernmost and larger lake of the two, their waters separated by a narrow causeway but linked by a lock and a weir. It is referred to on photographs from the 1870s as 'the New lake'.

The *Norfolk Chronicle* reporter was much taken by Mr Amherst's care of his estate and his workforce, which was an enormous 300 strong, calling him '... its princely owner – a prince in heart as in fortune. Would that there were more estates and men of this kind in the country.' This was not mere condescending flattery, William Tyssen-Amherst was an exceptionally enlightened employer, even paying pensions to his retired employees, and was a philanthropist and builder. The folly Tower was one of several ambitious architectural garden features he had constructed at Didlington. The Tower was sited on a mound, presumably formed from the material removed from the lakes during their construction. Although from a distance it appears round, it is octagonal and built of flint, not brick, but with extensive brickwork in it, which could account for the journalist's error. It is a splendid crenellated Gothic folly, and has a single-storey octagonal addition, which had a practical use as a summer house in which to take tea.

BELOW The nineteenth-century folly Tower, known as the 'Castle Cave' in the 1880s, and as it appears today (**RIGHT**).

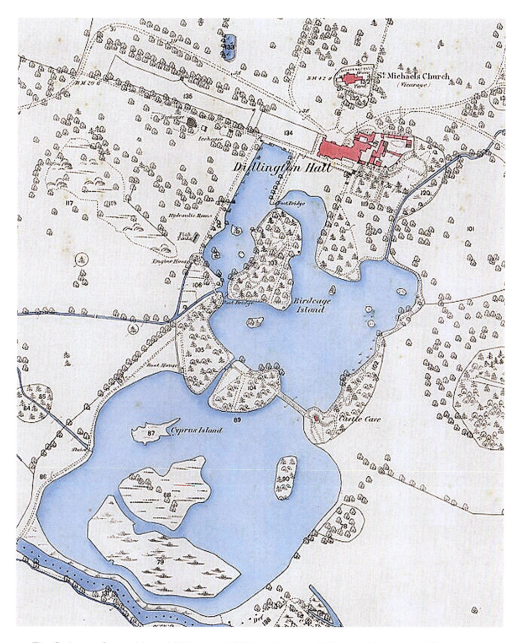

The Ordnance Survey Map of Didlington, 1884. At the top left, the double avenue of lime trees leads towards the hall's west façade, giving way to a rectangular lawn which adjoins the house. Below the top of the lake is the boathouse. The large Birdcage Island in the upper lake is reached by two footbridges. A causeway crosses between the upper and lower lakes. To the right of this on an elevation is the Castle Cave Tower.

The waters of two lakes are linked by a narrow channel with a lock, and a second boathouse serving the lower lake stands to the left of this. A series of meandering paths led through the woodland planting and round the upper lake, its island giving ever-changing views. The Rose Garden is on the south-east corner of the hall. The River Wissey runs below the lower lake.

The Tower conveniently boasted a kitchen with fireplace and chimney, which extended the season. Although both sections are now roofless, the single storey has had inserted a strong perforated grid allowing rain through and viewing access; the work, as all the restoration at Didlington, of the current ownership.

The other major construction to have survived at Didlington is indeed spectacular – a five-bay underground boathouse. It was a huge and typical large-scale Tyssen-Amherst undertaking. The upper of the two lakes was extended to the western section of the garden allowing the entrance to the boathouse to be built into the raised bank which terminated the lake. It then extended back under the garden, on which grass tennis courts were later installed. The long balustrade above the boathouse façade gives way to a flight of steps at either end leading down to the water.

Here passageways lead back into the building to reveal the five boat bays recessed behind arches level with the lake. The internal vaulting is of brick, the external facing in stone. The boathouse was built either in the 1860s or 1870s, though the architect is not known.

With his unquestioned aesthetic judgement, William Tyssen-Amherst could never have been satisfied with the compromised appearance of his house. In the 1880s he employed one of the leading architects of the day, Richard Norman Shaw (1831– 1912), to give the somewhat plain and ungainly structure a very substantial makeover, recladding and adding to it to achieve an architectural balance, transforming in particular the west front by extending it to provide a pronounced classical exterior, with fine

ABOVE The steps, arches and structure of the boathouse remain intact. Beyond is the current Didlington Hall designed by Julian Bicknell in 2004, built on part of the site of the demolished building. To the left is Norman Shaw's long garden wall in front of which ran Didlington's Herculean herbaceous border.

LEFT Today silted and unused, one of the boat moorings inside the boathouse.

The hall from the north-west, c.1870 prior to Norman Shaw's remodelling. The Italianate Tower was built in 1856, only five years after the completion of Osborne House. Royal patronage of Italianate style proved influential. The 60-foot tower at Didlington was in fact a water tower, the water raised by a ram powered by the streams in the grounds. The water was then piped throughout the house and used in the gardens. The tower was blown up using gelignite in 1956.

detailing. Today Shaw's work alone would guarantee that Didlington Hall would be listed. To the long south front he was asked to add a 'museum', in fact an opulent seven-bay ninety-foot-long saloon, complete with gallery and organ, to house part of the ever-growing Amherst collections, in particular to display their Gobelin tapestries in a custom-built space.

One of the unique features of the Amherst's garden, indeed jaw-dropping in any garden, was the row of seven Sekhmets – seated statues in diorite of the Egyptian lioness-headed goddess, each of them nearly seven feet in height and each weighing nearly two tons. They were bought in 1864–5 from Dr John Lee of Hartwell House near Aylesbury. Dating from 1390–1352 BC and the reign of Amenhotep III, they had originally stood in the Temple of Mut in Karnac and their translation to Norfolk as garden ornaments was extraordinary indeed. They reflected one of the main passions of William Amherst – Egyptology. Boldly he allocated one Sekhmet to each of his seven daughters. As Sekhmet was a brutal god, the goddess of war, violent storms and pestilence, this might seem foolhardy. However, when appeased, Sekhmet's powers could be used to protect, and she became a goddess of healing. Arriving in England in the 1800s, in 1833 the statues had been exhibited in the huge alcove recesses of John Rennie's original Waterloo Bridge. Now serenely placed along the frontage of the

ENTICING PATHS

'museum', this must have been accepted as considerable appeasement. Since 1915 the Sekhmets have been in the Metropolitan Museum of Art in New York.

Lord Amherst, as he became in 1892, and his wife Margaret, shared an intense interest in ancient Egypt. They amassed extensive and important collections of cuneiform tablets, papyri and Egyptian antiquities. Yet a far-reaching and more important connection links Didlington to Egypt. Samuel Carter was a reputed animal painter and illustrator based in London and Swaffham, who was born nearby in Dunham. In Norfolk, he was in demand by the gentry to paint their horses, pets and prize farm animals, as well as portraits and family groups. When invited to Didlington to paint, he brought with him his

BELOW c.1870s: the south front of the hall and terraces with the Sekhmets, to the right, before the building of the Saloon.
FACING PAGE The seven statues of the goddess Sekhmet.

ABOVE The Saloon. In addition to the Gobelin tapestries, here were many Egyptian and other antiquities (in display cases beneath the end window), French and English furniture, Limoges enamels, and English majolica; all of it sold by Christies in 1908.

BELOW The hall from the south-east, with the Flower Garden and the Sekhmets placed along the façade of the Saloon. From the Sale Catalogue of 1910.

Samuel Carter's 'Heronry at Didlington' which appeared in the *Illustrated London News* in 1868.
OVERLEAF The Swimming Pool and the classical central atrium of the changing rooms.

youngest son, Howard. The son's keen interest in the Egyptian artefacts he found there led to him being asked to catalogue the collection, and eventually to being found a job by the Amhersts to work under, and be trained by, the leading Egyptologist of his day, Flinders Petrie. Thus, they launched the career of the discoverer of Tutankhamen's tomb. Howard Carter was to write, 'It is to Lord and Lady Amherst that I owe an immense debt of gratitude for their extreme kindness to me during my early career. It was the Amherst 'Egyptian collection, perhaps the largest and most interesting collection of its kind then in England, that aroused my longing for that country. It gave me an earnest desire to see Egypt'.

There is a third architectural tour de force at Didlington which survives, but it post-dates the Amhersts. Built for Colonel Smith, it was a garden addition becoming very much in vogue in the Roaring Twenties – a Swimming Pool. The scale alone is impressive, with a rectangular open-air pool 144 feet long and 64 feet wide. But it is the pool house which remains extraordinary, conceived as a classical temple, complete with a central Roman-style atrium for relaxing. Within this is a small central pool and a changing room either side, one for the men, the other for the ladies. A colonnade with pairs of Ionic columns ran down the length of the building, with at its centre steps down to the water. From a distance, the pool house was designed to look like a temple sitting in the landscape. Today its roofs have gone, but for the rest it remains in

good condition and with a wistful air of romance, particularly in autumn as the Virginia creeper growing over part of it, reflected in the water, turns a deep red.

Alicia, the fifth of Lord Amherst's seven daughters, grew up with a love of gardening and was later famed in part for her garden writing. She recalled: 'From the earliest days I had my garden, several little beds designed by the eldest sisters and used to plant my pansies and tend my flowers with utmost care. We each had an island of our own in the lake and as we were allowed to go about in boats from an early age, we used to work on them, daffodils planted and dead leaves cleared and so on. My mother used to work in the garden too and I learnt much of my practical gardening and love of flowers from her. With father it was marking and planting of trees, thinning boughs and cutting vistas. From very early days till now, whenever I was at home with him, I used to walk out about the lake or round the courts, altering, planning, cutting or planting.'

This early interest in gardening and access to the many volumes relating to the history of gardening in her father's famous library led Alicia at the age of thirty to write *A History of Gardening in England*, 1895. This was and remains, an important work which laid the foundation for the later study of, and provided a method of approach to, garden history. It was very well received, although a review in the *Quarterly Review* in July 1896 was less complimentary: ' ... a clear and readable sketch of the history of gardening' was something of a put-down and it complained that Alicia had devoted too many pages to the earlier periods at the expense of the nineteenth century which had 'long outshone all that has gone before'. It is thought this was written by the then unknown, Gertrude Jekyll.

An indication of what life was like at Didlington for one of Lord Amherst's gardeners was given in a short account written by James Trimbee. He came to Didlington at the age of eighteen in 1902, to take up the job of second journeyman in the greenhouses and stayed for three years. Eventually he was given the job of raising in pots the forced strawberries, which when they reached their peak were sent down to the house to impress the guests, on this occasion Queen Victoria's youngest daughter Princess Beatrice of Battenberg and her daughter Princess Victoria Eugenie (later Queen of Spain). The two ladies tucked in, but soon complained about the odd taste, and refused any more. Later, when queries were made, it was discovered that Trimbee had been feeding the plants with a mixture of clay and London sewage. However, this did not stop the fruit being made into jam. He redeemed himself by nurturing Lord Amherst's many hundreds of chrysanthemum plants, then much prized, and in demand throughout the autumn to decorate the house. He produced the finest blooms yet seen at Didlington and was given due praise.

The Amhersts it seems were Renaissance polymaths, they could expertly turn their hand to almost anything. Margaret Tyssen-Amherst, apart from her love of and knowledge of gardening, was a good horsewoman, a fine archer, was efficient at

The prize Didlington chrysanthemums.

taxidermy, book binding and heraldic painting. According to *The Washington Post* in a 1906 article, 'Both Lord and Lady Amherst are wonderfully clever artificers in ivory, and in the turnery room is a tool of their own invention by means of which they solved the puzzle of how the Chinese intercarve one ivory ball within another. All the family are adept in mechanical art ...' Margaret became a member of the Worshipful Company of Turners. 'The grounds ...' the paper informed its readers, ' ... comprise a collection of emus, the only one in England, a heronry, a tremendous duck decoy establishment, and a farm, where all the animals, even to the very cats, are snow-white.'

The sale of the property in 1910, the close of the Edwardian era, saw an end to Didlington's true golden age. The Sale Particulars described the gardens as '... delightful old-world gardens ... arranged with perfect simplicity and good-taste'. And they decided that the grounds, 'are inexpensive to maintain owing to the natural beauty of the landscape'. It was not the gardens, but the sporting potential which was the main selling point. Everything was here to hunt and kill, including an otter hunt, and as a taster the boast was that '3,000 partridges and ... 7,000 pheasants have been turned down this season'.

William Amhurst Tyssen-Amherst, bibliophile, antiquarian, collector, Egyptologist, MP and philanthropist with his wife, Margaret. He is holding a book of stories, poems and illustrations edited by his wife, *In a Good Cause* published in 1885. She solicited all the especially commissioned material for free from friends and her contacts. The profits were to benefit the North Eastern Hospital for Children, Hackney Road in London. The book was dedicated to Alexandra, the Princess of Wales and included a short story by H. Rider Haggard and a poem, *Les Jardin de Tuileries* by Oscar Wilde.

ABOVE The upper lake from the 'Castle Cave' looking towards the new hall built on the south-west corner of the site of the original building.

OVERLEAF The lakes at Didlington Hall today. The new hall is at the top of the picture in the centre, with the original lake below it. William Amherst's lake is below that. The River Wissey, screened by trees, lies across the centre of the picture. At the bottom, are the extended gravel extraction lakes of the 20th century.

Today all of Lord Amherst's extensive ornamental gardens have gone, are dead, ploughed up or overgrown. A few tangible remains emerged after digging, some of the labels of the plants from the rock garden, but little else. However, the woodland remains, with drifts of aconites, snowdrops and daffodils and here and there fine specimen trees, many of them planted by royal visitors. Sandringham is only twenty miles to the north, and the excellent shooting brought the king, Edward VII and Queen Alexandra, the future George V and Edward VIII, and a host of lesser royals, all of whom planted trees. The two huge lakes are still here, silted in part and the lower one sometimes dry. Understandably it is the garden architecture which has, for the most part, survived; the long, ornamented garden walls, the folly above the lakes, the subterranean boathouse and the temple-like pool house with its clear reflective water. All of them giving a flavour of what was once a great Norfolk garden, and bearing witness to the ephemeral nature of such a creation and its inherent fragility.

19

Some Norfolk Gardens Illustrated by Edmund Prideaux

Tom Williamson

Edmund Prideaux (1693–1745) was an amateur topographic artist whose father, Humphrey, was Dean of Norwich Cathedral from 1702. His sketches, which remained unpublished until the twentieth century, are mostly of country houses; and of these, the majority have some connection with the Prideaux family. In addition, however, he illustrated some other seats, both in the West Country, and in East Anglia. Included among these latter sketches are six Norfolk houses: Narford (three pictures), Houghton (one), Melton Constable (one), Raynham (three), Blickling (two), and Earlham (one). The sketches are immensely important as a source for Norfolk garden history, for a number of reasons, but especially because they were made in or around 1725, at a time when a new style of gardening – still strongly geometric, but rather simpler than in earlier decades – was being adopted at the most fashionable residences. Prideaux's views provide a good flavour of gardens laid out in this 'late geometric' style, dominated by simple grass 'plats', turf terraces, clipped hedges, wide gravel paths, and ornamental 'wildernesses'. In addition, two of the places he drew – Narford and Houghton – were also illustrated in plan by Colen Campbell in Volume III of his *Vitruvius Britannicus*, published in 1725. The sketches provide us with an impression of what the kinds of gardens depicted by Campbell in plan would have looked like in three dimensions; that is, how they would have been experienced by contemporaries.

Four of the sketches are reproduced here. The full collection is presented in an article by John Harris, published in 1964 in the journal *Architectural History*.

Edmund Prideaux, 1643–1745, painted by
William Aikman, 1730. Prideaux Place, Padstow,
his family house, is shown in the background.

Houghton Hall

The West Front of Houghton Hall

The construction of Robert Walpole's new mansion at Houghton began in 1721 and continued until the early 1730s. A number of architects (James Gibbs, Thomas Ripley, Colen Campbell, and William Kent) were involved in its design, and modern authorities disagree about who was responsible for what, and when. Prideaux's sketch was probably made in 1725 or 1726 and shows the west front of the new hall nearing completion but still surrounded by scaffolding. It also shows that construction of the flanking pavilions, to north and south of the main house, had begun. The low building in front of the house may represent part of the earlier hall, converted into workmen's accommodation – the previous house occupied a position a little to the west of the new hall – but may be an entirely new, temporary structure erected for this purpose. Similar uncertainty surrounds the difference between the two corner turrets: one with a dome, as today, the other with a simple pyramidal roof. It has been said that the design of Houghton Hall was altered during construction, and that Campbell's original plan (as shown in the elevation presented in *Vitruvius Britannicus*), to give the turrets simple roofs in the correct Palladian manner, was changed by James Gibbs, with Walpole's support, in favour of Baroque-style cupolas. In fact, it is likely (as Harris has argued) that the original architect was Gibbs, that the cupolas were a feature from the start, and that Campbell's attempted 'correction' of the design along more correct Palladian lines was never adopted. The pyramidal roof shown by Prideaux is thus, in all probability, a temporary covering for this part of the building, rather than an earlier and more 'correct' form of roof.

The gardens shown were laid out (probably in the 1710s) in front of the previous hall, and Prideaux's sketch can be compared with a number of near-contemporary maps and plans, including Thomas Badeslade's estate map of 1720. Immediately in front of the house was a plain grass plat or lawn; beyond was a central axial path, flanked by topiary, to either side of which were strips of lawn and then hedged wildernesses (ornamental woods), only the edges of which can be seen in the sketch. What cannot be seen from this perspective but is clearly shown on the *Vitruvius Britannicus* plan (and less distinctly on Badeslade's map) is the 'fosse' or ha-ha which divided the gardens from the surrounding deer park. This was almost certainly the first to be created in East Anglia.

The ensemble is typical of gardens laid out in the simplified 'late geometric' style of the first two decades of the eighteenth century. Unfortunately, much uncertainty surrounds the identity of their designer. A plan, showing a layout similar in broad outline to that depicted by Badeslade and Campbell, survives in the Gough collection in the Bodleian Library at Oxford, amongst drawings which are otherwise largely by the famous landscape designer Charles Bridgeman, who was certainly working at Houghton by the end of the 1720s. However, Horace Walpole later attributed their design to 'Mr Eyre', probably Kingsmill Eyre, who features in Robert Walpole's correspondence (and in a painting which hangs in the hall). The main elements of this ensemble survived well into the eighteenth century and form the basis for the new design for the grounds made in the 1990s.

Research continues on the history of this important landscape. In particular, in April 2013 a pipeline trench some 680 metres in length, and a metre deep, was cut through the area around the hall, stables and kitchen garden, providing a rare opportunity to examine the below-ground archaeology of the area. It revealed, amongst other things, demolition rubble from the earlier hall, and the extraordinary amount of earth-moving and levelling which accompanied the creation of the eighteenth-century landscape.

Melton Constable Hall

Melton Constable Hall

Melton Constable Hall, built in the 1670s for Sir Jacob Astley, is one of the great country houses of Norfolk. The hall itself is designed in the rather loose, 'domestic' classical style usually associated with architects like Hugh May or Roger Pratt. It stood within a deer park with medieval origins and was surrounded by extensive walled gardens. Prideaux's sketch of Melton Constable is, in itself, perhaps less informative than the other illustrations discussed here. Its importance lies in the fact that it can be compared with the better-known aerial perspective of the house and its grounds – complete with axial canal, parterres and topiary – which was published by Kip and Knyff in their *Britannia Illustrata* of 1707 (see page 442): for there are a number of significant differences between the two representations.

To some extent, the differences may reflect real changes made to the grounds of the hall during the period between c.1707 and c.1725. Prideaux's sketch thus suggests that the south garden ran without interruption to the walls of the house, while the Kip/Knyff view shows that there was a small intervening court; while the cross-avenue which the latter shows running west from the gardens to the building later known as the Bath House is not illustrated by Prideaux. There are also hints (no more than that, given the angle of Prideaux's view) that the planting within the walled courts had been simplified since 1707. Sir Jacob continued to live until 1729 and, while he chose to retain his garden walls, he may have adopted some other elements of the new fashion for geometric simplicity. Other discrepancies between the two representations, however, probably reflect inaccuracies in the earlier, aerial view. Prideaux thus suggests that that the east wall of the west garden ran out from the corners of the house, whereas Kip and Knyff suggest, once again, an intervening court; and while Prideaux correctly shows the house raised up above the garden on a terrace, Kip and Knyff quite clearly do not. Doubtless mistakes were made when the ground-level views prepared by Knyff were combined and redrawn, back in London, as an aerial perspective. Prideaux's sketch provides a powerful reminder of the limits of pictorial evidence, especially aerial views like this. It must be emphasised, however, that the scale of the gardens shown by Kip and Knyff was not (as is sometimes assumed with their views) exaggerated. Fragments of garden walls exposed in drainage ditches cut through the park to the south of the hall show that the courts really were as extensive as their picture suggests.

Earlham Hall

Unlike the other places discussed here – Houghton, Narford, and Melton Constable – Earlham was a relatively modest residence which at this stage lacked any form of park. The house shown by Prideaux was originally erected in the late sixteenth century but was extensively altered in the 1640s. Purchased by Thomas Waller in 1657, it was at this time owned by his grandson Waller Bacon, MP for Norwich.

Prideaux's sketch shows the house from the north, framed by an avenue of trees and surrounded by farmland. No details of the gardens are visible but the block of trees to the west (right) of the house was probably a 'wilderness' or ornamental wood of some kind. This area is still occupied by trees, although none old enough to have been in existence when the sketch was made, and it is flanked by earthworks of terraces which form part of a more extensive complex of garden remains around the house, apparently the remains of a sophisticated garden of late seventeenth or early eighteenth-century date. A short length of avenue also survives, focused on the north front, but this is composed of nineteenth-century lime trees and does not appear to relate directly with the feature shown by Prideaux.

Prideaux shows a dovecote standing at the end of the avenue. This is almost certainly the building which still exists in Earlham Park, close to the bridge taking the Watton road across the river Yare. From Prideaux's vantage point this would have been hidden from view, so it has been moved several hundred metres to the east. Dovecotes were still important symbols of status in the 1720s: until legal changes at the end of the seventeenth century only lords of manors had been allowed to erect them. They were thus often proudly displayed, close to the main façade or, as here, beside a public road, and Prideaux obviously thought that this particular example should be included in

the view. Clearly his sketches were not direct representations, akin to photographs: but such manipulations of reality, rather than lessening the usefulness of the sketches as evidence for garden history, actually increases it, by throwing important light on how a man like Prideaux 'read' the symbols displayed in the vicinity of grand residences.

Earlham Hall

Narford Hall

Narford Hall

The construction of Narford Hall was begun by Sir Andrew Fountaine in 1702 but was completed by his son, another Andrew, who succeeded in 1706. The latter was Vice-Chancellor to the Prince of Wales, Newton's successor at the Royal Mint, a well-connected collector and dilettante and a friend of both Swift and Pope. The hall, built in stages, included a library (completed in 1719) which was an early exercise in astylar Palladian.

Not surprisingly, the grounds of the hall as depicted by Prideaux (in no less than three sketches) were at the cutting edge of fashion: something confirmed by the plan published by Colen Campbell in 1725. The gardens displayed all the key features of the late geometric style: there were few walls or brick terraces, and no fussy, complex parterres. Gravel paths, neat lawns, clipped hedges and areas of ornamental shrubbery and woodland ('groves' and 'wildernesses') predominated. Avenues ran through the surrounding fields but, again typically for the period, they were few in number and exclusively aligned on the principal façades of the house.

As Prideaux's drawing shows, the gardens at Narford also featured a number of garden buildings in which a knowledge of the newly fashionable Palladian style of architecture was displayed – in this case, a diminutive Roman tetrastyle temple, the 'Portico'. Typically, this is set within a simple geometric compartment, defined by hedges, the shape of which is mirrored by that of the ornamental pool or 'bason' within it. From Campbell's plan of the grounds we know that this ensemble lay immediately to the north of the hall. The temple is a useful reminder of the fact that the temples and other classical features that graced the simple, sweeping parklands of Capability Brown and his 'imitators' in the second half of the eighteenth century had first appeared in England as features of gardens designed in a very different manner.

Older symbols of elite status also had an appeal to Prideaux. As with Earlham, a dovecote, traditional badge of manorial lordship, is proudly displayed; and as at Earlham a degree of artistic license has been employed to achieve this, for Campbell's plan shows clearly that this structure really stood over 500 metres to the north and would hardly have been visible from Prideaux's vantage point.

Edmund Prideaux's illustrations are an important source for the study of Norfolk's gardens, and capture their development at a crucial point in time. Those he prepared of Raynham and Blickling, not discussed here, are equally informative. But, like all sources for garden history, they are particularly useful when they can be compared and contrasted with other representations, contemporary or near-contemporary.

20

Templewood

Roger Last

There is nothing quite like Templewood anywhere in Norfolk. It is one of the few noteworthy 1930s additions to the county – a country house and landscape, completed, if landscape can be so described, in 1938. Taking his cue from the small chateau built for Louis XV in the grounds of Versailles, its owner wanted a 'Petit Trianon' in the middle of woods, 'far away from the noises of the modern world'. He got just that. There were no fighter jets then.

Templewood is a mile to the south-east of Northrepps in north-east Norfolk. It was the *grand projet* of the politician, Sir Samuel Hoare (1880–1959) who was, in 1944, created Viscount Templewood of Chelsea. He was one of the leading politicians of his day, throughout the 1920s and 1930s holding a series of high cabinet positions, becoming both Foreign and Home Secretary. For some, despite his long and distinguished career, his reputation today is somewhat dimmed, as he is seen as a leading appeaser, although he helped build up Britain's aviation power as Secretary of State for Air, throughout much of the 1920s. During the period in which Templewood was built he was Home Secretary in Chamberlain's government.

FACING PAGE The entrance drive to Templewood.

LEFT Sir Samuel Hoare, Viscount Templewood of Chelsea (1880–1959). He held the posts Secretary of State for India, First Lord of the Admiralty, and both Foreign and Home Secretary, ending his diplomatic career as Britain's Ambassador to Spain.

Sidestrand Hall, the east front entrance. The original Georgian building was progressively extended in a similar manner by Sir Samuel's father in the nineteenth century to produce a long, and rambling house. The west front alone has 15 bays. By contrast, in Templewood, Sir Samuel wanted a house far more compact and functional. In 1935 Sidestrand Hall was sold and became a Methodist guest house; it is now a school for children with special needs.

His new Norfolk house was not to be a grand country mansion, but a shooting box. However, it was to be a grand shooting box. Tied as he was to London by his ministerial work, he originally intended it as a weekend retreat, rather than a permanent home. Sir Samuel wished to have a small house on a big site. His family home, like many English houses, had been the opposite. The original Georgian house had been much extended, and consisted of several long, and no doubt hard to heat, wings. He was born at Sidestrand Hall, just inland from the steep cliffs to the east of Cromer. This he owned until the mid 1930s, and described the house as having all the inconveniences of a big house but with 'none of the spaciousness that is so essential to country life'. Templewood would redress that.

The new house was designed by the firm of Seely and Paget. The choice of architects could not have been in doubt: Paul Paget was Sir Samuel's nephew. Apart from this fortunate connection, the Honourable John Seely, later the second Baron Mottistone, and Paul Paget, had already earned their spurs, despite their firm being new, and they both being young. Paul Paget had charm, and John Seely, the design skills. They also had all the right connections and immense good luck. Paul Paget wrote: 'You were just introduced to the right people, behaved in the right way and so commission followed commission.'

Six years earlier their first important commission had been an exceptional one indeed. This was the redesigning and additions to the remaining sections of the former medieval royal palace at Eltham in south-east London, for the extremely wealthy Courtaulds, Stephen and the highly eccentric Virginia. She was Romanian and even claimed to be, several generations removed, a niece of Vlad the Impaler. As if these high-profile clients were not demanding enough, the brief was equally so. In addition to a large new house, employing the very latest ideas and technology for the Modernist Deco interior, it called for the use of a raft of historical architectural elements and detailing, culminating in the incorporation, and major repair of, no less than Edward IV's great medieval dining hall from the 1470s. Not all contemporary critics liked the hybrid result, one deciding the new additions looked like 'a cigarette factory'. But today, the restoration work and lavish Art Deco interiors are seen as a masterpiece.

The Courtaulds hosted lavish entertainments in their new house. All high society, and every celebrity wanted to flock there. Queen Mary and Stravinsky both did, and Sir Samuel had doubtless been down to inspect, if not to actually like, what had been achieved. A somewhat cold man, he would have had politely to contend with the peccadilloes of Virginia's pet ring-tailed lemur, Mah-Jongg, which had free run of the house. Certainly not for him were the interiors in the latest Moderne, or the somewhat eclectic Renaissance stance of the new exterior work. His taste was for a clear-cut classical style, well suited to display his collection of French and English eighteenth-century furniture and paintings. However, after their Eltham success, clearly his nephew and his partner could be entrusted with the design of his new house, provided of course that Sir Samuel dictated the way forward. The building was to be impressive without being grand, decorative without being ostentatious, and was to incorporate a treasure trove of reclaimed architectural fragments.

Sir Samuel admired the Palladian villas of the Veneto, in particular Palladio's design for the Rotonda, Villa Almerico-Capra, at Vicenza. An early design for Templewood

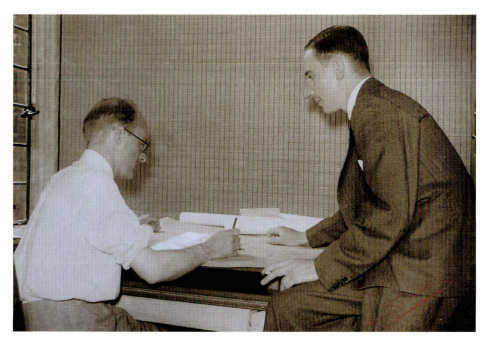

John Seely and Paul Paget in their offices in Cloth Fair, London. 1930s.

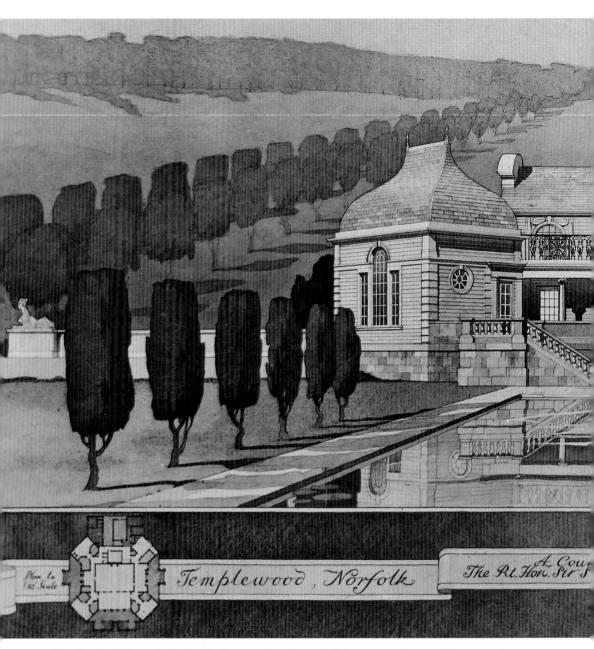

The first Seely/Paget design for the house at Templewood. This was a much more elaborate and grander, and therefore expensive, approach than the one adopted. Four large corner pavilions are set at angles to the main block of the house, with a formal rectangular pool placed directly in front. The double staircase, brought from Nuthall Temple after its demolition, descending from a columned terrace, was implemented. Although double avenues of trees were planted on the steeply ascending land behind the house, a circular classical temple as a focal point was not built.

Templewood under construction. Soane's ionic columns and the Nuthall Temple sphinxes are already in position. 1937.

featured large decorated pavilions on each corner of the central block, set at diagonals. A simpler, and far less costly, approach was adopted. With regard to cost, and limited intended use of the property, Sir Samuel pronounced 'Let it last fifty years to see me out. No one will want a house like this when I am gone.'

Although elements of the geometric cubes and linear approach of the contemporary modern thirties house were not called for, they were, at least in spirit, still cleverly incorporated. Albeit here dressed up by Ionic columns rescued from the western façade and southern loggia of Soane's Bank of England, and with stone, ironwork and sphinxes from an English Palladian villa, Nuthall Temple (1754) in Nottinghamshire – both victims of insensitive demolition. Seely and Paget were required to keep 'modern comfort in line with Palladian requirements'. Work began in 1937. The resulting house, its bricks originally painted a warm yellow 'after the manner of eighteenth-century Russia', is simple and easily read. Yet it was presented, with its attached entrance portico and pediment, south-facing loggia with columns, balustrading and double staircase, finial urns and coat of arms, as something with a superior presence and a degree of pedigree, which was most certainly not nouveau.

Into what gardens and landscape was such a singular building to be placed? Seely and Paget had drawn up garden plans for Eltham Palace, a modified version of a master plan developed by the firm of Thomas Hayton Mawson & Son. Mawson had died in 1933, the most eminent garden designer of the Edwardian and immediate post-war period. It came as no surprise that his designs were not Modernist, but offered varied styles along more traditional lines. It made no matter what they were. Sir Samuel had no quibbles about what was appropriate at Templewood: 'Of the general scheme we never had a doubt. It was to depend on straight lines and regular proportions.' So clear in his mind was he, that he had begun preparing the grounds and planting up the landscape in 1925 in anticipation of the construction of the house, thirteen years later. The house was therefore placed into an already well-defined landscape of restrained and linear planting.

Sir Samuel, as he saw it, had before him two clear approaches to the planting of his landscape. The Capability Brown one, in the English manner, with loose and natural tree 'clumps', further developed by Repton, or the French approach, with symmetrical straight avenues. Admitting himself 'constantly under the influence of the French traditions of my wife's family', he opted for the French. Lady Maud's family owned the Château de Coigny in Normandy. Here was a great avenue of elms, and the nearby estates had equally impressive avenues of sweet chestnut. Norfolk estates however, in Sir Samuel's view, were very inferior. 'We had often deplored the lack of such avenues in many Norfolk parks, and were determined to make them a central feature of our future plans.' He did.

Formal recognition came early, as in *Country Life*, (the pictures were taken in 1938), due to the celebrity of both the owner and his architects.

The approach to the house is from the west, down a long straight double avenue of sweet chestnuts and *Quercus ilex* (how fortunate that elms were not chosen). The avenue leads directly to the house with its entrance portico. Closer to, the Nuthall Temple sphinxes raised on podiums, reveal themselves, either side of shallow entrance steps. The house is then seen to be placed at the centre of a huge cross, the entrance drive being one of the arms. The ground is sloping, with the house sited halfway down the incline.

Sir Samuel may have rejected an English landscape approach, but he much admired Humphry Repton and took his advice to avoid a 'scene consisting of vegetable productions only'. He realized that the site 'needed water no less than avenues'.

Templewood

The approach to the house from the west, with its newly planted avenues of sweet chestnuts and smaller *Quercus ilex* behind. 1938.

ENTICING PATHS

ABOVE Templewood, the house from the north-east. 1938.

BELOW Templewood in winter, the Reflecting Pool. Behind the house the double avenues of sweet chestnut trees are imposing themselves on the landscape. 1948.

FACING PAGE A Nuttall Temple sphinx guards the house's entrance.

The southern avenue slopes down to a small chalk stream, which later becomes the Mundesley Beck, at under eight kilometres in length, the second shortest river in Norfolk. This he dammed to let it rise to a higher level and allowed it to flow through a simple, but large, square Reflecting Pool. This was highly effective, an eye-catcher designed to complement the simplicity of the overall layout by adding the animation of changing light on the water. Balustraded footbridges, the ironwork from Nuttall, were added crossing the beck on either side of the pool. Beyond it the land rises again giving the whole vista pleasing contours.

The house is placed in nearly 200 acres of woodland and Sir Samuel was helped to some extent to quickly create his avenues by cutting into the existing woods. However, considerable planting took place, and a wide variety of trees and shrubs were added to enliven the southern avenue in particular. Apart from chestnut, walnut, poplar, swamp cypress, acers, mountain ash, crataegus, bird cherry, and liquidambar were planted, with junipers, dogwoods, viburnum, berberis, and spiraea. These in turn tapered the

View from the terrace of the southern avenue. Either side of the Reflecting Pool are the wrought-iron balustrades of small bridges over the diminutive Mundesley Beck, which flowed through it.

avenue as it rose up the slope beyond the beck, giving a more dramatic perspective. The northern avenue, rising behind the house, boasts two impressive double avenues of sweet chestnut. The avenue to the east stretches away through rising woodland planted either side with chestnut and *Quercus ilex*. The *Quercus ilex* was chosen for its dark and contrasting colour. But these are no ordinary trees. All the Templewood stock was descended from the grand *Quercus ilex* avenue at Holkham Hall, a pedigree which particularly pleased Sir Samuel.

Near the house, at the start of the eastern avenue, was a further feature – a hard tennis court, with a York stone path leading to an octagonal tennis kiosk. The Seeley/Paget design for this was based on the two memorial kiosks Edwin Luytens had built in 1929 either side of the road which runs through the meadow at Runnymede in Surrey. Sport was a feature of this landscape with not only tennis, but in winter, ice-skating on the Reflecting Pool, and above all shooting.

Flowers were not a feature. There are no gardens or flower beds at all. Swathes of grass sweep up to the house on every side. Flowers would have been seen as an unnecessary excess for a shooting box, and would have been inappropriate, mindful of the overall ethos of the place, with its emphasis on clean lines and restraint. Neither

ABOVE The house from the south, 2019.
RIGHT The tennis kiosk.

were there flowers or plants in pots, apart from a large planted lead cistern. Lady Hoare did have plans made for an Erica Garden, but this never materialized. Sir Samuel wrote 'Designing avenues and vistas, adding colour with bright-leaved maples, scarlet oaks, liquid amber, and the scores of different shrubs that produce the best autumn tints, have made me as keen a woodscape gardener as any amateur of roses and herbaceous borders.'

He was a keen forester, and his natural predisposition was towards trees. Besides, on the practical front, the woodland planting was designed to foster pheasants and woodcock. This was essential, especially as Sir Samuel was said to be the finest shot in England. There was a distinct lack of sentiment in the Templewood layout. In addition to the colour provided by the variety of trees and shrubs, a walk through the woods, following close to the beck, led to a collection of azaleas provided by Lionel de Rothschild.

The Little Broad, created by damming the Mundesley Beck. An impressive piece of hydraulic engineering: the water is held in place by embankments and controlled by sluices.

These were planted close to a picturesque sheet of water known as the 'Little Broad', which had been created by Sir Samuel's father in the 1900s, by damming the beck.

The design at Templewood, with its emphasis on line, simplicity, and the bold massing of only a few elements, was part of a renewed interest at this time in the wider landscape. There had been a gradual return to favour of the eighteenth-century landscape, after a decline in the Victorian era. But there was no brief for exact historical revivalism. Besides, revivals are always tempered by the concerns of their own age. An eighteenth-century magnate would have found it irresistible not to have terminated his grand vistas with a monument. The landscape would have been incomplete without a column or a temple. Lord Templewood was not tempted. The palette of grass, trees and water, and the sky, was certainly enough. It has been suggested that the golf course, by the turn of the century already in place near every large town, was a spur to the renewed appreciation of landscape. The landscape in this instance was dedicated to sport, in which there was certainly no place for the indulgence of columns or temples.

Neither house nor landscape at Templewood is large, but what has been achieved is a fine sense of scale. The landscape appears to be large, and is carried out in the grand manner, and this in an age when grand gesture was not the order of the day. The most important new garden of the period which championed the open landscape, was Lord

Fairhaven's at Anglesey Abbey, in Cambridgeshire, although this was on a far greater scale and readily embraced architectural ornamentation. In style, no greater contrast could be found than with those two great twentieth-century garden icons, Hidcote and Sissinghurst. Both are intimate, and each, although highly planned and structured, celebrates plants and flowers. Templewood is expansive, and has a beauty wrought from an almost startling restraint. In line with what was then the latest architectural philosophy, it displays a confident fitness of purpose. But it is doubtful if Sir Samuel, unflinchingly his own man, was in the least influenced by that. The conflict between the modernist idiom 'less is more' and its enemies' riposte 'less is a bore', here reaches fever point.

To those who like their landscapes rich in form and structure, Templewood may seem a dull landscape. To them it is perhaps like its creator, who was described, albeit by his political opponents, as lacking 'charisma' and as 'irritating and unattractive'. Although, that said, there is a poetic streak in some of his descriptive writing. MP for Chelsea for thirty-four years, Sir Samuel loved to retreat to his beloved Norfolk, and no doubt to be temporarily relieved of the constant pressures of high government office. In the 1940s, after his retirement, it became his permanent home. As he looked out at all points of the compass to broad avenues, with what Sir Samuel described as their 'delightful symmetry', all of them backed by woodland, he must have been pleased enough by what he had created – a unique composition of miniature park and mansion. Its combination of style and restraint is impressive.

Sir Samuel and his wife, Lady Maud, on the loggia at Templewood. 1956.

Sir Samuel died childless and in 1962 his nephew, Paul Paget, the co-architect of Templewood, and the surveyor to the fabric of Windsor Castle and from 1966 of St Paul's Cathedral, inherited the property. He lived there until his death in 1985. He was no gardener or 'woodscape gardener' either. By the 1960s the Reflecting Pool had become silted and overgrown, the inevitable result of allowing a stream, which brought silt, to flow through it. The pool he now described as his 'malarial swamp' and he had it filled in. Whatever the pragmatism in that, it was a notable loss, robbing the south avenue of its main designed feature.

Sir Samuel's main problems when he laid out Templewood were rabbits and bracken. Over eighty years on they are now honey fungus, grey squirrels and a truly ubiquitous curse, muntjac deer. Added to which are a raft of imported tree diseases. Some of the trees in the avenues have become diseased, and others overcrowded, for the planting was carried out to be immediately effective. Where the sweet chestnuts in the approach avenue were planted in sticky clay, some have succumbed to honey fungus. These been replaced with oaks. Much of the form of the ornamental planting in the south avenue has been lost. It was inevitable that the crisp outline of the young planting would become blurred with age, and tree growth has narrowed the original spaciousness of the avenues.

TOP Paul Paget in 1985. After his retirement as the Surveyor to the fabric of St Paul's Cathedral, he was presented with a replica of the measuring pole used by Sir Christopher Wren during the construction of the cathedral.

ABOVE The house today, from the north, sheltered and secluded in its mature woodland.

ABOVE The restored Reflecting Pool.
OVERLEAF Templewood from the rising woodland to the south.

Since the 1980s, Templewood's current owner, Eddie Anderson, Paul Paget's stepson, lays an emphasis on the ecology of the site, and its rich flora and fauna. The grass is allowed to grow longer than before to encourage wild flowers and nesting pheasants. And he has reinstated the Reflecting Pool, although in a truncated form, not allowing the beck to flow through it. But for the rest, the prospects are still as tranquil and pleasing as Sir Samuel Hoare had intended. He wrote: 'As I look ... from the water in front and watch the ducks of varied species ceaselessly moving in graceful action, I think of the flights that I shall have near by on cold evenings, and of the woodcock that come with the north-east wind. For our Petit Trianon is much more than a summer house in which we sit in August and September. It is a winter home in the midst of migrant birds that grow tame in their seclusion and look curiously upon the two strangers who have settled in their preserves.' Templewood remains as hauntingly evocative.

21

Heyrick 'Tony' Greatorex's Garden, Snowdrop Acre

Richard Hobbs

Many years ago, when I worked for the Norfolk Wildlife Trust, I was approached by Broadland District Council asking if I would carry out a conservation assessment on a small piece of land they owned in the parish of Witton, which lies between Postwick and Brundall. I arrived at the site in the middle of summer to find a carpet of head-high nettles under trees. It did not look very exciting, but there were some unusual trees and shrubs in among the nettles. There was, and still is, a fine specimen of the Himalayan horse chestnut *Aesculus sinensis*, together with *Osmanthus* x *burkwoodii*, x *Mahoberberis aquisargentii* and very surprisingly the hermaphrodite form of butcher's broom, *Ruscus aculeatus*. It was clear that this had been a garden. Having handed in my very short report I was told that I should have visited earlier in the year when it is covered in snowdrops. When I asked how on earth the District Council came to own the site, I was told it had been acquired from the Greatorex family. Suddenly the site had become a lot more interesting because when I started collecting snowdrops, one of the first doubles to be acquired was 'Jacquenetta', soon followed by 'Cordelia' and 'Ophelia'; collectively these and many others are known as the 'Greatorex Doubles'.

It was on this site that Heyrick Greatorex, who was known as Tony, the diminutive of his middle name, bred more named varieties of snowdrop than anyone else has yet achieved in this country. It was done during a difficult war and post-war period of austerity when the breeding of *Galanthus* was neither fashionable nor profitable, in complete contrast to today.

Heyrick Anthony Greatorex was born on 28 February 1884, at 126 Loughborough Park, Brixton, the second of seven children born to Heyrick Anthony Greatorex senior and Mariane Lavinia Caunter, née French. His parents had both been married before. Their wedding took place in St John's Church, Brixton, on 4 December 1884. Heyrick

Galanthus 'Greenfinch' – one of the most spectacular, green-tipped cultivars, found in Snowdrop Acre. The site is one of only a few around the world where an excellent gene pool produces such natural crosses.

ABOVE Snowdrop Acre in February – the mass flowering of *Galanthus* in part of Tony Greatorex's garden.

LEFT Heyrick Anthony Greatorex, aged 31, and Janette Tillett on their wedding day, 1915.

FACING PAGE Heyrick Anthony Greatorex, c.1916, Second Lieutenant in the Royal Norfolk Regiment.

senior was a very successful stockbroker. The family moved around a good deal before, by 1901, taking up residence in Rowneybury House, a large Georgian house with extensive grounds in Sawbridgeworth in Hertfordshire. There the Greatorexes had six house servants, a gardener and 'estate labourers'. Some measure of the importance and size of this house can be gained from the fact that from 1999 to 2014 it was the home of David and Victoria Beckham, which owing to lavish additions and refurbishment was dubbed 'Beckingham Palace'. In 2014 the house and estate sold for £11.35 million.

In 1897, Heyrick junior, aged 13, was sent to Repton School in Derbyshire. The Greatorex family and their name originate in that county. In 1251 there are references to 'Great Reaches', which was a small farming community, now called 'Great Rock' farm in the Derbyshire High Peak between Buxton and Tideswell. Heyrick left school in 1901 and we know little about him until he appears in Norfolk in 1915, where he married Janette Isabel Tillett of Witton in the parish church on 25 October. He was thirty-one years old and the marriage certificate records his profession as 'gentleman'.

During the First World War he joined the Inns of Court and City Yeomanry Officers' Training Corps, in November 1915 attaining the rank of Corporal. The fact that he joined the Inns of Court and City Yeomanry suggests that between 1901 and 1915 he may well have been training as a lawyer. On 25 September 1916, he was commissioned into the Norfolk Regiment. He initially joined the 8th Battalion and then served as a lieutenant in France and Flanders with the 9th. He was wounded in action on the western front at Lagnicourt in April 1917 and was discharged, having been awarded the Victory Medal and the British Medal. He returned to Norfolk where he spent the rest of his life. During the Second World War he joined the Norfolk Battalion of the Home Guard based in the Great Yarmouth area. His platoon guarded Acle Bridge, but local rumour has it that he spent most of his time in the Bridge Inn next door. He was certainly a character and stories about him abound.

From his very fortunate and comfortable beginnings, Tony Greatorex's life spent in Norfolk was modest. He lived in a small single-storey home and the 'spare' room was an old railway carriage in the garden. In fact, he owned neither; both house and garden belonged via his wife to the Tillett family. Whatever the condition of his house, he did have a considerable sized garden of

ABOVE Greatorex's house at Snowdrop Acre in the 1930s.

RIGHT The only known picture of Tony Greatorex in his garden at Snowdrop Acre. 1930s.

FACING PAGE *Galanthus nivalis* 'Flore Pleno'.

six acres. We know Greatorex lived there from 1915 to 1954 thanks to a mountain of correspondence with the local District Council. He was constantly in dispute with them over planning permission, of which there was none, the drains, which were in short supply, and the rates. Although the house was pulled down in the 1970s, a small part of the foundations still remains. By the end of his life he was described as a 'retired poultry farmer'. When he died on 31 January 1954, aged 69, he was buried in an unmarked grave in Brundall churchyard. A decline to obscurity in marked contrast to his great-grandfather, from 1819–1831 organist and Master of the Choristers at Westminster Abbey, who was buried in the Abbey's cloisters. Yet today it is not his illustrious forebear who is remembered; the Greatorex name has gained recognition due to Heyrick Anthony and his snowdrops.

Tony Greatorex used his resources on developing his garden, a therapeutic pursuit after his experiences in the First World War. A hobby which over the years clearly became a passion. The land he occupied was much larger than the present Snowdrop Acre. The 1946 and 1948 aerial photographs show Snowdrop Acre as a densely planted garden, so much so that it is almost impossible to see the house. The six-acre site was grass with many trees and shrubs and what looked like orchard trees, with a complex system of paths radiating from the house. Many of these trees were rare and some Tony had grown from seed. This area today is totally different. The Tillett family eventually sold the bulk of the land to a Dr Hilton. The sale included all the land now

associated with the house Hilton built called 'St Andrews', the garden of which is now mainly lawns with some trees on the edges. Unfortunately, despite the Tilletts trying to stop it, many of Tony's rare trees were felled after the land changed hands. Growing up with gardens surrounding his father's large Hertfordshire house, Greatorex had an interest in gardens and plants beyond that of his passion for snowdrops. His grandfather, Thomas Greatorex, had been a Fellow of the Linnaean Society, so there was a clear family interest in natural history and taxonomy.

Despite his lack of planning permission, when Tony Greatorex died, his wife Janette continued to live at their house until her death in 1971. The Tillett family tried to get planning permission for a new house which was refused. A purchase order was served, and Broadland District Council became owners of the site in 1979. Today it is managed as a nature reserve by BADCOG, the Blofield and District Conservation Group, and is locally known as 'Snowdrop Acre'.

Snowdrop Acre is a rather shady site with a light, well-drained soil ideally suited to snowdrops. And it was here that Tony Greatorex produced more famous snowdrops than have come from any other garden in Britain. For his breeding purposes he grew *Galanthus nivalis* 'Flore Pleno' and *Galanthus plicatus*, but he had many others as well. *G. woronowii* occurs in several dense patches. It has little or no variation and sets seeds only rarely. This is somewhat surprising as there are many clones in cultivation that set

ABOVE *Galanthus plicatus.*

LEFT The Snowdrop Bible – Bishop, Davis and Grimshaw's *A Monograph of Cultivated Galanthus.*

seed regularly. The rabbits, however, do a good job in spreading them around. *G. ikariae* does very well here and sets lots of seed. Nearly every flower produces a pod, which is very unusual for snowdrops in Britain. Most of the population looks very close indeed to *G. ikariae* 'Butt's Form', but there are some seedlings with green patches on their outer segments. He also grew *G. nivalis* 'Sharlockii' with its large split spathes resembling donkey's ears and *G. nivalis imperati* which is a particularly large neat

ABOVE LEFT *Galanthus nivalis imperati* and (**ABOVE RIGHT**) *Galanthus* 'Hippolyta'.

form from southern Italy. This mixture of the best forms available at the time has, over the years, led to a vast number of interesting seedlings.

Twenty-four of the seedlings that have occurred on this site are named and described in what has become the 'bible' of snowdrop growers, Bishop, Davis and Grimshaw's *A Monograph of Cultivated Galanthus*. Fourteen of these plants were selected and named by Greatorex himself. He released 'Nerissa', 'Hippolyta' and 'Lavinia' before 1948, followed by more Shakespearian characters – 'Cordelia', 'Desdemona', 'Jaquenetta', 'Titania' and 'Ophelia', then finally 'Dionysus', 'Jenny Wren', and 'White Swan'.

All these plants have survived to this day and are widely available at, what for snowdrops, is a reasonable price. Today, rare snowdrops can be very expensive. In 2015, £1,390 was paid for a single *Galanthus plicatus* 'Golden Fleece'. The buyer was billed an extra £4 for postage. Snowdrops make excellent garden plants, which bulk up relatively quickly. The only problem is telling them apart. One rather curious character of these plants is that when first planted, they produce juvenile flowers that often look very different from adult ones. This also happens if a bulb produces a second flower. 'White Swan' and 'Jenny Wren' are less well-known, and it is thought that the

ABOVE *Galanthus nivalis* 'Flore Pleno' growing en masse at Snowdrop Acre.
FACING PAGE *Galanthus* 'Dionysus'.

Greatorex originals have been lost to cultivation and that two rather undistinguished snowdrops have taken on their names. Greatorex gave a seedling to Frank Waley, a well-known Hertfordshire bulb grower, which is now known as 'Poseidon' and two to Lewis Palmer known as 'L. P. Long' and 'L. P. Short'. Lewis Palmer was a very influential and respected gardener who gardened at Headbourne Worthy in Hampshire and is best known for the *Agapathus* Headbourne hybrids. Then in the 1970s Fred Bugloss, a senior member of the Royal Horticultural Society's Joint Rock Committee, visited the site and collected three more double snowdrops that are known as 'G. 71', 'G. 75' and 'G. 77'. Thankfully no more doubles have been named since then. Some of the above are rather similar to each other.

Greatorex transferred pollen deliberately from *G. nivalis* 'Flore Pleno' onto selected forms of *G. plicatus* to produce his seedlings. As with many double flowers, snowdrops are double because the stamens have become petaloid, rendering the plant sterile or nearly so. In a population of double snowdrops, a careful search will usually reveal a small amount of pollen.

Greatorex's achievement has also to be seen within the context of his time as for most of his life, there were no nurseries offering specialist snowdrops for sale. The first to do so was the Giant Snowdrop Company and they produced their first list in 1953. Until then snowdrops were largely passed around and swapped among an elite group of gardeners. Greatorex's plants were distributed this way and through the

LEFT Richard Hobbs examining the *Galanthus* in Snowdrop Acre.
BELOW *Galanthus* 'Bishop's Mitre'.
FACING PAGE *Galanthus* 'Clovis'.

Royal Horticultural Society's garden at Wisley. He predates twin-scaling which has revolutionized the growing and selling of snowdrops in the last twenty-five years. Commercial growers have obtained as many as 100 twin-scales from a single bulb. Greatorex had to wait for clumps to build up on their own and some do this very slowly. We can now increase them at least 10 times faster. Today many people are breeding snowdrops but Tony Greatorex was the first, and for many years, the only person to do so.

Although he was regarded as a recluse for the latter part of his life, he must have had contacts with many important and well-known gardeners in order to gather together his superb collection of rare and unusual snowdrops. By the same method he assembled some very good colchicums, which still grow in Snowdrop Acre including *Colchicum speciosum* 'Album', *C. speciosum* 'Atrorubens' and *C.* 'Dick Trotter' which were not available in the trade at that time.

Recently several interesting plants from Snowdrop Acre have been named. Probably the best and most famous is G. 'Greenfinch' (see page 406). A fabulous flower of great substance, 'Greenfinch' has large inner and outer marks of a very strong dark green. The outer marks are streaks rather than blotches and look as if they have been thickly painted on. The tips of the outer segments are somewhat pinched in.

When happy this is a big strong plant that is quite distinct and well worth growing. G. 'Mr Spoons' is a similar but less robust plant with smaller green marks and with distinctly spathulate outer segments, hence the name.

The site has produced many interesting oddities, five of which have been named. G. 'Barguest' and G. 'Bishop's Mitre' are both 'Sharlockii' types, but the former has no green markings on the outer segments and the ears of the split spathe are somewhat hooked at the tips. G. 'Bishop's Mitre' is very striking indeed with strongly split spathes and a good green mark on its outers. What makes this plant extraordinary is the very short scape and very long pedicel, which means that when the flowers first come out, they sit on the ground. 'Matt-adors' is even odder. It has good green marks on its outer segments, but the pedicel is so short that the flower remains within the spathe. This snowdrop does not dangle as they should, but remains, in an interesting and some may say rather ugly semi-upright position.

A rather lovely short, squat plant is 'Quintet' which when well-nourished will produce five outer segments. It is elegant and easy to grow, putting on weight relatively quickly. The last cultivar to mention is 'Clovis'. 'Clovis' sometimes has three outer segments and three inner segments, when it looks rather boring; other times one or two outer segments and five or four inner ones, when it looks very unusual but rather ungainly; and occasionally it has no outer segments and six inner ones when it looks magnificent! A typical clump will include all possible combinations. Bulbs will do different things in

different years, which is why the snowdrop is a fascinating plant and can become a real talking point.

If you visit Snowdrop Acre today, you will find a huge range of snowdrops including a small number with two flowers on each scape. An outstanding double-header has been named 'Saraband'. What at first seems like a rather dull and small garden, hidden away in Norfolk, is in fact a treasure trove, one of the most significant snowdrop sites in the country, and a lasting memorial to its fascinating and dedicated progenitor.

Galanthus 'Saraband'.

22

James Pulham & Son at Sandringham

Scilla Latham

The gardens at Sandringham are familiar to the many thousands of people who have visited them since they were first opened to the public in 1908. However, despite having such a public face their history is less well known since very few estate papers appear to survive in the Royal Archives. Additionally, the apparent absence of any references in correspondence or journals written by members of the royal family or their courtiers further clouds the story. This article examines the part played by James Pulham & Son in the development of the gardens during the half century following the purchase of Sandringham as the Prince of Wales's country house in February 1862.

In 1869 the construction began on a new house to designs by Albert Jenkins Humbert. Humbert was in royal favour having designed the Royal Mausoleum at Frogmore. There had been an Elizabethan house at Sandringham, to be replaced in 1771 by a Georgian one. Nineteenth-century alterations followed to leave a sprawling white stuccoed house which, although it boasted twenty-nine bedrooms, was considered no longer large enough to accommodate the royal household and regular substantial house parties that were so much part of life at Sandringham. The old house was

FACING PAGE *The Pulhamite Rocks and Planting by the Lake at Sandringham House.* Cyril Ward, c.1912.

ABOVE The west façade of Sandringham House.

Albert Edward, Prince of Wales, and Princess Alexandra by the lake at their newly purchased house at Sandringham, 1863.

demolished, except for the mid nineteenth-century conservatory by Samuel Teulon. A further concern was the inherent damp in the house that was thought to have contributed to Princess Alexandra's rheumatism, which no doubt prompted the filling-in of the lake which ran in front of the property and constructing a new one at a lower level to the south. Works on such a scale presented the opportunity to redesign the entire garden between 1868 and 1870.

William Broderick Thomas (1811–98), one of the leading landscape gardeners of the day, whose work at Felbrigg Hall, Norfolk, and Henham Hall, Suffolk, may have been familiar to the Prince of Wales, was commissioned to create a garden in the latest naturalistic style of which Princess Alexandra was an enthusiastic admirer. James Pulham (1820–98) whose company specialised in the construction of picturesque rockwork gardens and watercourses was brought in to design and construct rockwork around the lake and watercourses. He may also have advised on its planting.

The Pulham family business originated in Woodbridge, Suffolk, where the first James Pulham (1793–1838) worked for Lockwood's, a family building firm that developed

Portland Stone Cement for use in the manufacture of architectural ornaments, fountains, statues, and vases. A son, also called James, was born in Woodbridge in 1820, but the family soon moved to Spitalfields when Lockwood's opened a second London branch that was run by James Pulham. In the mid 1840s, the business moved to Broxbourne in Hertfordshire, where local clay was more easily accessible for the manufacture of a wide range of terracotta products for his own factory. These included monuments, tombs, bridges, and balustrades made from stone-coloured cement, which by 1845 was referred to as Pulham's Stone Cement, as well as traditionally coloured garden terracotta work.

The swift success of the company is demonstrated by the exhibition of their terracotta products in the 1851 Great Exhibition in London, and later in the 1862 International Exhibition, London, and the Exposition Universelle in Paris in 1867: this led to them becoming an even more desirable adornment to any fashionable garden. The International Exhibition catalogue said: 'Mr Pulham of Broxbourne is a large exhibitor of Terracotta, not only for architectural purposes, but for those of gardens, conservatories and general ornamentation of the grounds. They are of excellent design, carefully and skilfully modelled, and so 'baked' as to be uninfluenced prejudicially by weather.'

In 1877, Pulham published a prospectus titled *Picturesque Ferneries and Rock-Garden Scenery* which describes their rockwork and includes a 'list of some of the places where the Pulhamite System of forming Rock has been adopted during 28 years in Ferneries, waterfalls, Alpineries, Rock Gardens ...' There is no doubt that being able to include

Turn-of-the-century advertising for Pulham & Son.

Sandringham House in the early 1880s, showing part of the Pulhamite rockworks by the end of the re-sited Upper Lake.

'HRH the Prince of Wales, Sandringham: Waterfalls, Rocky Stream and Cave for Boathouse in a Cliff open to a Lake, 1868, 1875 & 1876' increased demand for the firm's services. This booklet and the 1915 company catalogue – *Garden ornament, vases; terminals; pedestals; sundials; seats; fountains; balustrades; figures etc.* – are invaluable sources of information about Pulham's products and work because when the company closed during the Second World War, virtually all the company records were destroyed.

It seems that even before his father's death in 1838, James Pulham II had devised the system of manufacturing artificial rocks to create the picturesque garden rockwork features for which he is undoubtedly now best known. His earliest garden rockwork, in the gardens at Hoddesdon Hall, in Hertfordshire, dates from 1838, but although a few other sites from the 1840s and 1850s are recorded in the 1877 prospectus, it was not until the 1860s that Pulham rockwork was in high demand for naturalistic landscape gardens. A notable surviving example of his early work is the garden at Highnam Court, Gloucestershire, where he worked intermittently between 1847 and 1862.

The rockwork features around the lakes at Sandringham as well as the Dell and stream feeding the lakes from it. These started in 1868 with work on the Upper Lake.

A photograph from the Royal Archives from 1882 shows the extent of the rockworks. The planting is mainly birch trees before the introduction of any conifers.

What Pulham achieved is typical of his work and provides good examples of many of the features described in his prospectus. In it he states that an early interest in geology was the basis of his skill in imitating the characteristics of local stone so he could adapt 'Pulhamite' to match any naturally occurring stone. 'Where no real stone or rock exists, or too expensive to get it to the place, it may be artificially formed on the spot, with burrs, rough bricks, or concrete for the core, which is then covered with cement, to imitate the colour, form and texture of the real rock as of red, yellowish, grey or brown sandstone whichever is desired or most consistent with the geology of the district?'

Close inspection of the rockwork at Sandringham reveals that it is a carefully constructed mixture of local carstone and Pulham's custom-made artificial rock. The effect of prolonged weathering on carstone is to accentuate the naturally occurring orange iron oxide, whereas the Pulhamite stone remains relatively unaffected by weather, demonstrating the marketing pledge 'Durability guaranteed' for their stone. This is particularly evident around the 'cave' created to be used as a boathouse at the top of the Upper Lake, where large slabs of light-coloured Pulhamite form the roof of the cave and darker carstone the sides. Another indicator at Sandringham is that

ABOVE The upper of the two lakes. Today the dense planting obscures some of the drama of Pulham's extensive rockworks, with its boathouse cave or grotto.

LEFT The Cave boathouse. The Pulhamite boulders were a less expensive alternative to natural stone. Their lighter weight saw cost savings too in their transport and erection.

the soft carstone blocks, quarried and carted from Wolferton, are smaller than the manufactured Pulhamite blocks.

Sandringham's 1868 garden with a formal area retained around the house, but increasingly naturalistic landscaping beyond it incorporating the lakes and streams, rockwork, and naturalised planting, exemplifies the naturalistic style of garden design first associated with Robert Marnock in the 1850s and brought to maturity by William Robinson in *The Wild Garden*, published in 1870. 'It is not generally known that rocks cropping up or out, are desirable to produce rugged picturesque effects in gardens

such as we see in the natural landscape.' Princess Alexandra's enthusiasm for this new style is recognized in *The Gardeners' Chronicle*: 'The Queen's Wild Garden is a little spot screened in a plantation: a grassy path leads through this, and on either side wildflowers are growing. The gardeners are unable to make this spot appear more wild than Her Majesty would like it to be. It is the extreme opposite of the formal garden in front of the mansion.'

An 1871 photograph album in the Royal Archives includes two views across the Upper Lake when the rockwork and associated planting had just been completed. The photograph looking towards the house has a distinctive bearded figure in highland dress proudly standing on the rocks by the boathouse: as yet not satisfactorily identified, it is tempting to suggest he is the Head Gardener, William Carmichael. It is interesting to note that no concessions were made to creating an instant garden by planting mature plants, and it must have been several years for the full effect of the planting to be appreciated. Even so, William Broderick Thomas's appreciation of Pulham's work is expressed in a letter: 'I am very much pleased with your work, and I consider the Boat-house quite a work of art. I will say again, I was very much pleased with everything

and hope His Royal Highness will be.' An article in *The Gardeners' Chronicle* in 1892 notes: 'These stretches of water upon which Mr Pulham was engaged some few years ago, are being thoroughly cleansed, are furnished with rockeries at certain points, and they are connected with each other by rocky rivulets constructed in a very natural and pleasing manner.'

James Pulham returned to Sandringham in 1875 and 1876, which is almost certainly when the rocky outcrops and a waterfall feeding water from the Upper Lake into the newly dug Lower Lake were made. A reference to the work being 'under the guidance of a fee earning specialist named Thomas' described by the Prince of Wales as 'a gentleman, not to be described as inexpensive' confirms William Broderick Thomas's

TOP The planting here succeeds in making the artificial stone look like part of a natural rocky outcrop.

ABOVE The Lower Lake. Here the individual rocks are even larger but the conifer planting, successful and dramatic as it is, has now hidden much of the work and lessened the intended impact.

FACING PAGE Steps were added to the south of the boathouse to reach the edge of the lake. The cascade is a later addition and the summerhouse, not by Pulham, is from 1913.

role in this project. There can be little doubt that Pulham's rockwork at Sandringham was a success, but it was not until 1895 that the firm received a royal warrant from the Prince of Wales, which may provide a clue to later work at Sandringham by Pulham & Son.

The Pulham 1877 prospectus lists Sandringham as one of the places where their terracotta-work had been supplied, however without documentation it is impossible to say exactly what or where these examples of terracotta garden 'ornamentation' were. The Pulham terracotta 'Forty Thieves' vases (two of which have the company stamp) on the terrace to the west of the house, overlooking the former parterres, are not in the 1871 views of the terrace, but this may be because this area does not appear to be finished yet. The large oval 'basket weave' planters on the terrace, which in summer are planted with heliotrope, are not illustrated in the 1915 Pulham catalogue; however, their similarity to other work suggests they were from the company.

ABOVE 'Forty Thieves' vases on the west terrace.
LEFT 'Basket weave' planters.

A page from the Pulham's *Garden Ornament Catalogue*, 1925, illustrating some of the numerous designs for urns, tazzas, pedestals, fountains, tubs, pots, vases, sundials, balustrades, finials, figures, and garden seats. Although long postdating the firm's Sandringham work, a large number of items in this and earlier catalogues had been available over many years.

In the 1890s, there was a resurgence of activity in the gardens that coincided with the arrival of the new Head Gardener, Archibald Mackellar, and the restoration and extension of the house following the fire in December 1891. On stylistic grounds, fountains, balustrading and other ornamental stonework made for Sandringham at this time can be attributed to the company. In late summer of 1891, correspondence between the Prince of Wales and Lord Ferdinand Rothschild refers to a circular fountain that was to be installed the following spring. It could be the impressive stone fountain with an ornate bowl on a pedestal standing in a large circular red scagliola basin, which dominated the intersection of the walks bisecting the Kitchen Garden, until it was removed in the 1980s. That such a grand fountain positioned at the pivotal point was not described in earlier lengthy articles about the Kitchen Gardens, suggests that the fountain marked in this

ABOVE Two ornamental features thought to be supplied by Pulham's: a ram's head planter in the centre of the North Garden and a well head on the south-west lawn.

BELOW The fountain at the centre of the long herbaceous walk in the Kitchen Garden. c.1955.

position in the 1st Edition Ordnance Survey map (surveyed 1883/4), may have been replaced as part of a major reorganisation of the Kitchen Garden in 1892. The new fountain incorporated a number of decorative motifs used by Pulham elsewhere.

Pulham & Son may also have supplied the columnar fountain supporting St George set in a large circular basin that stood in the middle of the Rosary Garden, which was laid out by Archibald Mackellar in 1896 to replace the tennis court. One other piece of work that may have been by Pulham & Son at this time is the large armorial cartouche and associated balustrade on the north side of the new upper level to the Billiard Room, which was added following the fire in December 1891. Although on a larger scale, the cartouche is similar to those made by Pulham in Belle Vue Park,

The armorial cartouche and a section of balustrade, both possibly the work of Pulham & Son.

Newport (1893), and Madeira Walk, Ramsgate (1894), at this time. The balustrade is similar to the 'Frimley Balustrade' illustrated in the Pulham 1915 catalogue; however, it can also be interpreted as a reworking of the Teulon ornamentation so admired by the Prince of Wales when he bought the house.

The final chapter of the development of the gardens during this half century was initiated by the gift of a pair of wrought-iron gates from the Prince and Princess of Wales to the King and Queen in 1903 on the occasion of their fortieth wedding anniversary. Echoing the gift of the Norwich Gates by the people of Norfolk on their wedding, these gates enter the formal Square Garden before reaching the walled Kitchen Gardens. The ornamental brick gate piers surmounted by terracotta urns, are typical of the Pulham's work on other walled gardens.

In conjunction with the gates, a 210-foot-long Pergola with brick piers matching the gates was built in 1905 to continue the impressive approach to the walled Kitchen Garden. The pergola is made up of fourteen cubes each measuring fifteen foot in height, width and distance between each of the piers, which supported massive oak timbers. Similar to pergolas built by the Pulhams, it too can be confidently attributed to them on stylistic grounds, although without the benefit of documentary evidence

this remains unconfirmed. A postscript to the 1905 work are two semicircular stone seats designed in 1909 by Sir Lawrence Alma-Tadema PRA in exedra either side of an Italian well head at the midpoint of the pergola. Since Pulham & Son manufactured garden stonework to other artists' designs it is very possible that these seats were manufactured by them.

There can be no doubt that the gardens laid out at Sandringham between 1868 and 1909 are an outstanding example of the English Landscape School and Gardenesque,

ABOVE The entrance to the Kitchen Garden, seen from the inside, with its ornamental brick piers and urns.

LEFT One of the Sir Lawrence Alma-Tadema designed seats thought to be made by Pulham & Son.

ABOVE AND BELOW A watercolour by Cyril Ward with the pergola in its prime, 1912, and a section of the piers, minus their crossbeams, today.

epitomizing the naturalism and informality that was key to Edwardian garden design. Sandringham remains a rare example of the grand Edwardian country house and garden, which after the First World War was an anachronism that most families could no longer afford. The continuing employment of James Pulham & Son in the gardens at Sandringham not only illuminates their career, but also illustrates the development of garden design and ornamentation during the half century that Sandringham was the country house of Edward VII and Queen Alexandra.

FACING PAGE Part of the gardens and grounds at Sandringham House from the 1906 Ordnance Survey map.

The Upper Lake with its rockworks is here called 'Fish Pond'. The terrace with its vases is immediately below the long west front of the house, and the Kitchen Garden, with its ornamental piers and seats, is the huge walled enclosure, upper right, in part labelled 'Sandringham Dairy'.

ABOVE Sandringham House from the south-west.

23

Norfolk's Gardens in Art

Roger Last

Monet's series of paintings of his water garden at Giverny in Normandy are considered by many to be the supreme examples of the depiction of a garden in all its moods being transcended into art. Such pictures are rare. For the most part depictions of gardens are competent and often beautiful, although few are of serious artistic merit. However, these sketches, oils, watercolours, and etchings can say more than words in evoking a period and giving information. In that sense they are invaluable. As a local and historical record, they are highly prized, and to garden historians, treasure indeed.

On a national level the record is thin on the ground for the sixteenth century. In the seventeenth, garden depictions do start to appear, although often as a background to portraits, sections of garden layouts apparent over the shoulders of the sitters. Their inclusion testifies to their importance, besides intending to signal the sophistication, taste and wealth of their owners. Unfortunately, none of these portraits depict any Norfolk gardens, and there is no artistic record of any Norfolk garden at all, until suddenly in c.1680, there is a full-blown oil painting of one. This is of Sir Roger Pratt's new house and garden at Ryston Hall. He designed the house, and four other highly influential ones in England. As a gentleman-architect of such proven ability, indeed he was Britain's first architect to be knighted, it

FACING PAGE A detail from *Stiffkey Old Hall*. Anthony Green, 2008. Oil.

LEFT *Ryston Hall*. Artist unknown, c.1680. Oil. The oldest surviving painting of any Norfolk garden.

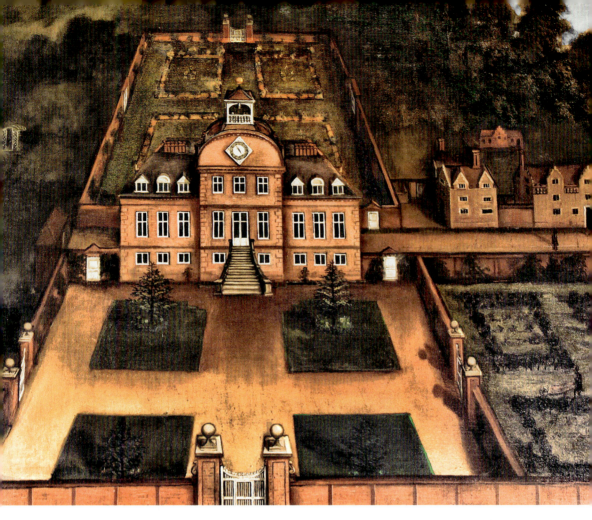

ABOVE *Ryston Hall*, the central section of the painting, digitally enhanced to show more detail.

Apart from the North and South Gardens, the picture shows the walled, the east or Kitchen Garden, not banished to some distant hidden location, but conveniently close to the house. Here fruit trees are trained round the walls and small trained trees or bushes enclose the rectangular beds with their neat rows of vegetables. Approaching the gate is the shadowy figure of a gardener with a hat pushing an elongated wooden wheelbarrow. To the left, outside the walls, is a white-painted arbour or summer house, with criss-cross trellising and a curved roof set to the side of a large rectangle of grass enclosed by trees.

LEFT The figures in the foreground, placed outside the formal gardens to give them maximum size, presumably are dark-haired Sir Roger Pratt with his hand to his beard, and his wife Ann with a hooded cloak, right, and their dogs. A man points to the landscape or to a rather Biblical-looking figure with a long stick, white beard and cloak.

seems inconceivable that he did not devise his own garden layout. The painting, which still hangs in the hall today, judging from the settled nature of the depicted planting must have been painted half a dozen or so years after the hall's completion in 1672. Its technical and artistic merit is not high, but the clarity of the evidence is excellent. The viewpoint is elevated, looking down on the hall and both walled North and South Gardens, and part of the south-east enclosure, a walled Kitchen Garden. The South Garden was gravelled with four large square plats of grass, each with a central conifer, surrounded by a circular bed of flowers. The North Garden had grass not gravel paths, again with four square grass plats, but these are bordered by plat bands, raised flower beds in which, as was the custom of this period, the plants were planted with generous intervals between them. Plants could be expensive, and this method of display enabled all their attributes to be fully appreciated.

About ten years later comes a picture of the garden at Aylsham Old Hall. Again, an elevated perspective shows the formal layout either side of the house. Flowers play no part at all in this geometrical plan of grass beds bisected by gravel paths. Brick walls contain the enclosures with pleached fruit trees grown against them. Apart from decorative gates, the only other ornamental features are, to the west, an exceptionally large statue of Justice on a plinth at the centre of the cross walks, and to the east, a narrow canal with a brick garden house at its head. Although somewhat austere, this

Aylsham Old Hall. Artist unknown, *c.*1690. Oil.

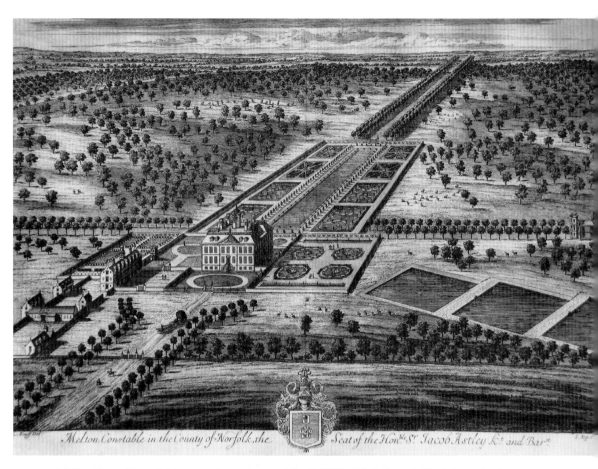

Melton Constable Hall, Johannes Kip and Leonard Knyff, 1707. This is the only Norfolk garden to appear in the two Dutch draughtsmen's *Britannia Illustrata*. The brilliantly deduced aerial perspective was the only way to adequately depict a huge Baroque garden of this kind, with its long axial avenues of trees, and to the south of the hall its eight huge parterres flanking a formal canal. To the bottom right are tiered fishponds.

formal layout perfectly complements the symmetry of the house. It is not known who painted either the Ryston or the Aylsham painting.

Once into the eighteenth century the garden pictures are attributable, but it has to be said that Norfolk boasts little of any particular artistic merit from this period featuring any of its gardens. The view of the vast garden and landscape layout of the grounds of Melton Constable Hall, by Johannes Kip and Leonard Knyff from *Britannia Illustrata*, 1707, is highly impressive, both pictorially and technically. As a record of a Norfolk example of a huge Baroque garden it could not be bettered, but it is a record, not Art. The same can be said of Edmund Prideaux's invaluable depictions of Norfolk gardens (see pages 376-385). While the lost gardens at Raynham Hall from the 1720s in particular are a unique record, their artistic merit is minimal. William Kent's illustrative

Sketch of Denton Rectory. Francis Cufaude, 1747.

proposals for part of the grounds at Holkham Hall are far more accomplished, as indeed would be expected from a garden and interior designer and a painter. Horace Walpole, however, deemed his skills as a painter to be 'below mediocrity'. But then Walpole was the master of the putdown.

There are fine oil paintings of Norfolk designed landscapes and the halls they enhanced. John Wootton's painting of Langley Park of c.1749, although largely designed to show off the posing Beauchamp-Proctor family with their horses and state-of-the-art carriage, does still depict the sweeping parkland and trees and even a circular temple in the distance. What is missing from the record are the smaller estates and gardens of the Georgian age. One notable exception is the 1747 oil painting by Francis Cufaude of Denton Rectory and gardens in south Norfolk. It was commissioned by the rector, the Revd Mathew Postlethwaite, who also commissioned two portraits of himself. He could afford to as he was appointed archdeacon of Norwich in 1742. Francis Cufaude (c.1701–c.1750), from King's Lynn, was apprenticed to the Painter-Stainers' Company in London, but by the early 1740s returned to work in Norfolk and Suffolk. His Denton painting is the only known oil painting which depicts a Norfolk domestic garden in the eighteenth century. His small preliminary sketch shows his intentions for the oil, which was worked up to four feet wide. Taking an elevated perspective, it depicts the rectory with its walled and hedged gardens and the church, set in an undulating

ABOVE *Denton Rectory*. Francis Cufaude, 1747. Oil.

FACING PAGE Detail of *Denton Rectory*, believed to be the owner, the Revd Mathew Postlethwaite, standing in his parterre with its formal flower beds.

BELOW Detail of *Denton Rectory*, a gardener at work in the Kitchen Garden.

well-wooded landscape. As a painting it has great charm and character. However, it is the eighteen figures in it, strolling and working, which give it such energy, and its interest is compounded by the detail of the garden. Mathew Postlethwaite stands beside his formal flower beds while in front of him two men are pulling on the ropes of presumably a net, dragging it across a rectangular pond. A gardener digs in the Kitchen Garden, two gentlemen with ladies walk from the walled forecourt with its four grass plats. Another cleric arrives on horseback followed by a haywain pulled by two horses, startling the geese.

Denton, its church and rectory, is further celebrated in a fine pencil and watercolour by Paul Sandby RA (1731–1809). A founder member of the Royal Academy, Sandby has been called 'the father of the English watercolour' and is particularly noted for his landscapes and topographical scenes. His Denton picture shows a large central oak tree framing both the church on its elevation and the rectory with a foreground pond with a single cow. It is landscape rather than garden but an excellent complementary piece to the earlier Cufaude.

Humphry Repton (1752–1818) was nowhere as talented an artist as Sandby. But his work is competent. His pen and ink drawings of 'Noblemens & Gentlemens' seats in Norfolk, 1779–80, are often the earliest pictorial account of these locations and

FACING PAGE *Denton Church and Rectory*. Paul Sandby.

ABOVE *Catton Park, View to the South-West*. Humphry Repton. Pen and wash, 1788.

With the spire of Norwich Cathedral seen rising between the trees, Repton depicts himself seated with his sketch pad. The two onlooking ladies are thought to be the daughters of the owner of the park, Jeremiah Ives.

BELOW *Sheringham Park*. The approach to the house as proposed in Repton's Red Book for Sheringham. Watercolour. 1812.

Fishing in the Lake, at Kimberley Hall. Humphry Repton. Pen and wash, 1779–80.

Repton added to their interest by frequently peopling his sketches. At Wolterton the grass is being scythed and rolled, and at Kimberley ambitious fishing with a boat and a drag net is in full swing. Repton provided sketches, turned into engravings, for the many halls in their landscapes in south and north Erpingham and Eynsford for Mostyn John Armstrong's *History and Antiquities of the County of Norfolk*, 1781, which are an invaluable record. As a landscape designer his proposals for his client's grounds were presented in his well-known Red Books. Repton's first and last major commissions were in Norfolk, where he is thought to have worked on twenty-three sites. His Red Books remain for seven Norfolk gardens among them Sheringham, Holkham, Barningham, and Wood Hall, Hilgay. At Catton Park, his first commission, no Red Book survives but he produced delightful paintings of the park. Undoubtedly the Sheringham Red Book is one of his finest, as is the landscape he produced, his last and favourite commission. Unlike an independent artist who might concentrate on mood and feeling, Repton wished above all to produce pleasant well-lit scenes of landscape and gardens which

Detail of *Horsford Rectory*. William Burton, 1791. Watercolour. The couple's baby wears an identically styled hat, plus feather, as its mother.

would appeal to his clients. His views were commercial tools. They do give us excellent reference material however, and the best do have artistic merit.

A charming amateur watercolour from 1791 shows the rectory at Horsford. It was painted by the rector himself, William Burton. He has his back to the viewer with his wife in profile. He had just moved there, and no doubt wished to celebrate that fact. The house is comfortable, although as rectories then went a trifle modest, and the garden in a typical late eighteenth-century style, lawns and trees, including conifers, and the house itself festooned in climbing plants. They could be roses or trained fruit. The whole offset with white-painted low wooden fencing with chain link above.

From c.1800 comes a remarkable watercolour of a collection of town gardens in Rose Lane in Norwich. Remarkable in that this sort of study is rare. From the early 1800s, it gives a detailed account of gardening styles, design, and horticultural interests in this period. Larger gardens and parks are well documented, but smaller domestic gardens such as these are not.

Another Norwich garden appears in the etching John Crome (1768–1821) made of Chapelfield gardens. It is unrecognizable. The trees are dense, bisected by a rough broad path through which cows are being driven, no doubt on their way to market. It is hard to believe that this scene is within the former medieval walls of the city. Its woodland would seem delightful to us now, but the Victorians, who had more than their fair share of this type of country beyond the city, did not want it, seeing instead

Gardens in Rose Lane, Norwich. c.1805. Artist Unknown. Watercolour.

In the foreground a formal rectangle hedged garden. Throughout the various garden enclosures are tunnel arbours, what appears to be a laburnum tunnel, generous beds of herbaceous planting, seats, even a raised viewing pavilion with balustrade, and an extensive Kitchen Garden. Liberal use in made of the walls for trained fruit. To the right, from an open window on the first floor of the house, a man holding a book looks out. Beneath him, attached to the wall is a single bird in a cage within a larger enclosure. A gardener with a rake over his shoulder walks down the central path. In the Kitchen Garden to the left, a second gardener with upturned hat is shown digging. Among the trees beyond the Kitchen Garden are various houses, some of them thatched, and two windmills stand on the horizon.

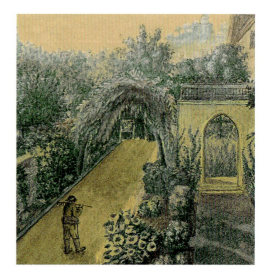

View in Chapel-Field, Norwich. John Crome, Undated. Etching.

chronic civic neglect, describing Chapelfield as 'well-nigh wilderness'. In 1880 in went the municipal gardens instead.

Again, from the second decade of the nineteenth century, John Sell Cotman (1782–1842) made a series of pencil and wash illustrations from which engravings were made, of many of the seats of the Norfolk gentry. These were published in *Excursions in the County of Norfolk* in 1819. They form an important architectural, garden and landscape record. Here are Earlham Hall, Stratton Hall, Shotesham Park, Earsham Hall, Quidenham, Wolterton, Narborough and Blickling Halls among many others. The open parkland around these halls, with rich woodland beyond, looks remarkably similar – noble, but somewhat monotonous. No monuments or follies enliven the views. Large herds of deer, cattle or sheep show what was considered preferable, certainly in economic terms. Cotman for artistic and compositional advantage showed no hesitation in transforming the slightest hint of undulation into highly energetic contours. His scenes appear to be a well-wooded Wiltshire rather than Norfolk. Wolterton is viewed from an impressive and boastful eminence. Indeed such a vantage point does exist in Blickling woods, beautiful, although in no way as dramatic. And although Kimberley does sit on a hill above its lake, its slopes are far from being as roundly embellished as Cotman depicts them.

Cotman's *In the Bishop's Garden, Norwich* (1824–5), has a hopeful-sounding title. What careful prospect could he have devised, especially with the subject matter so close to his house, across the road in St Martin-at-Palace Plain. Alas, from a topographical and garden design perspective he disappoints. But this was never his interest. His small

Wolterton Hall. John Sell Cotman, 1819. Etching from the pencil and wash original.

painting is a study of bushes and trees, the latter gaunt and leafless, with rook's nests. The painting, impressionist, and remarkably so at such an early date, with a thick use of paint, and texture, ignores the garden and concerns itself with exploring the form and mood of its limited subject. The same applies to John Middleton's *The Avenue, Gunton Park* (1840s). It does not aim to add to our knowledge of the park, instead it is a fine study of a closely planted avenue of autumnal trees, with two felled trunks, and a receding figure.

John Sell Cotman's *From the Front Garden of my Father's House at Thorpe*, was reworked as a lithograph by his son, Miles Edmund, (1810–1858). The 1841 lithograph is a clear and bold version of the impressionistic original. It depicts a typical late Georgian, early Victorian, villa garden. The scene is bucolic. The foreground creeper-clad balustrade sports three peacocks looking out, as

In the Bishop's Garden, Norwich. John Sell Cotman, 1824–5. Oil.

From the Front Garden of My Father's House at Thorpe. John Sell Cotman, reworked as a lithograph by his son, Miles Edmund Cotman. 1841.

the viewer does, onto the broad reflective River Yare beneath. The garden is lush with shrubs at the height of summer and backed by trees beyond. A series of terraces, with grass banks and steps descend to the river. By the water's edge, just seen, are the tops of two fishing pavilions or summer houses. It is a picture of tranquillity and order, testament to the unsullied positive intervention of man. No wonder that even by the 1780s Thorpe was known as Norfolk's Richmond.

The mid nineteenth century proved a low point in depictions of Norfolk's gardens. The outstanding garden paintings of that period belong to Edward Adveno Brooke (1821–1910). Romantic and opulent they were, charged with well-being and atmosphere, but great art, unfortunately not. Twenty-five of his paintings appeared in *The Gardens of England*, 1857, reproduced as chromolithographs. The expensive volume, which took Brooke years to complete, concerned itself with only the grandest

A Summer Afternoon – Ladies Boating on the Lake at Thurning Hall, c.1860. Artist unknown. Watercolour.

of gardens, nineteen of them. Included was the parterre at Trentham, the terrace at Harewood House, from Suffolk the theatrical architectural drama of Charles Barry's Shrubland Park with the sun setting in the west. Norfolk managed only one garden which lived up to the exacting brief, Holkham. Brooke's depiction of the then new *St George and the Dragon* fountain on Nesfield's latest terrace, is not his finest work, (see page 274/275) being rather flatly lit and sketchy when compared to his far more engaged compositions.

For the serious artist, gardens were not a natural subject. This may seem odd for, of man's creations, gardens are among the most alluring. But gardens have already been designed, pictures consciously made within them, their views contrived, and vistas terminated. The artist is not inspired to merely copy a ready-made form. He looks for the unusual, or more often the commonplace, turning it into art by his unique perception. Amateur artists on the other hand have found the garden a prime source of subject matter. All those long Victorian and Edwardian summer afternoons with little to do, or so we imagine, what better than to seek out some shade and sit down and paint the garden. Such luxury of course applied only to the financially stable, but there must be thousands of such amateur depictions up and down the country, hidden in attics or decorating some lesser part of the house, much of it dubious art, but all invaluable reference material.

From its hesitant beginnings in the late 1830s, photography has become the backbone of pictorial reference material. In addition, there is no doubt that in the hands of great photographers their work transcends into art. One of the earliest photographs of a Norfolk garden was taken by William Bolding of Weybourne. A corner of his garden probably taken in the 1850s, showing beneath an ivy-clad wall two circular skeps (wicker beehives), an acanthus in flower, and a large planted pot. It is just such a corner a painter would have relished. The photograph is pleasing, but this one could not claim to be art, although the photographer may well have chosen this fragment precisely to mirror an artist's choice of composition.

Some of P. H. Emerson's work could be thought in its composition and evocation of atmosphere and place, to rise above the mere capturing of an image, and he himself believed in the power of the photographic medium as a fine art. In Norfolk he is famed for his beautiful portfolio of pictures published under the title *Life and Landscape on the Norfolk Broads*, 1886. The few gardens he chose as his subject matter were in Suffolk. Norfolk needs to look to the work of Walter Clutterbuck (1853–1937). His fine photographic output is yet to be properly evaluated. Born in Chippenham, he had the wealth and time to travel extensively – he wrote travel guides to locations as diverse as Borneo and the Arctic. He also became a plant collector and an accomplished amateur photographer, often using a stereoscopic camera. In 1898–9 he travelled and photographed extensively in Japan. When not travelling, he lived in Norfolk, first at

Northrepps Cottage then at Marsham Hall. In the county he photographed a diverse range of topics: marshmen, fishermen, the interior of churches, harvesting, the coast, and gardens. Two calm and sensitive studies portrayed his wife, Violet, herself a talented amateur artist, in a cottage garden in Blakeney. In one she looks out to sea amid of mix of plants, with alliums growing

Corner of a Garden in Weybourne. William Bolding, c.1850s.

A Blakeney Garden. Walter Clutterbuck, c.1900.

or laid out to dry in the foreground. The path she is standing on leads to a curious garden shed, fashioned in part from an upturned boat. Walter Clutterbuck also photographed Blickling and the grounds and topography of both his Norfolk homes.

A largely self-taught artist was Catherine Maude Nichols (1847–1923). Norwich born, she depicted Norfolk landscapes and many Norwich street scenes and buildings, including some gardens. She worked across a broad range of mediums, but it is through

Carrow Abbey. Catherine Maude Nichols, 1905. Drypoint etching.

her drypoint etchings that she is best known, over 200 of them, some of excellent quality. She produced titles such as *Shady Garden Scene* and *Garden with Flower Beds*. Her painting of the Bethel Hospital in Norwich, then still a mental institution shows much of the building, including one bay window, clad in creepers or ivy. There is a clipped yew hedge with semi-circular arches, flower borders, paths and lawn. Other scenes show Crown Point, Eaton and Carrow Abbey.

The period 1880–1920 is seen as the golden age of English garden painting, certainly in quantity. To the fore, along with Birkett Foster, Helen Allingham, Ernest Chadwick, must rank Ernest Arthur Rowe, George Samuel Elgood and Beatrice Parsons. Not in their league, Cyril Ward's (1863–1935) works can at best be described as competent period pieces. Predominantly working in watercolour he specialized in landscapes, topographical scenes and gardens, including his own in Surrey. In his book *Royal Gardens* (1912), he produced six views of the garden at Sandringham. There are early colour photographs of Sandringham at exactly this period, but it needed the eye of the watercolourist to record the opulent mood of the gardens then at their peak. He depicts the huge swathes of herbaceous planting weaving their way through the trees near the house, like everything at Sandringham, on a prodigious scale. The walled garden of sixteen acres boasted a monumental pergola, fragments of which remain, (see page 435), which Ward depicts dripping and swagged with climbers – roses, jasmines, and honeysuckles which grew here to perfection. Beyond the pergola lay one of the garden's wonders, the double herbaceous borders, these truly Herculean, each four yards wide

ABOVE *Herbaceous Planting to the West of Sandringham House.* Cyril Ward, 1912. Watercolour.
BELOW *August Flowers, The Pleasaunce, Overstrand.* Beatrice Parsons, c.1910. Watercolour.

and over 300 long. Such floral opulence as this has never been bettered.

That opulence was depicted in paint by Beatrice Parsons (1869–1955). She was born in London, studied at the Royal Academy schools, and later set up her studio in Hertfordshire. Cyril Flower, Lord Battersea, commissioned her to paint views of his garden at The Pleasaunce in Overstrand. Edwin Lutyens had extended the house and given architectural garden advice, but it was Cyril and Constance Flower who designed the garden. It was not the design but the planting which interested Beatrice. Not for nothing has she been described as 'the Queen of the blazing border'. She painted the Edwardian garden and those of the inter-war period when they were at their luxuriant zenith, the borders overflowing and brilliant. Her depiction of those at The Pleasaunce could have become a formless blur of gawdy colour, but her draughtsmanship and precision saw each flower clearly delineated.

She would return many times to The Pleasaunce recording a period of labour-

A Border in the Parterre Garden at Blickling. Beatrice Parsons, c.1925. Watercolour.

intensive garden exuberance, now long gone. She also painted frequently at Blickling Hall. Her watercolour of the parterre shows the planting in the garden as designed by Constance, Lady Lothian, before the simplification in the 1930s carried out by Norah Lindsay. Massed banks of flowers of every hue tumble on to the lawns in a superabundance of late summer colour, with the Oxnead fountain and the east front of the hall behind. This, and others Blickling compositions such as the more muted *Entrance to the Kitchen Garden* and *Garden Steps*, although verging on chocolate-box material, are skilfully controlled into accomplished pieces of garden painting.

It was not only the photograph which rendered the literal pictorial recording of gardens unnecessary. In the twentieth century the camera, from box brownie to the revolution of digital, was joined by newsreel, home cine-camera, video, and importantly – in the second half of the century – television, all of which were left to record the century's gardens. This freed the artist to dwell on garden atmosphere or detail. Although some chose to abstract the landscape, particularly Paul Nash (1889–1946), John Nash (1893–1977), and Graham Sutherland (1903–1980), unfortunately for Norfolk, none of these artists worked there. The garden itself was rarely treated as a subject for abstraction. The twentieth century concentrated on painting the ordinary in the garden; corners of the suburban garden, and views over unremarkable and often neglected back plots. Here unruly nature, and often very untidy man, presented fruitful compositions: a section of a half-dug allotment, apples trees, a crowded washing-line, a broken gate, abandoned bike or pram and the ubiquitous garden shed. The ordered designed garden was ignored as the garden in paint was marginalized. It would be difficult indeed to judge the twentieth-century's garden achievements through its art.

There were exceptions. John Piper's (1903–1992) highly distinctive work typically has architecture as its main subject matter, in particular, churches, halls and manor

The Potting Shed. Kate Gabriel, 2017. Acrylics on canvas board. The artist was born in Leeds, and this is her own garden at Manor Gates, Ludham. Interest here is derived from a working corner and its detail, rather than a whole garden scene.

Holkham. John Piper, 1939. Oil.

houses. In Norfolk he painted many churches, as well as East Barsham Manor and the neo-Gothic of Shadwell Park. Gardens are a theme, but not as frequent. However, just before the outbreak of the Second World War he produced a marvellously 'abstract' depiction of the Holkham grounds, with the hall (turned a haystack yellow), the *St George and the Dragon* fountain, lake, Leicester Monument, the church and dark woods, all under a complex faceted sky, blocked with white and black cloud. It is Piper at his best. Later he returned to paint William Kent's Triumphal Arch. Originally this was the main gateway into the estate from the south and sets the tone for what is to come. Taking a straightforward symmetrical viewpoint Piper shows through the arch's high central opening the long avenue, bordered by *Quercus ilex*, leading to Kent's obelisk in the far distance. The execution of the work is far from straightforward with Piper's seemingly relaxed but fast strokes employing his highly original palette of colours. In his screenprint much black is used, the trees and grass highlighted with oranges and greens.

His second Norfolk garden was Sandringham; *View Across the Lake to the House* was painted in 1970. An obvious viewpoint, but always a good one, this is a strong piece of garden design, with the foreground lake, a rich planting of shrubs and waterside plants and trees, framing the house beyond. Again, it is carried out in the distinctive Piper manner. The red brick of the house dominates, balanced by the greens of the planting. A typical touch, the waters of the lake are black. It is a lively and free interpretation. The picture was commissioned by Queen Elizabeth the Queen Mother.

ABOVE *The Triumphal Arch, Holkham*. John Piper, 1976. Screenprint on paper.
BELOW *Sandringham*. John Piper, 1970. Drawing in pencil, pen and ink, wax resist, indian ink, bodycolour and coloured chalks.

Art of a very different kind is the quirky and often humorous work of Brian Lewis. Born in Surrey, he moved to Norfolk in 1981, and has his home and studio in Sheringham. His paintings of the seals at Blakeney Point have achieved iconic status, prints of which sell round the world. The seals, like so many plump and elderly gentlemen propped up against a sandbank, stare at the boats of tourists, who stare back at them. Other subjects include many Norfolk buildings and landscapes, and several gardens. Typically Lewis's work is brilliantly lit, the colours are pure technicolor, and the whole is laced with humour. He is much quoted as saying he only paints the sunny days and not the dull ones. 'I leave the grey days and angst for others.' His work certainly adds to the variety of depictions of Norfolk gardens in art. Among them are aerial perspectives of both Blickling and Voewood, the latter faithfully depicting what Pevsner described as the 'violently idiosyncratic' butterfly house of 1905 and its garden design, with beyond, the fields and woods, and a ribbon of sea. The lodges at Felbrigg also appear, a corner of the Old Vicarage garden at East Ruston and several works commissioned by garden owners, among them the hall and garden at Swafield.

Voewood. Brian Lewis, 2017. Acrylic.

East Ruston Old Vicarage. Brian Lewis, 2000. Acrylic.

And that variety was enhanced in 2008 by Anthony Green RA. He chooses as his prime source material his own middle-class life, set in ordinary domestic interiors. These figurative and narrative works are highly distinctive and recognizable by their irregular-shaped canvasses, the use of bright colour and the often extreme, manipulation of perspective. So, his depiction of the Old Hall and gardens at Stiffkey, although in subject matter not unique in his output, comes as something of a departure. Although basically rectangular, the edges of his canvas have his characteristic irregularity and the perspective is distorted too, although not compound as is often the case. The view is from high up revealing the hall, its terraced gardens and its various outbuildings, running from the sea and Stiffkey church at the top of the canvas, down to the River Stiffkey which runs along the bottom. The work was commissioned by the then owners of the hall, John and Anne Bell, who refurbished much of the hall and commissioned Arne

Maynard to recreate the terraced gardens in the spirit of the original seventeenth-century layout. Whereas in the seventeenth century the garden was usually glimpsed in the background of a large portrait of its owner, here the opposite is the case, the owner (and his dog) is glimpsed, a small figure standing in the foreground on a bridge, plan in hand, highly subservient to his house and garden, but nonetheless proudly showing it off and his achievements. This drones-eye view, which in fact is nearly possible from the top of the steep hill opposite the garden, clearly depicts its layout and chief features, in much the same way as the earliest of Norfolk's surviving garden paintings, that of Ryston Hall. There too its owner is seen as a small figure at the bottom of the canvas. Garden depiction over more than three centuries turned full circle.

It is noticeable over the centuries how infrequently Norfolk gardens have been painted or used for inspiration, especially considering how many there are. Among those works which do exist, there is no Monet or great art here, however, there is a richness and diversity of both style and treatment of subject matter. The twenty-first century will certainly add its own unique artistic view of the ever-increasing creative flair and variety displayed in the county's gardens. The camera can accurately record the image, but it takes the unique vision of the artist to add insight and perceptive creativity, and to capture more intensely the mood and feel of the garden.

Stiffkey Old Hall. Anthony Green, 2008. Oil.

Acknowledgements

All books are the product of collaboration and I am most grateful to all of those who have helped to bring this book together. My thanks must go to Matthew Martin, the chair of the Norfolk Gardens Trust for suggesting the idea for the book, and to the Trust's committee for their backing in what has proved to be an extended period. My particular thanks go to Sally Bate for her encouragement and help in many ways; to Hetty Burdon for her precision in proofreading and constant querying in the pursuit of exactitude, and to Kaarin Wall for her visual flair and design skills in putting this book together. There would be no book if it was not for my fellow contributors and their generosity in giving their time to research and write the articles. I give my special thanks to them and to all those who helped provide material, who allowed access to their properties, and who allowed images in their possession to be copied. My specials thanks here to David Clarke who put his extensive archive at our disposal; and to those who assisted in finding material or allowed their images to be used; to Gerard Stamp for his addition of atmospheric images of Gunton, to Eddie Anderson for access to his Templewood archive, to the Brundall Local History Group, to Angela Reid for the use of her Didlington archive, to Mike Page for his aerial shots and to John Fielding who took especially commissioned new ones. Among those also to thank are: Erica Bailey, Wednesday Batchelor, Penelope Billington, Barbara Bryant, the Marquess of Cholmondeley, Paul Clarke, Tom Cook, Charlotte Crawley, Keith Day, Colin de Chair, Rosemary Dixon, Clare Everitt, Kate Gabriel, Simon Gaches, Adrian Gamble, Sam Garland, Annie Green-Armytage, Jon Haggerwood, Fi Hitchcock, Debbie Hooks, Derek Kemp, David King, the Earl of Leicester, Brian Lewis, Kit Martin, Hugh Mason, Michael Mason, Frank Meeres, John Morley, Janet Muter, Shirley Place, Jonathan Plunkett, Nigel Pope, Chris Poole, David Pulling, Peter Sheppard, John Simmons, Mark Spires, Geoff Stebbings, Tony Stimpson, Elizabeth Stretton, Nigel Surry, Charles and Virginia Temple-Richards, the Marquess and Marchioness Townshend, the Rt Revd Graham Usher, Bishop of Norwich, Chloe Veale, Norma Watt, Peter Woodrow, Geoffrey and Etta Wyatt.

While every effort has gone into checking the facts and dates, errors do occur, and I apologize to those readers who find any as I know how irritating such mistakes can be, to them and to me in particular.

Sources and Further Reading

1 Norfolk's Switzerland
Brundall Local History Group, *The Book of Brundall & Braydeston*, 'Brundall Gardens' by Doreen Oliver (Halsgrove, 2007).
Muter, W. G. and J. C., *A Hundred Years in Brundall Gardens* (1987).
Patterson, A. H., *Brundall on the Broads* (pamphlet, 1920s).
Peart, Stephen, *The Picture House in East Anglia* (Terence Dalton Limited, 1980).
With special thanks to Janet Muter for her source material, and to the Brundall Local History Group.

2 The Leicester Monument
Documentary sources
Holkham Archives: Architectural Plans by Donthorn; Estate Office Letter Books, including Agricultural Letter Book.
Published sources
Bacon, R. N., with foreword by Robert Leamon, *A Narrative of the Proceedings regarding the erection of the Leicester Monument* (Norwich, 1850).
Stirling, A. M. W., *The Letter Bag of Lady Elizabeth Spencer Stanhope* (London, 1913).
Further reading
Hiskey, Christine, *Holkham: the social, architectural and landscape history of a great English country house* (Unicorn Press, Norwich, 2016).
Wade Martins, Susanna, *A Great Estate at Work: the Holkham Estate and its Inhabitants in the Nineteenth Century* (Cambridge, 1980).
Wade Martins, Susanna, *Coke of Norfolk, 1754–1842: A Biography* (Woodbridge, 2009).

3 My Lord's Garden
Beer, E. S. (ed.), *The Diary of John Evelyn*, 6 vols., (Oxford Clarendon, 1955).
Blomefield, Francis, *An Essay towards a Topographical History of the County of Norfolk*, 5 vols. (Lynn, W. Wittingham, 1739–75).
Doubleday, Herbert A. (ed.), *The Victoria History of the County of Norfolk*, vol. ii, (London, 1901).
Historical Manuscripts Commission – *Portland*, vol. ii, (London, HMSO, 1893).
Kent, E. A., 'The Houses of the Dukes of Norfolk in Norwich' (*Journal of the Norfolk and Norwich Archaeological Society*, 24, pp. 73–87, 1931).
www.gilliandarley.com
   The full text of this article which includes three paragraphs relating to Albury Park in Surrey can be found in *Garden History: Journal of the Garden History Society*, winter 2006. 34:2, pp. 249–253, entitled 'John Evelyn's Norwich Garden'.

4 The Eastern Arboretum
Advertisements and multiple references (*Gardeners' Chronicle and Agricultural Gazette*).
Advertisement for the Eastern Arboretum (*Norwich Mercury*, October 1841).

Advertisement for the sale of stock on 17th and 18th November at Town Close Nursery (*Norfolk Chronicle and Norwich Gazette*, November 1848).

Census Return for Norwich (1841).

Grigor, James, *The Eastern Arboretum, or Register of Remarkable Trees* (Longman & Co., 1841).

Grigor, James, *To the Planters of England and Lovers of the Picturesque*, advertisement with reference from the Duke of Newcastle and quote from Wordsworth's letter (*Gardeners' Chronicle and Agricultural Gazette*, 1 February 1845).

Grigor, James, *Report on Trimingham & Runton Plantations in the County of Norfolk, Belonging to Sir Edward North Buxton Baronet*.

Loudon, John Claudius, *Arboretum et Fruticetum Britannica* (1838).

Loudon, John Claudius, *Reviews of the Eastern Arboretum* (*Gardeners Magazine*, 1840 and 1841).

Minute Book (Norwich Union Archive, 1847–51).

Obituary (*Norfolk Chronicle and Norwich Gazette*, 6 May 1848).

Obituary (*Inverness Courier*, 9 May 1848).

Obituary (*Aberdeen Press & Journal*, 17 May 1848).

OS First Edition map, Norwich (Ordnance Survey, 1883).

Probate, Birth, Marriage and Death Records (Public Record Office).

References to Grigor's prize-winning essay on 'Classes of Farm Fencing in Nottinghamshire' (*Journal of the Royal Agricultural Society*, 5 April 1845 and 16 August 1845).

Rosary Cemetery Norwich; Burial Records and Cemetery Plan, Section E, Plot 780 (Norfolk Record Office).

Strutt, Jacob George, *Sylva Britannica; or Portraits of Trees, Distinguished for Their Antiquity, Magnitude or Beauty* (1830).

Transactions of the Highland Agricultural Society of Scotland, vol. 6, pp. 557–574 (January 1847).

5 The Maharajah is Well Satisfied

Boulton and Paul catalogues (1866–1898).

Boulton and Paul pamphlets, *Distinctive Buildings for Garden and Estate* (1935).

Corporate authors, *The Leaf and the Tree, the Story of Boulton and Paul Ltd, 1797–1947* (1947).

Gurney-Read, Joyce, *The Trades and Industries of Norwich* (Gliddon Press, Norwich, 1988).

6 George Skipper's Sennowe Masterpiece

Aslet, Clive, *The Last Country Houses* (Book Club Associates, London, 1982).

Bryant, A., *Map of the County of Norfolk 1826* (Norfolk Record Office).

Country Life, 24 December 1981, pp. 2242–2245; 31 December 1981, pp. 2298–2301.

Elliott, Brent, *Victorian Gardens* (Timber Press, 1986).

Faden, W., *A new topographical map of the county of Norfolk 1797* (Norfolk Record Office).

Jolly, David, and Skipper, Edward (eds.), *One Hundred Years of Architecture, 1880–1980: George Skipper, Edward Skipper and Associates, 'George Skipper – Architect Exuberant'* (Norwich, 1980).

Journal of Horticulture and Cottage Gardener (December 1892, p. 507).

Kenworthy-Browne, J., et al., *Burke's and Savills Guide III* (1981).

Map of the Sennowe estate, accompanying 1898 sale particulars (dated 1887).

OS Maps: 6" to 1 mile:
first edition published 1891;
second edition published 1907;
third edition published 1905.
OS 25" to 1 mile: first edition published 1885; second edition published 1906 (Ordnance Survey).

Pevsner, N., *The Buildings of England: North-West and South Norfolk* (1962).

Sale Particulars, Sennowe Park 1850 (MC30 MS 18622/185, Norfolk Record Office).

Sale Particulars, Sennowe Park 1887–1898; *Norfolk Local Studies Library Map of the parish of Guist 1785* (46 BCH, Norfolk Record Office).

Thomas, Steven, *The Architecture of George Skipper*, unpublished thesis for DipBldgCon. (RICS), College of Estate Management (Reading University, 2005).

Tithe Map of the Parish of Great Ryburgh, undated c.1845 (PI50 b/5, Norfolk Record Office).

Unpublished report on Sennowe Park (UEA Centre of East Anglian Studies, 1988).

Williamson, Tom, *The Archaeology of the Landscape Park: garden design in Norfolk, England c.1680–1840* (BAR British Series 268, 1998).

7   The Business of Gardening

Clark, K., *What the Nurserymen Did for Us: The Roles and Influence on the Landscapes and Gardens of the Eighteenth Century* (Garden History, 40, pp. 17–33, 2012).

Harvey, J. H., *Early Nurserymen* (Phillimore, Winchester, 1974).

Harvey, J. H., *Leonard Gurle's Nurseries and Some Others* (Garden History 3, pp. 42–9, 1975).

Williamson, T., *The Archaeology of the Landscape Park: garden design in Norfolk, England, c.1680–1840* (Archaeopress, Oxford, 1998).

8   The Pleasure Gardens of Norwich

Darley, Gillian, 'John Evelyn's Norwich Garden' (*Garden History*, Journal of the Garden History Society, Winter 2006).

Darley, Gillian, 'My Lord's Garden' (*Norfolk Gardens Trust Journal*, 2008).

Doderer-Winkler, Melanie, *Magnificent Pleasures* (Yale University Press, 2013).

Downing, Sarah Jane, *The English Pleasure Garden 1660–1820* (Shire Publications, 2009).

Fawcett, Trevor, 'The Norwich Pleasure Gardens' (*Norfolk Archaeology*, vol. XXXV, part 111, 1972).

Stevens Curl, James, *Spas, Wells and Pleasure-Gardens of London* (Historical Publications Ltd, 2010).

Winstanley, Roy (ed.), *The Diary of James Woodforde, vol. 9, 1780–1781* (The Parson Woodforde Society, 2000).

9   Botanic Connoisseur

'Cool Greenhouse Plants for Everyman' (*Journal of the Royal Horticultural Society*, vol. LXXXV, pp. 440–7).

Fletcher, Harold R., Initial quotation from *The Story of the Royal Horticultural Society 1804–1968*, p. 352 (Oxford University Press, 1969).

Hellyer, Arthur, 'The Gardens of a Great Collector' (*Country Life*, 4 Mar 1982).

Lees-Milne, Alvilde and Verey, Rosemary, *The Englishman's Garden* (Penguin, 1982).

Lloyd, Christopher, 'Friends Remembered' (*The Guardian*, 24 December 2005).

Mason, L. Maurice, 'Trip to Madagascar, January–February 1965' (*Journal of the Royal Horticultural Society* vol. 91 (3), pp. 121–6., 1966).

Mason, L. Maurice, 'The Travels of a Plant Collector' (*Journal of the Royal Horticultural Society*, vol. 94, pp. 481–9, 1969).

Morrison, Alasdair, 'Maurice Mason, a Tribute' (*The Garden*, vol. CXIX, pp. 102–3).

Simmons, John, 'A Living Memorial' (*The Garden*, vol. CXIX pp. 368–371).

10 Hortus Episcopi

Dean and Chapter, 1859, Lease map of Bishop's palace grounds (Norfolk Record Office).

Fernie, E., *An Architectural History of Norwich Cathedral* (Oxford: Clarendon, 1993).

Maps of Norwich: Clere 1696, Hochstetter 1789, Millard 1830, Morant 1873, Ordnance Survey 1885 and later editions.

Muir, Dorothy Erskine, *Lift the Curtain* (1955).

Norfolk Archaeology, 186, vol. VI, pp. 27–37.

Pevsner, Nikolaus, and Wilson, Bill, *The Buildings of England – Norfolk 1:*

Norwich and North-East (Penguin Books, 1997).
Whittlingham, A. B., *Plan of Norwich Cathedral Priory of the Holy Trinity* (1938).

11 A Parterre by Two Ladies

Blickling, Garden, Park and Estate (The National Trust, 1999).
Blickling Hall (The National Trust, 1987, revised 2003).
Brown, Jane, *Eminent Gardeners* (Viking, 1990).
Butler, J. R. M., *Lord Lothian (Philip Kerr)1882–1940* (Macmillan & Co Ltd, 1960).
Country Life (vol 67., 7 June 1930, p. 821).
Eastern Daily Press, 12 October 1901, MC3/985, (Norfolk Record Office).
'Gardens Old and New' (*Country Life*, 1900s).
Gardening World, The (vol. IV, 17 September 1887).
Gardeners' Chronicle, The (3 November 1894, p. 534).
Hadfield, M., Harling, R., Highton, L., *British Gardeners* (A. Zwemmer Ltd, London, 1980).
Hayward, Allyson, *Norah Lindsay* (Frances Lincoln Limited, 2007).
Pevsner, Nikolaus, and Wilson, Bill, *The Buildings of England – Norfolk 1: Norwich and North-East* (Penguin Books, 1997).

12 The War Memorial Gardens, Norwich

The Architectural Review: A Magazine of Architecture and Decoration LXXXIV (Norwich Heritage Library).
Dixon Hunt, John, *Greater Perfections* (Thames and Hudson, 2000).
Minutes of the Norwich Markets Committee; Minutes of the Norwich Parks and Gardens Committee; Minutes of the Norwich City Council; Lord Mayors' papers (Norfolk County Archive).
Morton, Tim, and Gliddon, Gerald, *Lutyens and the Great War* (Frances Lincoln, 2010).

Nobbs, George, *Norwich City Hall* (1988).
Pevsner, Nikolaus, and Wilson, Bill, *The Buildings of England – Norfolk 1: Norwich and North-East* (Penguin Books, 1997).
The Times; The Eastern Daily Press; and *Norwich Evening News*.

13 Lakes in Norfolk Landscaped Parks

Bate, S. (ed.), *Capability Brown in Norfolk* (Norfolk Gardens Trust, 2016).
Bishop, W., *The Origins and Evolution of Ornamental Lakes* (Unpublished PhD thesis, University of East Anglia, 2017).
Williamson, T., *The Archaeology of the Landscape Park: garden design in Norfolk, England, c.1680–1840* (Archaeopress, Oxford, 1998).

14 Art and Industry

Barnards Ltd, a retrospect (Norwich 1911).
Bethel Hospital papers: 'Orders for the Reception of a Private Patient' (Norfolk Record Office).
Eastern Daily Press, 5 November 1880.
Eastern Daily Press, 24 October 1983.
Evening News, 8 November 1997.
Norfolk Annals, 1880, vol. II, 1851–1900.
Pevsner, Nikolaus, and Wilson, Bill, *The Buildings of England – Norfolk 1: Norwich and North-East* (Penguin Books, 1997).
Weber Soros, Susan, and Arbuthnott, Catherine, *Thomas Jeckyll, Architect and Designer* (The Bard Graduate Center for Studies in Decorative Art, Yale University Press, 2003).

15 The Holkham Fountain

Holkham Archives, documentary sources: Estate Office Letter Books, Architectural plans, Account books.

Published sources
Stacy, Henry W., *Guide to Holkham* (Norwich, 1861).
Gardeners' Chronicle, The, 16 October 1858.
James Easton's obituary, 1871: http://www.greenandcarter.com/main/obituary.htm (accessed 2016).

On the fountain's recent history: https://www.holkham.co.uk/visiting/the-hall/the-fountain (accessed 2019).

Raymond Smith, Charles, *Mapping the Practice and Profession of Sculpture in Britain and Ireland 1851–1951* (University of Glasgow History of Art and HATII, online database 2011: http://sculpture.gla.ac.uk, accessed 2019).

Roscoe, Ingrid; Hardy, Emma; and Sullivan, M. G. (eds.), *A Biographical Dictionary of Sculptors in Britain 1660–1851* (Yale, 2009, for Charles Raymond Smith).

Further reading

Hiskey, Christine, *Holkham: the social, architectural and landscape history of a great English country house* (Unicorn Press, Norwich, 2016).

16 Carrow and the Colmans

Cantell, Judith, *Norfolk Gardens Trust Journal*, 'Carrow Conservatory' (Spring 2005, pp. 25–29).

Carrow News, Carrow Magazine (quarterly 1905–1992, various).

Colman, Helen Caroline, *Jeremiah James Colman, a Memoir* (Privately printed at the Chiswick Press, 1905).

Colman, Helen Caroline, 'Carrow House Past and Present' (*Carrow Works Magazine*, April 1922, pp. 51–54).

Colman's of Norwich, Information Guide No. 3 (Unilever Archives & Records Management).

Edgar, S. H., *The Story of Carrow Abbey; The History of J. & J. Colman* (1970s).

Gurney-Read, Joyce, *The Colman Family; Trade and Business Colmans* (1990).

Jones, Henry, *List of Trees and shrubs planted in Carrow Garden, Norwich* (Unilever, Port Sunlight, 1924).

Pevsner, Nikolaus, and Wilson, Bill, *The Buildings of England – Norfolk 1: Norwich and North-East* (Penguin Books, 1997).

Rye, Walter, *Carrow Abbey* (limited edition, 1889).

Story of Colman's Mustard-Growing, The.

Taigel, Anthea, *Town Gardens Survey, Norwich* (Norfolk Gardens Trust, 1997).

17 The Renaissance of Gunton Park

Armstrong, M. J., *History and Antiquities of Norfolk* (1781).

Carter, G., et al., *Humphry Repton Landscape Gardener 1752–1818*, pp. 158–9 (Sainsbury Centre for Visual Arts, 1982).

Country Life, no. 179 (9 June 1960), pp. 1296–9; no. 51 (21 December 1989), pp. 48–53; no. 1 (2 January 1997), pp. 24–5.

The Grove, Gunton Park, Norfolk: Assessment of Importance [addendum to restoration plan prepared in 1990] (Debois Landscape Survey Group, 1997).

Jones, B., *Follies & Grottoes* (Constable, 1974).

Journal of Garden History, vol. 11, nos. 1 and 2, pp. 45–7 (1991).

Landscape No. 1, pp. 36–41 (October 1987).

Pevsner, Nikolaus, and Wilson, Bill, *The Buildings of England – Norfolk 1: Norwich and North-East* (Penguin Books, 1997).

Williamson, T., *The Archaeology of the Landscape Park: garden design in Norfolk, c.1680–1840* (BAR British Series 268, pp. 237–8, 1998).

Willis, P., *Charles Bridgeman and the English Landscape Garden* (Elysium Press Publishers, 2001).

18 Didlington's Golden Age

'The Didlington Hall Estate and its Owner' (*Norfolk Chronicle*, 21 November 1885).

Duggan, Brian Patrick, *Saluki: The Desert Hound and the English Travelers Who Brought It to the West* (McFarland, 2009).

Minter, Sue, *The Well-Connected Gardener* (The Book Guild, 2010).

Particulars of Sale, Didlington Estate, 1910 (Norfolk Record Office).

Sydney Morning Herald (19 January 1909, p. 7).

Taranaki Herald (21 January 1909, p. 3).

Trimbee, James William, *Memories of Didlington Hall* (Norfolk Record Office).

Trimbee, James W., and Trimbee McKenzie, Jean, *A Trail of Trials* (The Pentland Press, 1995).
The Washington Post (21 August 1906, p. 6).

19 Some Norfolk Gardens Illustrated by Edmund Prideaux

Campbell, Colen, *Vitruvius Britannicus*, vol. iii (c.1722, London).
Harris, J., *The Prideaux Collection of Topographic Drawings* (Architectural History 7, pp. 17–39, 1964).
Harris, J., *The Architecture of the House* (1996).
Moore, A. (ed.), *Houghton Hall: the Prime Minister, the Empress and the Heritage* (Norfolk Museums Service, Norwich).
Kip, J., and Knyff, L., *Britannia Illustrata* (London, 1707).
Taigel, A., and Williamson, T., *Some Early Geometric Gardens in Norfolk* (Journal of Garden History vol. 11, nos. 1 and 2, 1991).
Walpole, H., *Essay on Modern Gardening* (London, 1784).
Williamson, T., *The Archaeology of the Landscape Park: garden design in Norfolk, England, c.1680–1840* (Archaeopress, Oxford, 1998).
Williamson, T., 'A Pipeline Trench at Houghton Hall' (*Norfolk Archaeology* XLVI, 4, pp. 526–37, 2013).

20 Templewood

Hoare, Sir Samuel, 'Templewood, Norfolk. The Shooting-Box of the Rt. Hon. Sir Samuel Hoare ... described by himself' (*Country Life*, 4 February 1939).
Templewood, Viscount, *The Unbroken Tread* (Collins, 1949).

21 Heyrick 'Tony' Greatorex's Garden, Snowdrop Acre

Bishop, M., Davis, A., and Grimshaw, J., *A Monograph of Cultivated Galanthus* (The Griffin Press, Maidenhead, 2001).
Thanks are due to Sonia Greatorex, Penelope Billington and Erica Bailey for research into and information about Heyrick Greatorex's life.

22 James Pulham & Son at Sandringham

The Art Journal Illustrated Catalogue of the International Exhibition, 1862, p. 162 (Published 1863).
Cathcart, Helen, *Sandringham: the Story of a Royal Home* (1964).
Gardeners' Chronicle, 3 September 1892, p. 268.
Gardeners' Chronicle, 21 June 1902, p. 407.
Hitching, Claude, *Rock Landscapes – The Pulham Legacy* (Garden Art Press, 2012).
Journal of Horticulture, Cottage Gardener (Royal Photograph Collection, Windsor Castle).
Pulham Company Catalogue, *Garden ornament, vases; terminals; pedestals; sundials; seats; fountains; balustrades; figures etc.* (1915).
Pulham, James, *Picturesque Ferneries and Rock-Garden Scenery* (1877).
1871 Photograph Album in the Royal Archive, Windsor Castle (No. 22 in the illustrated Pulham catalogue, 1915).

23 Norfolk's Gardens in Art

Hobhouse, Penelope, and Wood, Christopher, *Painted Gardens* (Pavilion Books, 1988).
Turner, Peter, and Wood, Richard, *P. H. Emerson: Photographer of Norfolk* (Gordon Fraser Photographic Monographs, 1974).
Ward, Cyril, *Royal Gardens* (Longmans, Green & Co, 1912).
Williamson, Tom, and Taigel, Anthea, *Gardens in Norfolk* (Centre of East Anglian Studies, 1990).

Picture Credits

The Norfolk Gardens Trust is most grateful to all those individuals and institutions who allowed access to and use of their illustrative material: prints, etchings, paintings, archive photographs and original contemporary photographs. Every effort has been made to contact the owners of the material. Where this has failed, the Trust hopes they will take pleasure in seeing their photographs used in this book.

Picture Research, Principal and Archive Photography by Roger Last

2/3, 4–6, 13–16, 32, 33, 36/37, 39, 41, 43, 44, 46, 47, 60, 61, 102/103, 107, 108, 109 bottom, 111 middle, bottom, 112 insert, 114, 116–118 top, 119, 121, 160, 161, 164, 166, 172, 176–179, 181, 182, 184–187, 200, 202/203, 204, 205 bottom, 206, 216 top, 218, 220–227, 228/229 top, 230, 231 bottom, 239 bottom, 240/241 bottom, 241 centre, 244 bottom, 247 bottom, 254, 255, 257 bottom, 258, 267 top, 269–272, 280–288, 290–293, 294/295 bottom, 303, 307, 312 top, 315 top, 316, 318–322, 324, 328–331, 333, 342/343 top, 344–346, 358 top, 362, 368–370, 373, 386, 388, 397, 399 top, 400, 402 bottom, 403–405, 421, 426–429, 432 top left, 436/437, 473, 475, 480.

With the exception of, or material provided by:

Agnews 446. **Eddie Anderson** 387, 389, 390–396, 398, 399 bottom, 401, 402 top. **Archant Norfolk** 148, 152, 213, 214/215, 219. **Penelope Bailey** 408 bottom, 409, 410. **Sally Bate** 29, 195 top, 134/135 bottom, 256/257 top, 266 top, 327 top, 367, 435 top, 452 top. **Courtesy the Bodleian Library, Oxford** 234 top. **Brundall Local History Group** 17–28, 30/31. **David Clarke** 62–64, 68–74 top, 76–83 top, 84, 85, 87–101, 103 insert, 299, 300 bottom, 301, 302, 313, 314. **Val Corbett** 201, 205 top. **Country Life** 192, 197, 198. **Colin de Chair** 337, 338/339. **John Donat** 332, 336 top. **Clarissa Dormer** 249. **His Grace the Duke of Norfolk, Arundel Castle/Bridgeman Images** 48, 58 top. **Brian Ellis** 412 bottom, 413 right, 416 top. **John Fielding** 112/113, 174, 183, 242/243, 244 top, 246 bottom, 298 bottom, 325. **Valerie Finnis/RHS Collections** 146. **The Francis Frith Collection** 432 bottom. **Kate Gabriel** 460. **Annie Green-Armytage** 180. **Pauline Harrold** 454. **Allyson Hayward:** Courtesy of Allyson Hayward author of *Norah Lindsay:*

The Life and Art of a Garden Designer 188, 191, 199 right. **Christine Hiskey** 289. **Richard Hobbs** 406, 408 top, 411, 412 top, 418. © **Holkham Estate** 34, 36 insert, 45, 238/239 top, 276, 277, 279, 295 top. **Jstor.org** 350. **Courtesy of Judy's Snowdrops** 417. **David King** 413 left, 416 right, 419. **Scilla Latham** 74 bottom, 83 bottom, 430, 432 top right, 433, 434, 435 bottom. **Brian Lewis** 463, 464. **Local Studies Library, Norwich** 140 bottom, 141. **Ludham Community Archive** 306, 317. **Hugh Mason** 150. **Michael Mason** 154, 156, 159, 162, 163. © **National Portrait Gallery London** 208. **National Trust** 190, 193, 194, 199 left, 236, 237 bottom, 376, 447 bottom. **Norfolk and Norwich Archaeological Society** 57 right. **Image courtesy of Norfolk County Council at www.picture.norfolk.gov.uk** 86, 106 right, 142, 144/145, 173, 196, 217, 248, 250, 251, 253, 261, 264/265, 298 top, 300 top, 304 top, 323, 347, 356, 360/361, 455–457. **Norfolk Museums Service (Norwich Castle & Art Gallery)** 67, 296, 310, 311, 447, 448, 452 bottom. **Norfolk Record Office** 125, 228 bottom, 252, 263. **Oak Springs Garden Library, Virginia** 450. **OS Maps reproduced by kind permission of Ordnance Survey** 175, 312, 359, 436. **Mike Page** 35, 167, 231 top, 232/233, 237 top, 240 top, 246/247 top, 374/375. © **The Piper Estate/DACS 2020** 461. **George Plunkett – by kind permission of Jonathan Plunkett** 57 left, 59, 135 top, 137, 170, 209, 211, 212, 216 bottom, 266 bottom, 267 bottom, 268. **Collection of Peter Prideaux-Brune, Prideaux Place, Padstow** 378, 380, 383, 384. **Private Collection** 104, 105, 106 left, 110, 111 top, 115, 118 bottom, 120, 122 (courtesy of Pamela Clarke), 140 top, 228 bottom (courtesy of David Brown), 241 top, 438–441, 443, 444/445, 465, 469. **David Pulling** 449. **Angela Reid** 348, 349, 351–355, 357 top, 358, 363–366, 371, 372. **Royal Collection Trust/© Her Majesty Queen Elizabeth II 2021** 256 bottom, 422, 425. **Royal Collection Trust/All Rights Reserved** 462 bottom. **RHS Lindley Library** 274/275. **RIBA Collections** 210, 278. © **The Royal Society** 50. **Gerard Stamp** 326, 334/335, 340/341, 342, 466. **Geoff Stebbings** 149, 151. **Suffolk Museums** 260 bottom. **Will & Elsie Tjaden/RHS Lindley Collections** 158. **Michael Warren** 157. **Courtesy of The Weiss Gallery, London** 10, 49. **Tom Williamson** 126. **Courtesy of the Christopher Wood Gallery** 459. **Yale Center for British Art** 234 bottom. From *A Prospect of Britain*, Samuel and Nathaniel Buck, 54, 55, 128 top, 130. Boulton and Paul Catalogues 1880–1911, 84, 85, 87–97, 100, 101. From *Country Seats of the Noblemen and Gentlemen of Great Britain and Ireland* (1870), illustration by Alexander Lydon, 327. From *The Eastern Arboretum*, James Grigor, 62–64, 68–74 top, 76–83 top. From *The Gardens of England*, E. A. Brooke (1857) 274/275. From *The Gardens of England in the Midland and Eastern Counties*, Ed. Charles Holme (1908) 305, 315 bottom, 317 top. From *Royal Gardens*, Cyril Ward (1912) 420, 435 top, 458 top. From *Sandringham*, Mrs Herbert Jones, 424.

Index

Entries in **bold** refer to the Illustration captions

Aberconway, Lord **156**
Acer pseudoplatanus 'Brilliantissimum' 157
Adam, Robert 327, **328**, 329
Aesculus sinensis (Himalayan horse chestnut) 407
Aikman, William 377
Albert Edward, Prince of Wales 87, 90, **91**, 256, 257, **258**, 422, **422**, 424, 429, 431, 433
Alexandra, Princess **422**, 422, 427
Allen, William 332
Allingham, Helen 457
Alma-Tadema, Sir Lawrence **434**
Almey, Philip **339**
Amherst, Lady Sarah 357
Amherstia nobilis (the Pride of Burma) 357, **357**
Anderson, Eddie 403
Anglesey Abbey, Cambs 401
Aram, John 124
Aram, William 124
Araucaria excelsea (Brazilian pine) **80**, 80
Arisaema candidissimum 165
Aristolochia clematitis (birthwort) 319, **322**
Armstrong, Mostyn John 448
Arum maculatum (lords-and-ladies) 319
Atkinson, Robert 210
Aylsham Old Hall **441**, 441

Bacon, Lady Priscilla 150, 161
Barnard, Bishop and Barnards **249**, 250, **251**, 252
Barnard, Charles 250, **250**
Barningham 448
Barron, William **105**, 106, 114, 116

Basire, J. 56
Baskerville, Thomas 57, 59, **61**
Bayfield Park, water in 225, 245, **246–7**
Beales, Peter 181
Beck, William **41**
Bedford, Duke of **41**
Beeston St Lawrence, lake at **228–9**, 229, 245
Begonia masoniana, the 'Iron Cross' begonia 154–5, **155**
Bethel Hospital, Norwich 457
Beverley, Dr Michael 20, **20**, **21**, 22, **23**, 25, **25**, 26
Bicknell, Julian **362**
Bignold, C. R., Lord Mayor of Norwich 207
Birch, Steph **339**
Bishop Bridge, Norwich 54, **55**
Bishop, John 250
Bishop's Garden, the, Norwich 167, **167**, 168, **170–1**, 171, **174–7**, **183**, 451–2, **452**
Bishop Alnwick's Gate **169**, 170, 174
Bishop Reynolds' chapel 169, 174, **178**
Bishop Salmon's porch **168–9**, 169–70, 174, **178**
double herbaceous borders **172**, 172, 176, 183, **186–7**
exotics **181**, **182**, 182–3
greenhouse 183
Holly Walk 177
Kitchen Garden 174, 183, **184–5**, 183
Labyrinth and wild-flower meadow 174, 176, **179**, 179, 183
main lawn 177, **178**

public opening 184
reduction in size 174–5, 176
Rose Garden 174, 176, **180**, 181, 183
Bishop's House, Norwich 170, 174, 176
Bishop's Palace, Norwich 168, 170, **173**, 174
Blackett, Sir William **52**
Blakeney Point 463
Blickling Hall **195**, 203, 205, 377, 451, 463
 lake 235–6, **236–7**, 245
 Parterre 189, 190, 192, 194, 196–7, **196–8**, 198–9, **200**, 200–1, **201–3**, 202–3, **459**, 460
Blomefield, Francis 59, 235
Boardman, Edward 302, 313
Boardman, Edward T. 305, 313, 325
Boileau, Sir J. P. **41**
Bolding, William 455
Bolwick Hall, Marsham, lake at 225, **225**
Boulton and Paul 86–8, 90–1, 98, **100**, 101–2, 250, 252, 302, **303**, 305
 factory **85**, 98, 101, 102, **102–3**
Boulton, William 87
Braka, Ivor 337, **337**, 336, 338, 343–4
Brettingham, Matthew, the Elder 231, 327
Bridgeman, Charles 231, **234**, 327, 343, 379
Brooke, Edward Adveno **275**, 453–4
Brown, Lancelot 'Capability' 230
Browne, Dr Edward 53, 61
Bruister, Samuel 131

Brundall Gardens 18–19, **28**
　creation of 20, 22, 25
　development as tourist attraction 28–30
　Log House **23**, 25, 27
　Mere (Lily Lake) **16**, **19**, 25, **26**, **30–1**, **33**
　Museum **21**, 22
　plan of **28**
　Redclyffe/Redcliffe House **26**, 27, 29, 31, 32, **33**
　restoration 31–2
　Rock Garden **21**, 22, **22**
　Roman Dock 22, 31, **32**
　Rose Walk **29**, 29
Buck, Samuel and Nathaniel **130**
Buckenham Tofts Park, water in 230
Bunn, James 136
Bure, River 330
Burn, William 280
Burton, Decimus **105**, 106, 108, **112**
Burton, William 449

Campbell, Colen 377, 378, 379, 384
Carmichael, William 427
Carrow Abbey 297, **298**, 299, 301, 305, 309, **309–11**, 311, **312**, 313, **313–14**, 316, **320–1**, 323, **342–5**, **457**
　gardens 311, 313, 314, **315**, **316**, 316, **317**, 319, 325
　mural 319, **320–2**
Carrow House, Norwich 91, 102, 297, **298–9**, 299, **300–1**, 301–2, 305–8, 323
　gardens 301–2, 316, 325
Carter, George 335
Carter, Howard 367
Carter, Samuel 365, **367**
Castanea sativa (sweet chestnut) **77**, 77, 394, **395–5**, 398, 402
Catton, Charles, the elder **171**
Catton Park **447**, 448
Cedrus atlantica (Atlas cedar) 177
Cedrus libani (Cedar of Lebanon) **70**, 70
Chadwick, Ernest 457
Chaplin, Charlie 17
Charles II, HM King 54
Cheston, Charles 348–9
Christian, Ewan **173**
Clere, Thomas 57
Clutterbuck, Violet 455
Clutterbuck, Walter 455–6

Coke, Thomas William, 'Coke of Norfolk' 35, 36, **36**, 37–8, 47, 278
Coke, Thomas, 1st Earl of Leicester 35, 273
Coke, Thomas, 2nd Earl of Leicester 35, 38, 40, **277**, 278, 287
Colborne, Lord **41**
Colchicum speciosum 416
Colman, Alan 302
Colman, Caroline 299, 301, **302**, 302, 305, 311, 314, 325
Colman, Ethel 302, 305, **306**, 316, 325
Colman, Florence 302
Colman, Helen 302, **306**, 316
Colman, Jeremiah James **296**, 297, **298**, 299, 302, 302, 313
Colman, Laura 302
Colman, Russell 302
Constance, Marchioness of Lothian **192**, **193**, 194, **196**, **199**, 200, **205**
Cook, Thomas Albert **106**, 106, **115**
Cooper, Frederick Holmes 17, **17**, 18, 26–7, **27**, 31
Corbridge, James **236**
Corder, Edward **25**
Costessey Hall 123
　Park, water in 225
Cotman, John Sell **195**, **234**, 451, 452, 453
Cotman, Miles Edmund 452, **453**
Courtauld, Stephen 388, 389
Courtauld, Virginia 388, 389
Cow Tower, Norwich 54
Crataegus (hawthorn) **74**, 74
Crome, John **67**, **311**, 449, **451**
Cufaude, Francis 443, **445**
Cunninghamia lanceolata (Chinese fir) 159
Curtis, William 133

de Faxthorn, A. **110**
de Grey, Thomas 124
de Losinga, Herbert 168
de Monchaux, Paul **220**, 221, **222**
Decker, James 137–8, **139**
Denton Rectory **443–5**, 446, **446**
Didlington 351, 357–8, 359, 370–2
　boathouse 359, 360, **360–1**, 362, **362**

folly Tower 358, **358**, 359, 360
gardens **351–3**, 353–4, 363, 373
glasshouses **356–7**, 357
Hall 347, **347**, 348–9, 362–3, **363**, **364–6**
lakes 238, 245, 353–4, **354–5**, **359**, 359, 373, **373–5**
Sekhmets 363, **364**
Swimming Pool **346**, 367, **368–70**, 370
Ditchingham Park, lake at 229–30, **230**, 238
Dixon, Nigel **339**
Donthorn, William **35**, 40, 42, 46
Ducker, Brian **339**
Duke's Palace, the, Charing Cross, Norwich 49–50, 53, 54, 55, **56–7**, 57, **58**, 59, 131

Earlham Hall 377, 382, **383**, 451
Earsham Hall 451
East Barsham Manor 461
East Ruston Old Vicarage 463, **464**
Easton, James 288–9
Elgood, George Samuel 457
Ellis, James **339**, 344
Elsing Hall 253
Elveden Hall 90
Emerson, P. H. 455
Emes, William 236
Elizabeth, Queen Consort of George VI **213**, 216, 461
Elizabeth II, HM Queen **156–7**
Erpingham 448
Evans, Simon **339**
Evelyn, John **50**, 51, 52–3, 55–6, 59, 61
Eynsford 448
Eyre, Kingsmill 379

Fagus sylvatica 'Pendula' (weeping beech) 314, 316, **318–19**
Fagus sylvatica f. *purpurea* (purple beech) 179
Felbrigg 127, 226, 463
Felthorpe park **63**
Ffolkes, Sir W. **41**
Fincham Hall 147
Fitt, Frederick 126
Flower, Cyril, Lord Battersea 459
Footner, Francis Amicia de Chadwick Biden 190
Foster, Birkett 457
Foster, Sir W. **41**
Fountaine, Sir Andrew 384

Fraxinus excelsior 'Pendula' (weeping ash) **79**, 79, **82**, 82
Funnell, Barre **339**

Gabriel, Kate **460**
Gaches, Simon 179, 183
Galanthus **408**, 413, 415, 417
   'Bishop's Mitre' **416**, 417
   'Clovis' 417, **417**
   'Dionysus' 413, **414**
   G. ikariae 413
   G. ikariae 'Butt's Form' 412
   G. nivalis 'Flore Pleno' **411**, **415**, 415
   G. nivalis 'Sharlockii' 412
   G. nivalis imperati **413**
   G. plicatus 411, **412**, 413, 415
   'Greenfinch' **406**, 416
   'Hippolyta' 413, **413**
   'Saraband' 418, **419**
Garland, Sam 183
Gawdy Park, water in 226
Gear, Nick **339**
George V, HM King **269**
George VI, HM King **213**, 216
Gibbs, James 378, 379
Giles, Will 182
Gilpin, William Sawrey 238, **240**, 329, 336
Gladstone, Henry **302**
Gladstone, Mrs Catherine **302**
Gladstone, Mrs Henry **302**
Gladstone, W. E. **302**, 302, 316
Great Exhibition, 86, 252, 423
Greatorex, Heyrick Anthony 407, **408**, 409, **409–10**, 410–11, 415–16
Green, Anthony **439**, 464, 465
Griffin, William 126–7
Grigor, James 63, 65–6, **67**, 69, 73, 75, 238
   The Eastern Arboretum **62**, 63, **64**, 65, 66–7, **68**, 69, **70**, 71, **71**, 72, **72**, 73, 76–7, **76–83**
Guist 105
Gunthorpe Park, lake 238
Gunton
   bridge **328–9**, 329
   church **328**, 329, 338
   Hall 327, **332**, 332, 343
   lake 231, **232–3**, 245, **334–5**, **340**
   Park 329, **333**, 333–5, 337–8, **342–3**, 343–4, **344**, 452
   sawmill 329, **330**, 338
   Tower 329, **330–1**, **336**

Gurney, Daniel **82**

Hammond, Joseph 133
Hanneman, Adriaen 49
Harbord, Edward **330**
Harbord, Sir William 327, 329
Harbord-Hamond, Charles 337, **337**, 338
Hare, John 238
Hebe brachysiphon 181
Hedychium (ginger lilies) 153
Herkomer, Sir Herbert von 297
Hethel Thorn, the **74**, 74
Hevingham **77**
Heydon **77**
   Hall 124
   lake 238
Hilborough Park, water in 225
Hilgay, Wood Hall 448
Hillier, Harold 149, **160**
Hillington Hall 40, 124
   lake 238
Hoare, Lady Maud 393, **401**
Hoare, Sir Samuel 387, **387**, **388**, 389, 392–3, 394, 399, **401**, 401–2, 403
Hochstetter, Anthony **135**, **137**, 170, 171
Hodgson, David **168**
Holkham Hall 35, **35**, 36, **47**, **276**, 443, 454, **461**, 461
   fountain **272**, 273, **274–6**, **279**, **280–1**, 281, **282–3**, 283, **284**, 285, **288**, **290–1**, 291, **293**, 293–4, **294–5**, 454
   grounds 47, 276, 278, 281
   lake 231, 235, 236, **238–9**, 245
   water system **286–7**, 287–9, **289**, 291–2, **292**, 293
Honing 123
Hooke, Sir Robert **56**
Horsford Hall **81**
Horsford Rectory **449**, 449
Houghton
   gardens 379
   Hall 377, **378**, 378–9
   Park 227–8
Hoveton 126
Hoveton Hall, lake at **227**, 229, 245
Howard, Henry, 6th Duke of Norfolk **48–9**, 49, 52, 54–5, 56, **58**
Howard House, King Street, Norwich 53, **59**, 60
Hudson, John **41**
Humbert, Albert Jenkins 421

Hussey, Christopher 189

Indigofera (indigo) 182
Ives, Jeremiah **447**

J. & J. Colman Ltd 297, 307, 322–3, 324
James, C. H. 210, **210**
James, Graham, Bishop of Norwich 184
Jeckyll, Thomas 249, **249**, 250, 253, 254, **260**, 261, 262
   Norwich Gates 254, **255–7**, 257, **258**, **269**, **270–1**, 433
   Pavilion **248**, 249, 261, **261**, 262–3, **263–6**, 266–8, **268**
Jedburgh Abbey **193–194**
Jekyll, Gertrude 190
Johnson, Hugh **147**, **164**
Jones, Alan and Linda 32
Jones, Henry 311, 314, 325

Kemp, Derek 155
Kent, William 35, 235, 378, 442
Kerr, Philip, 11th Marquess of Lothian 189–90, **190**, 191, 203
Kerr, William Schomberg Robert, 8th Marquess of Lothian 194, **194**, 196
Kett's Oak, Wymondham **83**
Ketteringham Hall 254
Ketteringham Park, lake 238
Keymer, John 138, 141
Kimberley **448**, 448
   lake 230, **231**, 235, **238**, 245
Kip, Johannes **53**, 381, 442
Kirkpatrick, John **56**, **173**
Kneller, Sir Godfrey 50
Knyff, Leonard **53**, 381, 442

Ladbrooke, Robert **140**
Lakenham 124
Lakey, Chris **339**
Langley Park 443
   lake 230
Larchwood, Beachamwell 147, 148, 157, **160**, 161, **161**, 162, 165
Leicester Monument, the **34–5**, 35, **36–7**, **39**, **43–4**
   bas-relief scenes 40, **41**, 42, 44–5, **45**
   construction of 42
   design of **34**, 35, 38, 40
   funding of 38, 46
   inscription 40, **46**, 46

Lely, Sir Peter 58
Leslie, Sir John **193**
Letheringsett 299
Lewis, Brian 463, **464**
Lexham **41**
Lexham Park, water in 225
Lilium lankongense 165
Lindley, John 67
Lindsay, Norah **188**, 190–1, **191**, **199**, 200, 202
Liriodendron tulipifera (tulip tree) **178**, 179
Lloyd, Christopher 153, **155**
Loudon, John Claudius 63, **244**, 245
Lutyens, Sir Edwin 208, **208**, 459
Lyminge, Robert 205
Lynes, Judy **339**
Lynford Park, lake 238

Mackellar, Archibald 431, 433
Mackie family 124
Mackie's nursery **122**, 123, 124–6
MacLintoch, David **339**
Marnock, Robert 426
Marsham, Charles **195**
Marsham Hall 455
Marsham, Robert **70**
Martin, Amy **339**
Martin, Kit 331–3, 334, **336**, 338, **340**, 343–4
Mason, Hugh 165
Mason, Leonard Maurice **146**, 147–8, **148**, 149, 150, **150**, 152–4, **154**, 155, **156**, **157**, 159, **159**, 161–2, **163**
Mason, Margaret **150**, **155**, 161, 162, **164**
Maynard, Arne 464–5
Melton Constable **442**, 442
 Hall 91, 377, **380**, 381
 lake 230
Merton 124
Minns, James **107**
Middleton, John 452
Moore, John 131, 133
Moore, William 87
Morley, John 153
Mundford 126
Muter, Gerry and Janet 31, **32**
'My Lord's Garden', King Street, Norwich 51, 53, 54, 59, 61, 130, 131, 133, 134, **135**, 135
 modern redevelopment of 57, **60–1**

Narborough Hall 451
Narcissus bulbocodium 165
Narcissus cyclamineus 165
Narford
 grounds 384–5
 Hall 377, **384**, 384
 lake 238, **242–3**
Neech, Samuel 141
Nesfield, Markham 194, 196
Nesfield, William Andrews **276**, **278**, **279**, 280, **294**
Nichols, Catherine Maude 456–7
Ninham, Henry 65, **67**
North Elmham Park, lake 235, 245
North Runcton 82
Norwich Cathedral 168, 250, **447**
Norwich, Chapelfield 263, **264–5**, 266, 449, **451**, 451
Norwich, City Hall 210, 211, 213, 216, **216**
Norwich Gates **256**, **257**, 258, 262, 263, 268, **269**
Norwich, Heigham Park 266, 267
Norwich, marketplace 212, 213, **214–15**
Norwich, Pleasure Gardens **128**, 129, **130**, **135**,
 Greyhound Gardens 143
 New Spring Garden 130, 131, 133, 135, **135**, 136, 141
 Prussia Gardens 141
 Richmond Hill Gardens 130, **140**, 141
 Rural Gardens/Ranelagh/Royal Victoria Gardens 133, 134, 136–7, **137**, 141, **141**, 143, 144, **144**
 Wilderness **130**, 131, 133, 134, 141
Norwich, Rose Lane 85, 87, 88, 98, **99**, 101, **102–103**, 449, **450**

Osmanthus x *burkwoodii* 407

Paeonia emodi 165
Paget, Paul 388, **389**, 402, **402**
Parsons, Beatrice 457, **458**, 459–60
Paul, Joseph John Dawson **86**, 87, **98**
Pevsner, Nikolaus 268
Phibbs, John 337
Pickenham Park, water in 225
Pinus sylvestris (Scots pine) **81**, 81
Piper, John 460–1, **462**

Platanus x *hispanica* (London plane) 177
Platycerium wandae (New Guinea stag's horn fern) 157
Pleasaunce, The, Overstrand **458**, 459
Populus nigra 'Italica' (Lombardy poplar) **78**, 78
Port Lympne, Kent 191
Postlethwaite, Revd Mathew 443, **445**, 446
Pratt, Sir Roger 123, 439, **440**
Prideaux, Edmund **376**, 377, 442
Pseudopanax (lancewood) 182
Pulham and Son 422–4, 428, 433, 434, 437
Pulham, James 422, 424, 425, 429
Pyrus communis 'Uvedale's St Germain' (pear) **179**, 179

Quantrell, William 134, 141
Quercus (oak) **72**, 72, **76**, 76, **83**, 83
 Q. frainetto (Hungarian oak) 301
 Q. ilex (holm oak) 394, **395–5**, 398
Quest-Ritson, Charles **154**
Quidenham Hall 451

Rackheath Park, water in 225
Ravingham Hall 102
 lake at **246**
Raynham Hall 377, 442
 lake at **226–7**, 227, 231, **234**, 235
Repton, Humphry 229, 245, 329, 446, **447**, 448–9
Richardson, David **339**
Richmond, George **277**
Richmond, Nathaniel 229
Riddlesworth Park, water in 225
Ripley, Thomas 378
Roberts, Ian **339**
Robinson, William 426
Rosa 'Norwich Cathedral' 181
Rosa 'Penelope' **166**
Rowe, Ernest Arthur 457
Rowland Pierce, S. 210, **210**
Rowlandson, Thomas **131**
Ruscus aculeatus (butcher's broom) 407
Ryston Hall 123, 439, **439–40**, 441

Sackville-West, Vita 190
Sandby, Paul 446, **447**

Sandringham 25, 90, **91**, 254, **256–7**, 257, 437, 461, **462**
  Cave boathouse 425, **426**
  gardens 421, 426–7, 429, 433–4, **434–5**, 457, **458**
  house 421, **421–2**, 422, **436–7**
  lake 422
  Pulhamite rockworks **420**, **424**, 424, **425**, 425, **426–9**, 429
Sandys, Anthony 67
Sandys, Frederick 250
Sassoon, Sir Philip **191**, 191
Sayer, Bob **152**
Seely, John 388, **389**
Sennowe 105
  approaches **112**, 112, 113–14
  Boathouse **104**, **111**, 119
  gardens 105, 119, **120**, 121
  House **105**, 106, 108, **109**, **114**
  Italian Gates **109**, 113
  lake **111**, 112, 117, **119**, **242**, 243
  park 110, **112–13**, 113, 116
  terracing 117, **117**
  Winter Garden 117, **118**, 119
Shadwell Park 461
  lake 243–4, **244**
Shaw, Richard Norman 353, 362, **363**, 363
Sheringham 127, **447**, 448
Shotesham Park, water in 225
Sidestrand Hall **388**, 388
Simmons, John 159
Sims, Pippa **339**
Singh, Maharajah Prince Dhuleep 90
Skipper, George John **106**, 106–7, **109**, 110, **112**, 113–114, 117, 119, **121**
Smith, Charles Raymond 281–2
Snowdrop Acre, Witton **408**, 410, 411, 416, 418
Spencer, Earl 40, **41**
Sprowston **82**
Sprowston Hall 261
Squier, James **339**
SS Victorious **27**, 28, 30
Stamp, Gerard 338, 340, **341**
Stark, James **309**
Stiffkey Old Hall **438**, 464, **465**
Strachan, James, gardener 18, **18**
Stradsett Hall, lake at **244**, 245
Stratton Hall 451
Stratton Strawless **70**, 71

Strutt, Jacob George 63
Stuart, James **302**, 305, 313, 314, 316, 325
Surrey House, Norwich 107
Swafield Hall 463

Talbot Manor, Fincham 147, 148, 149, 153, 157, 165
Templewood 386, 387, **390–2**, **393–6**, **399**, 400–1, **402**, **404–5**
  approach 394, **394–5**
  design 389, 392, 400
  grounds 393, 397–8, **398**, 399–403
  water at **396**, 397, **398**, 400, **400**, 402–3, **403**
Tetrapanax (rice paper plant) 182
Teulon, S. S. 243, 280, 422
Teulon, William 332
Thirtle, John **311**
Thomas, William Broderick 422, 427, 429
Thorpe Abbots Hall 86
Thorpe Market 72
Thurning Hall **454**
Thurston, David **339**
Thurston, Mick **339**
Thwaite 123
Tilia (lime) **82**, 82
  T. dasystyla subsp. *caucasica* (weeping lime) 316
Tillandsia (air plants) 153, **154**
Tillett, Janette **408**, 409, 411
Townshend, Charles, 2nd Viscount **234**
Trimbee, James 370–1
Tuke, Samuel 51–2, 54, 56
Turner, C. **79**
Tyssen-Amherst, Margaret 365, 371, 372, **372**
Tyssen-Amherst, William Amhurst 348–9, **350**, 351, 362, 365, **372**
Tyssen-Amherst, William George 351

Upcher, Abbot 127
Usher, Graham, Bishop of Nowich 179, 184, **184**

Victoria, HM Queen 85, 87, 181
Voewood, Kelling 463, **463**

Walker, Arthur George **205**
Walpole, Horace 379, 443
Walpole, Robert 378
Walsingham Abbey, water at 225

War Memorial Gardens, Norwich **206**, **214–17**, **222–3**
War Memorial, Norwich 208–9, **209**, 212, 213, **220–1**, 220, 221, 222
  changes to 220–1
  construction of 207, 210, **211–12**
  debate over 219, 220
  design of 212–13
  listing of 219
  planting of 216–17, 222
  upkeep of 218–19, 220
Ward, Cyril **421**, **435**, 457, **458**
Ward, Keith **339**
Watling, Charles **213**
Watson, James, stonemason 42
Watts, George Frederick **194**
Weaver, David **339**
Weaver, Kate **339**
Weaver, Thomas **36**
Webb, John 236
Wensum, River **54**, 55, **57**, 59, **60**, 110, **112**, 131
West Tofts 127, 226
Westwick Park, water in 228
Weybourne 455
Whitbread, Madeline **199**
Wilkins, William **327**
Willmott, Ellen 190
Windham, William 127
Winfarthing Oak, the **76**
Wissey, River 373
Wodehouse, Thomas 105
Wolterton Hall 80, 448, 451, **452**
  lake at **224**, 231, **234**, 235, 238, **240–1**, 245
Woodford, James **218**
Woodforde, James 125, 126, 136, 138
Wootton, John 443
Wordsworth, William 75
Wright, John Michael **49**
Wyatt, Samuel 245, 327, 329
Wyatt, Sir Matthew Digby 194, 196
Wymondham **83**

x *Mahoberberis aquisargentii* 407

Zanthoxylum (Szechuan pepper) 182

Additional Picture Captions

Jacket cover Templewood
Title page The Avenue, Holkham Hall
Above Sennowe Park

Banner Pictures

Foreword The Carrow Mural (p. 4), Houghton Hall (p. 5, cf. page 378)
Contents Hoveton Hall lake (p. 6)
Contributors Detail, Henry Howard by John Michael Wright (p. 10), Sawmill Pond, Gunton (p. 13)
Introduction The Bishop's Garden (p.14), Sennowe Park, Boathouse (p. 15)
Acknowledgements Gunton Park (p. 466)
Sources Detail, Denton Rectory, by Francis Cufaude (p. 467)
Picture credits Holkham Hall (p. 473)
Index Blickling Hall garden (p. 475)

Norfolk Gardens Trust 2021
Norfolk Gardens Trust is a Registered Charity No. 801894
www.norfolkgt.org.uk
All rights reserved. No part of this publication may be reproduced, stored in a retrieval system, or transmitted in any form by any means (whether electronic, mechanical, photocopying or recording) or otherwise without the written permission of the Norfolk Gardens Trust.

ISBN 978-0-9556728-7-3

Designed by Kaarin Wall, Wiz Graphics
Printed by Swallowtail Print, Norwich